Bounded Lives, Bounded Places

BOUNDED

·

LIVES,

·

Free Black Society in Colonial New Orleans, 1769–1803

·

BOUNDED

·

PLACES

Kimberly S. Hanger

Duke University Press *Durham & London* 1997

3rd printing, 2006

© 1997 Duke University Press

All rights reserved

Printed in the United States of America on acid-free paper ∞

Typeset in Galliard by Tseng Information Systems, Inc.

Library of Congress Cataloging-in-Publication Data appear on the

last printed page of this book.

To the memory of my mother,

Marillyn Gloria Wells Stuckenschneider

Contents

List of Abbreviations

―――――■―――――

AGI PC   Archivo General de Indias, Papeles Procedentes de la Isla
             de Cuba
AGI SD   Archivo General de Indias, Audiencia de Santo Domingo
AGS GM   Archivo General de Simancas, Guerra Moderna
HTML   Howard-Tilton Memorial Library, Tulane University
LHC   Louisiana Historical Center, Louisiana State Museum
LLMVC   Louisiana and Lower Mississippi Valley Collections,
             Louisiana State University Libraries
NOPL   New Orleans Public Library, Louisiana Division
OPNA   Orleans Parish Notarial Archives
PDLC   Petitions, Decrees, and Letters of the Cabildo, NOPL
RDC   Records and Deliberations of the Cabildo, NOPL
1778 Census "Censo de Nueva Orleans del mes de junio de 1778," AGI
             PC 191
1791 Census Census of the City of New Orleans, 6 November 1791,
             NOPL
1795 Census "Recensement du 1er, 2me, et 3me quartiers," July 1795,
             AGI PC 211
SJR   Spanish Judicial Records, Record Group 2, LHC

List of Figures and Tables

————◼————

Acknowledgments

—■—

As I reach the end of a road long-traveled but full of rewarding and interesting side-trips, I have many individuals and institutions to thank. My
husband, Greg, insisted upon being named first and last in this list of ac-
knowledgments, so here is the initial installment. He has been my number one fan for finishing this book, cheering and prodding me on so that
someday we could spend more time together.

On the financial front, several institutions provided the funding that is
so vital to the research and writing efforts of scholars. They make public
dissemination of our ideas possible. Among those whose generous grants
helped support this study are the Program for Cultural Cooperation between Spain's Ministry of Culture and U.S. Universities, the Spain-Florida
Alliance, the University of Florida Department of History, the American
Historical Association, the American Philosophical Society, the Oklahoma
Foundation for the Humanities, the University of Tulsa Faculty Development Summer Fellowship Program, and the University of Tulsa Faculty
Research Grant Program.

Research is also made possible and enjoyable through the efforts of archives, libraries, and collections whose staffs locate, preserve, and organize
the documents, maps, books, and artifacts that contribute to our interpretations of the past. Those institutions that provided materials for my interpretation of colonial New Orleans include the Archivo General de Indias
in Seville, the Archivo General de Simancas, the Louisiana and Lower
Mississippi Valley Collections of Hill Memorial Library (Louisiana State
University), the Center for Louisiana Studies (University of Southwestern
Louisiana), the Louisiana Historical Center of the Louisiana State Museum, the Archives of the Archdiocese of New Orleans, The Historic New
Orleans Collection, Orleans Parish Notarial Archives, the New Orleans Pub-
lic Library, Howard-Tilton Memorial Library (Tulane University), the Loy-
ola University (New Orleans) Archives, and the Family History Library in
Salt Lake City, Utah. I especially appreciate the services of James F. Sefcik,

Charles E. Nolan, Kathryn Page, Alfred Lemmon, John Barbry, Sally K. Reeves, Wilbur E. Meneray, Carl A. Brasseaux, and Glenn R. Conrad.

Numerous people helped guide and shape my work, first as a thesis, then a dissertation, and finally this book, which is by no means perfect (with the usual caveat that I am entirely to blame) but is much improved as a result of their assistance. I owe a particular debt of gratitude to the late Roger M. Haigh and to Ronald G. Coleman for introducing me to my eighteenth-century friends in New Orleans when this project began as a master's thesis at the University of Utah. Larry R. Gerlach acquainted me with the entice-ments of historical detection. Several mentors at the University of Florida further sharpened my scholarly skills and guided me through a maze of theoretical constructs, demographic analysis, and the use and evaluation of primary and secondary source materials: Cheryll Ann Cody, Lyle N. McAlister, David Bushnell, Kermit L. Hall, David P. Geggus, Jeffrey D. Needell, Gláucio Ary Dillon Soares, Patrick J. Geary, and James Amelang. Murdo J. MacLeod, chair of my dissertation committee, has provided ad-vice, criticism, and encouragement; his thoughtful insights and continuing friendship are greatly appreciated. Fellow scholars of Louisiana and the greater Caribbean also served to inspire and challenge me with their own excellent research. Among them are Jane G. Landers, Gwendolyn Midlo Hall, Daniel H. Usner Jr., David J. Weber, Paul F. Lachance, L. Virginia Gould, Stephen Webre, Paul E. Hoffman, Light Townsend Cummins, Patri-cia Brady, Judith K. Schafer, and James H. Dormon. To my dear friend and colleague at the University of Tulsa, James P. Ronda, go special thanks for reading an early version of this manuscript and concocting a title for it. Thanks also to Jeanne Ronda for preparing the index and sharing her friendship as well. Another colleague at the University of Tulsa, Thomas M. Buoye, read and commented on the manuscript, proffered his friendship, and with volleyball games and bicycling trips relieved my mind of mundane academic matters.

Credit for the nuts and bolts of putting this book together and producing it in its final form goes to the able staff of Duke University Press. It has been a pleasure to work with two fine editors, first Rachel Toor and then Valerie Millholland. Managing editor Jean Brady and copyeditor Joan E. Howard helped improve the text immensely. The manuscript especially benefited from the insightful criticism of two reviewers, one anonymous and the other self-identified. You know who you are; thank you. Additional accolades go to Patty Eischen at the Louisiana State Museum and John Magill and Sally Stassi at The Historic New Orleans Collection for helping to obtain illustrations.

Finally, and most important, I would like to acknowledge the material and mental support of friends and family too numerous to list here. My father, mother, sister, brother, and in-laws gave me much love, encouragement, and assistance which I can never hope to repay. Heartfelt thanks go to my parents for instilling in me the belief that I could do and be whatever I wanted. And now for his second and final billing: words cannot convey the gratitude I feel for my husband Greg—or his delight that I finished this book. With much devotion, personal sacrifice, and understanding he endured months of separation while I visited archives in Spain and the United States, entered data into the computer, and pounded away at the keyboard.

Introduction

Colonial New Orleans' free blacks (*libres*) inhabited a complex, ambiguous world with which many of their contemporaries in other late-eighteenth-century slave societies were familiar. The dilemmas that libres faced in forming their identities are also similar to those which Americans confront in today's multicultural, multiethnic, complicated society. Their position within New Orleans' hierarchy was not well defined, and in fact most free blacks did not choose to be demarcated as a separate group, preferring instead to be admitted to and accepted by white society. In searching for identity, libres found their lives and the places in which they lived those lives bounded. On a daily basis they tested the boundaries of race, phenotype, occupation, status, religion, and gender—some evident, others more indefinite. Most free blacks desired that the distinctions between themselves and whites be dissolved altogether, claiming to be "free like you" and asserting "a universal equality among men," with only "their method of thinking, not color," differentiating them. Libre women would extend that equality beyond the confines of gender. Most free black men and women, however, did want to maintain the barriers of bondage, although with mechanisms provided for manumitting enslaved relatives and friends. Once freed and over generations libres distanced themselves from slavery and even took a vested interest in it by owning their own slaves. Theirs was an intricate, ambiguous place.

It was also a vital one. Free blacks played an important role in New Orleans society during the era of Spanish rule (in name from 1763 to 1800 and in effect from 1769 to 1803). It was over this period that the libre population grew to assume the "critical mass" needed to establish a distinct sense of identity. This development of a group consciousness among the leading libre families was a long, complex process that was begun but not completed by the end of Spanish rule in the early nineteenth century. It served as a foundation for the emergence of New Orleans' many, prosperous, and much-acclaimed Creoles of Color in the antebellum era of the United

States South.[1] Although several scholars have studied this population, few have looked at it closely in the colonial period, instead projecting findings for the nineteenth century back into the eighteenth, using a tactic ethno-historians call "upstreaming."[2] By the turn of the nineteenth century, New Orleans libres—like many of their counterparts in slave societies through-out the Americas and in the Caribbean in particular—had begun to come together as a separate group within a primarily three-tiered social order, distinct from whites *and* slaves.[3] This growing sense of group identity was based on several factors: phenotype (increasingly *casta* or mixed-race), occu-pation, family networks, military service, religious and leisure activities, and political expression, especially in pursuing citizenship rights in the face of increased discrimination and legal restrictions during the so-called Revolu-tionary Era.

Free blacks, however, continued to occupy an anomalous position in New Orleans society. Libres inhabited what Arnold A. Sio has termed "two psychological worlds": free and nonwhite. To this could be added the third dimension of gender. And they inhabited these worlds to different extents. Never acting as one, free blacks did not constitute a monolithic group in New Orleans or elsewhere; rather, "their consciousness largely coincided with their position in society."[4] In other words, some identified more with whites, some more with slaves, and an increasing number with each other, hence the creation of a group consciousness. In the fluid frontier com-munity of colonial New Orleans—what Gwendolyn Midlo Hall sees as "a complex, changing society" exhibiting "more chaos than order"[5]—very few individuals, white, slave, or libre, coalesced into a group with a common worldview. As Hall, Daniel H. Usner Jr., and others have recently shown us, there was no one dominant force in Louisiana's multicultural milieu, although libres definitely represented a subordinate element within that society.[6] Whether a particular free black identified more with whites, slaves, or other libres was due in large part to generational factors, with those who were newly freed associating more with friends and relatives still enslaved or with white consorts, fathers, or benefactors and those who were second- and third-generation libres creating networks among themselves. Because of Spanish legislation and their own efforts, slaves continuously entered the libre population, in larger and larger numbers toward the end of the eigh-teenth century. This and other characteristics of the demographic regime in New Orleans meant that free blacks had to interact with both whites and slaves. As time went on, however, libres' connections with each other made the creation of a distinct sense of group consciousness more and more likely. The free black population experienced demographic growth, urban concentration, regeneration by way of an increased percentage of freeborn blacks, economic success (at least for some libres), and involvement in such corporate entities as the church and the militia. This process of consciousness building was beginning to bear fruit by the end of the Spanish era and would help New Orleans' Creoles of Color organize to resist or avoid rising discrimination under American rule.[7]

The role of free blacks in American slave societies, the nature of these societies, and race relations within them have long fascinated historians and other scholars. Frank Tannenbaum's broad generalizations about comparative slave societies initiated the debate in the 1940s. Drawing on sociologist Gilberto Freyre's interpretation of slavery in Brazil, Tannenbaum asserted that a colonizing nation's institutions, laws, and traditions exerted the greatest influence on slave treatment in that nation's American dominions and that this treatment in turn influenced the quality of race relations between free persons and freedpersons. Both the tenets of Catholicism and Spain's legal system, founded on Roman and Visigothic law and encoded in Las Siete Partidas (The law of seven parts, compiled by the court of Alfonso the Wise in the thirteenth century), emphasized the slave's humanity, favored freedom as the ideal state of humankind, and promoted stability through paternalism and family formation. At the other extreme, Anglo common law and Protestantism placed the individual and the protection of property rights above all other considerations. Tannenbaum thus ranked Spain and Portugal first, followed by France, Holland, and, last, Britain, with respect to favorable slave treatment and race relations.[8] Like Tannenbaum, Stanley Elkins attributed the harshness or mildness of slave societies to the cultural values of various colonizing nations and linked conditions under slavery to freedmen's acceptance in the postemancipation order.[9]

Other scholars have charged that the Tannenbaum-Elkins school bases its assertions on ideal rather than actual circumstances; they point instead to material factors in assessing American slave systems.[10] Such variables included demographic profile, economic cycles, type of crop produced or labor performed, size of the production unit, absentee or resident ownership, climate, distance from the center of authority, and major historical events such as wars and revolutions, with ideological as well as political, economic, or social changes. All these factors varied temporally and spatially; they defy the neat categorization of slave systems by national worldview. A leader in this challenge to the Tannenbaum-Elkins thesis, David Brion Davis, agreed with Tannenbaum that "American society took a great variety of forms," but, unlike Tannenbaum, Davis attributed this diversity to "economic pressures and such derivative factors as the nature of employment, the number of slaves owned by a typical master, and the proportion of slaves in a given society."[11]

Scholars have used as one measure of a slave system's relative openness or repressiveness the ease of manumission and acceptance of free nonwhites in the dominant white society. Some, such as Tannenbaum, see a positive and others, such as Carl N. Degler, a negative relation. In the latter case, abused slaves found allies among government and ecclesiastical authorities who readily supported their claims to freedom or sale to a more lenient master and thereby curbed the power of hostile planter elites. Such paternalistic institutions characterized Latin countries, whereas Anglo cultures touted individualism, modernization, and laissez-faire principles that discouraged public interference in private matters.[12] Yet another group has argued that there was no correlation between slave treatment and race relations among former slaves and masters at all.[13] On one point, however, all agree: "Racism was a part of every American system that held African slaves and did not disappear when blacks and mulattoes became free citizens and economic and social competitors."[14] Only its intensity has varied.

The anomalous position of free African Americans within larger slave societies has attracted the attention of numerous investigators.[15] As noted above, however, few students of Louisiana have searched for the origins of antebellum New Orleans' large, influential, and prosperous free black population, unique to the United States South, in the Spanish colonial period. This lack of adequate, in-depth analysis holds true for many aspects of Spanish Louisiana's history. Jack D. L. Holmes correctly notes that "too few historians have analyzed the Spanish period" and that there is "a virtual neglect of the Spanish period from 1762 to 1806 in the text-books of American and even local and state histories."[16] Even more recently, Hall has lamented that "the history, especially the colonial history, of Louisiana has been badly neglected."[17] If free blacks inhabited two (or more) worlds, so too has Louisiana history, its colonial era in particular. It does not fit neatly into either Latin American or United States history and has been neglected by scholars of both fields. The few who venture into the colonial past of Louisiana have to be well versed in French, Spanish, *and* British/United States imperial aims (not to mention languages and paleography), but for those who do, the rewards are well worth the effort. Louisiana serves as a laboratory for the researcher interested in all the above-mentioned nations, in which the slavery and racial policies and practices can be tested, as well as the economic and material effects of integration into a capitalistic commercial world market system during the late eighteenth and early nineteenth centuries. The cultural exchange and accommodation that were typical of colonial Louisiana also constitute rich ground for investigation.

General scholarly and popular histories, works on specific topics in colonial Louisiana history, studies of free blacks in the southern United States, and broad studies of libres in Louisiana from its founding to the Civil War constitute the literature that deals in some respect with free blacks in New Orleans during the Spanish era. These works devote only a chapter or part of one or intermittent, random comments to this topic, however. In addition, many researchers rely on earlier, undocumented narratives of Louisiana, use such abstract phrases as "quite typical" rather than concrete figures, present varying population figures, and ignore the possibility that the conditions, size, fortunes, and makeup of the free black population changed over the last half of the eighteenth century. Fortunately, exciting new scholarship from Hall, Usner, Ulysses S. Ricard Jr., Paul F. Lachance, L. Virginia Meacham Gould, Carl A. Brasseaux, Gilbert C. Din, Light Townsend Cummins, and Thomas Marc Fiehrer—to name a few—is remedying these shortcomings.[18]

Within the debate over the comparative characteristics of slave societies, my own work discerns a combination of cultural-legal traditions and material conditions, with the latter having greater influence, in assessing the role of libres in Spanish New Orleans.[19] Spain installed its officials and institutions in Louisiana for only a short time and had to compete with firmly entrenched French cultural patterns. Spanish traditions, however, had their most lasting effect in New Orleans, the colony's administrative center. It was in New Orleans that Spanish laws protecting slaves and free blacks and advancing their interests came to full force, and it was New Orleans' urban environment that fostered economic and demographic conditions favorable to the rise of a notable libre population. Even though a chasm often separated legal and institutional ideals from material reality, as Jane Landers makes clear, "the emphasis on a slave's humanity and rights, and the lenient attitude toward manumission embodied in Spanish slave codes and social practice," did make it possible "for a significant free black class to exist in the Spanish world," a world that encompassed New Orleans in the last four decades of the eighteenth century.[20]

In New Orleans slaves and free blacks had more rights and opportunities, exercised those rights more readily, and received better treatment under Spanish rule than under either French or United States rule, but more on account of material than cultural factors. Spanish New Orleans' small-scale society facilitated personal, often intimate relationships that encouraged familiarity among all races, nationalities, and classes. Only when lower Louisiana's plantation system matured and slavery intensified with the rise of sugar during the last years of Spain's dominion and into the nineteenth century did state officials and planters together limit access to manumission and free black activities. The specter of slave revolt in Saint-Domingue, Louisiana, and other parts of the United States fueled white paranoia, as discrimination escalated and race relations deteriorated.[21] The findings presented in the following chapters accord with Fiehrer's analysis of trends in the region: "Louisiana (simultaneously with Cuba) underwent the same cycle of expansion and intensification of slavery after 1800 which had occurred in Saint-Domingue between 1750 and 1794." They also provide evidence from one region to support Eugene D. Genovese's generalization that "during the slave period in all countries intensification of racial antipathy followed commercialization and the ascendancy of bourgeois slaveholding classes."[22] As sugar and cotton production and Anglo-Americans gradually dominated the state's economy and political structure, libres found their rights and privileges reduced, their free association limited, and their strategic worth devalued.

The colony's early history provides a context for the changing status of free blacks in New Orleans and their increasing sense of group identity. First France and then Spain ruled the colony named in honor of France's "Sun King," Louis XIV. It encompassed a vast territory that stretched from the Gulf of Mexico to Canada and from the Appalachian to the Rocky Mountains.[23] Envisioning a giant arc of settlement stretching from Canada into the French Caribbean islands, Louis encouraged exploration of the Mississippi River in order to enlarge his empire and prevent British and Spanish expansion. France claimed and held Louisiana from 1699 until 1763. Over these six decades Louisiana passed from crown to proprietor and back to crown control; it never flourished economically or demographically, primarily owing to royal neglect and apathy. Louisiana was to form part of a mutually dependent system of colonies in the Caribbean, supplying the French islands with naval stores and lumber for the sugar industry and in turn receiving sugar and slaves. Louisiana's commercial crops (indigo, tobacco, and rice) were of lower quality than those produced in other French possessions, however. In addition, French slave traders sent their cargoes where prices and profits were highest and where they could obtain valuable goods for the return voyage — definitely not Louisiana. Thus there were few laborers to plant and harvest crops or process natural resources, and what goods they did generate often rotted on the wharves at New Orleans, especially when all too frequent wars disrupted commerce.[24]

The French crown welcomed the opportunity to rid itself of such an economic burden in the secret Treaty of Fontainebleau, signed on 3 November 1762, and the public Treaty of Paris that ended the Seven Years' War in 1763. That Spain was an ally and would most likely resist any Anglo-American expansion beyond the Atlantic seaboard sweetened the deal. Both Bourbon monarchies viewed Louisiana as useful primarily within a context of larger geopolitical considerations; neither wanted Britain to seize it. Spain in particular sought a buffer for New Spain, its richest kingdom in the New World. Although Spain, like France, considered Louisiana an economic burden, the crown hoped to utilize it as a protective barrier between mineral-rich New Spain and the increasingly aggressive North American colonies. Under both French and Spanish rulers the colony's purpose was primarily strategic.

Preoccupied with restoring order in its war-torn kingdom, Spain did not officially establish its laws and military power in Louisiana until 1769. The task of governing its newest province proved difficult. In 1765 the provincial superior council sent Jean Milhet, a prominent New Orleans wholesaler, to France in order to persuade the crown to retake Louisiana. The colony's merchants and planters especially feared strict Spanish mercantile provisions and currency devaluation. Unsuccessful, Milhet returned with news that Spain intended to institute its regime in the near future. In the spring of 1765 the crown appointed the renowned scientist Antonio de Ulloa y de la Torre Guiral first Spanish governor of Louisiana and instructed him to leave existing French customs and laws intact.

Ulloa's turbulent reign lasted a mere two and a half years. His unpopularity, indecisiveness, and refusal to exert authority confused and alienated influential Louisianians; the colony's deteriorating economy fueled their discontent. In November 1768 distraught French planters, farmers, merchants, and officials banished Ulloa from the colony. When Spain sent General Alejandro O'Reilly and twenty-one hundred troops a few months later to restore order, punish the rebellion's ringleaders, secure loyalty oaths from the population, and implement the laws and institutions of Castile and the Indies, it conveyed a definitive message that Louisiana now belonged to His Most Catholic Majesty. Thus Spain's initial experiment with a flexible colonial policy for Louisiana failed; only when a more rigid routine also failed did the crown reluctantly, and often unofficially, relax its stern mercantilist strictures.

Spain sought to attract settlers to the region in order to defend it, balance the somewhat hostile French population remaining in the colony, and promote agricultural and commercial growth. Its immigration policy was more successful than France's, but population flow and economic prosperity worked to the advantage of the United States rather than Spain. With generous grants of land, tools, and foodstuffs the crown enticed Isleños, Malagueños, and refugees from Acadia and Saint-Domingue to Louisiana. Despite efforts to keep acquisitive Anglo-Americans out of the Mississippi Valley, hundreds of them poured into the rich farmlands of upper Louisiana after 1783. Finally recognizing its inability to halt Anglo penetration, Spain in 1789 adopted a new strategy to incorporate its enemies rather than futilely struggle against them. The crown's imaginative yet ironic solution was to encourage former Anglo-American subjects to settle in Spanish Louisiana, swear an oath of loyalty to the Spanish crown, and work for Spain rather than oppose it. To attract these immigrants Spaniards guaranteed religious toleration, liberal land grants, and the right to navigate the Mississippi River. Gradually farmers and merchants from the eastern seaboard took over Louisiana, until by 1795 "it was too late for Spain to take effective steps against the Americans." [25]

Spain governed Louisiana until 30 November 1803. On that day officials marked the colony's transfer from Spanish to French rule; a mere twenty days later France in turn transferred Louisiana to the United States. Spain had actually secretly ceded the colony to France on 1 October 1800 in exchange for an Italian kingdom for the Duke of Parma. In this exchange, transacted in the Treaty of San Ildefonso, France's Napoléon Bonaparte also promised King Carlos IV that he would never transfer the colony to another party. Carlos thus rid himself of this economic burden called Louisiana, a dependent possession that required a larger *situado* (subsidy) each year, and won assurances that neither Britain nor the United States would gain easy access to the valuable New Spain.[26] At least he was correct in one respect.

During the colonial era government and private promoters failed to exploit the great potential of Louisiana's natural resources and population, much to the relief of a majority of settlers, slaves, and native inhabitants.[27] Reality never met expectation, at least not from an imperial perspective; Louisiana remained a poor colony, a peripheral region of both the French and the Spanish empires, valued primarily for its strategic position between Anglo-America and New Spain. Feverish searches for mineral wealth yielded nothing but a little copper. Dependent on Indians and Africans for foodstuffs and labor, settlers from Europe's urban centers refused to soil their hands doing menial tasks. Even as late as 1777 one contemporary observed that "the inhabitants neglect agriculture and generally employ themselves in hunting and fishing," preferring instead to engage in what one scholar has termed a "frontier exchange economy."[28]

Colonial interests did not recognize or realize the economic promise of the lower Mississippi Valley until the close of the eighteenth century. Sugar and cotton then became significant, highly profitable crops, and the people needed to produce these crops flowed into the region. The plantation system was slow to mature in Louisiana and did not really blossom until the nineteenth century. As indigo production declined across lower Louisiana in the early 1790s, sugar concomitantly emerged as the primary staple and spurred the consolidation of land, labor, capital, and technology. Though the rise of sugar occurred relatively late, "the agricultural basis of slavery in Louisiana parallele[d] the development of the institution in the circum-Caribbean region, from San Salvador on the Central American isthmus across to the British Leeward islands."[29]

Economic developments at the close of the colonial period foretold an increasing—at times stunning—material prosperity for Louisiana. Several trends coalesced to transform Louisiana from an economically depressed colony in the late 1780s and early 1790s into a flourishing territory and state of the antebellum era. Unprecedented exportation of sugar and cotton saved Louisiana from financial ruin and in turn attracted people and investments to the area. In terms of population alone, the colony experienced a higher growth rate during the last fifteen years than in all of the preceding years of the eighteenth century.[30]

The main beneficiary of this demographic increase was New Orleans, Louisiana's primary urban center and port. The furs, hides, timber, and agricultural products of the region's interior flowed through New Orleans on their way to the French, British, and Spanish West Indies, the North American colonies/states, New Spain, and occasionally Spain. New Orleans also served as the entrepôt for slaves and various goods such as flour and cloth that colonials could not supply on their own. Culturally and racially diverse, the New Orleans population labored as dock and transportation workers, domestics, agricultural processors, peddlers, shopkeepers, artisans, doctors, lawyers, merchants, and military and civilian government employees.

Free and slave persons of African descent performed many of the city's manual and skilled tasks.[31] Wholesale importation of slaves from Africa began in 1719, when ships under the employ of John Law's Company of the Indies deposited five hundred Guinean slaves on the banks of the Mississippi. These slaves, along with indentured servants, salt and tobacco smugglers, debtors, soldier farmers, and colonists who immigrated of their own volition, labored to construct the new colonial capital and produce crops for subsistence and export. Although enslavement of Native Americans continued well into the Spanish period, that group never met Louisiana's labor demands. One French governor even proposed to Saint-Domingue officials an exchange of three of his Indian for two of their African slaves.[32] He and other officials and settlers could not convince slave traders to send the numbers of bondpersons needed to exploit colonial resources to their full potential, primarily because in economic terms Louisiana constituted one of the least significant members of both the French and the Spanish colonial systems.

The traffic in slaves to Louisiana accelerated during the last two decades of the eighteenth century, with most of them coming from Senegambia, the Bight of Benin, the Bight of Biafra, Central Africa, Cuba, and Saint-Domingue. Although there was active smuggling of slaves in Louisiana mainly on the part of Scot slave traders in the 1760s and 1770s, a renewed and legalized slave trade under Spanish rule contributed to what one scholar has identified as the "re-Africanization" of Louisiana.[33] During the 1780s Spain and its governors in Louisiana encouraged merchants to import slaves of African descent from the West Indies. A royal *cédula* (decree) of 1782 admitted slaves disembarked from French West Indies ports duty-free. Two years later another decree modified that cédula, allowing certain slaves to enter duty-free but charging a 6-percent duty on other bondpersons. A liberal proclamation in 1789 granted freedom to black slaves who fled from alien lands and sought sanctuary in Louisiana. In light of the Saint-Domingue revolt that erupted in 1791 and Louisianians' fears that black slaves from the French islands would inspire their own slaves to rebel, the Spanish governor François-Louis Hector, baron de Carondelet et Noyelles banned slave imports from the West Indies. Carondelet lifted restrictions in 1793 but reinstituted them in June 1795, to last for the duration of the Franco-Spanish war. Even though the war ended one month later, the rebellion in Saint-Domingue continued; Carondelet issued a new proclamation forbidding the entrance of any black slaves, even those coming directly from Africa, into the colony. Although Louisianians continued to smuggle slaves in order to meet their rising labor needs, local authorities did not again sanction the foreign slave trade until 1800.[34]

Such material conditions as a flexible, diverse economy and a scarcity of white women, artisans, and soldiers contributed to the emergence of a free black population in colonial Louisiana. Because there were few white women, white males engaged in forced and consensual relations with Indians, Africans, and castas. Local officials, ecclesiastics, and settlers rarely condemned these interracial unions. Although most of the resulting offspring remained enslaved, the few French colonials who did free their slaves usually manumitted their mixed-race children and mistresses. French law stipulated that only the slaveholder could initiate manumission proceedings. Thus if a master refused to allow his or her slaves to purchase themselves or did not free them by donation or testamentary disposition, they had no recourse before the law. Urban slaves, especially skilled ones, most frequently purchased their freedom. As white artisans increasingly deserted the colony, free black artisans replaced them. The French crown also granted freedom to a few slaves for defending Louisiana from foreign invasions and native attacks. Placing libres in a middling position, strategically poised economically, legally, and socially between slaves and whites, French officials intended to utilize, and at the same time control, the growing number of free blacks in Louisiana.

From the very beginning of the city's history, libres resided in New

Orleans, but their exact numbers were unknown because French census takers did not indicate whether persons of African descent were slave or free. They consolidated free blacks with either hired hands or black slaves. The 1721 census of New Orleans enumerated 145 white men, 65 white women, 38 children, 29 white servants, 172 blacks, and 21 Indian slaves. By 1726 New Orleans' black population had risen to 300 but dropped to 258 in 1732 (28.9 percent of a total population numbering 893).[35] Only when Spain effectively took over Louisiana in 1769 did census takers begin to distinguish between libres and slaves, *pardos* (light-skinned blacks) and *morenos* (dark-skinned blacks).[36] Undercounting of libres continued, however, in both urban and rural areas of the province.

It was during the Spanish period that libres in New Orleans made their greatest advances in terms of demographics, privileges, responsibilities, and social standing. They jumped from 7.1 percent of the city's African American population in 1769 to a high of 33.5 percent in 1805. Over this period the free black population also expanded in absolute numbers; the immigration of Saint-Domingue refugees and natural reproduction fueled this growth well into the antebellum era.[37] Contrary to demographic trends found for many Spanish American regions at the beginning of the nineteenth century, libres never outnumbered slaves in New Orleans; they nevertheless made up a substantial proportion of the nonwhite population, just as they did in South Carolina and Florida.[38]

I have reconstructed the world of late-eighteenth-century New Orleans from the perspective of its free black residents with the help of a wide variety of primary sources, most of them housed in archives in Louisiana and Spain.[39] Numerous (albeit all too often unreliable) census materials, abundant collections of civil, ecclesiastical, and military records, and contemporary correspondence and travelers' accounts provide insights into the origins, growth, family formation, military and political participation, economic and social activities, and attitudes of free blacks. Fortunately for colonial scholars, Spain has a rich legal tradition. Its government, military, and church officials recorded and preserved almost every piece of information concerning Spanish Louisiana, although some data have been lost to time, neglect, and natural disaster. It is hoped that the strengths of many records make up for the weaknesses of a few and enable us to delve into the "foreign country" that is the past.

The most useful and utilized sources for analyzing the activities of "common folk" are notarial, judicial, and sacramental records. They constitute the most essential and numerous documents for the study of daily life in colonial New Orleans. For almost any business transaction to be legitimate according to Spanish law, it had to be recorded before a notary and paid for with the appropriate fee. When Spain assumed judicial control of Louisiana, royal officials reorganized its legal system and specified the duties of various notaries. In order to prevent fraud and malpractice Governor Luis de Unzaga y Amezaga declared on 3 November 1770 that

> no person, whatever be his or her rank or condition, shall henceforth sell, alienate, buy, or accept as a donation or other wise, any slaves, plantations, houses and any kind of sea-craft, except it be by a deed executed before a Notary Public; to which contracts and acts of sale and alienation shall be annexed a certificate of the Registrar of Mortgages; that all other made under any other form shall be null and void.[40]

These notaries (two in the 1770s and 1780s, three in the 1790s and early 1800s) recorded wills, antenuptial contracts, obligations, receipts, realty and personalty transactions, slave manumissions, and slave rental and apprenticeship agreements. They are organized by notary and located in the Orleans Parish Notarial Archives (OPNA), with those pertaining to the Spanish period and containing information on free blacks as follows: Juan Bautista Garic, nos. 2–12, 1771–79; Andrés Almonester y Roxas, unnumbered volumes, 1771–79, 1782 and nos. 1–2, 1781; Leonardo Mazange, 12 of Garic and nos. 1–7, 1779–83; Rafael Perdomo, last volume of Almonester y Roxas and nos. 1–16, 1782–90; Fernando Rodríguez, nos. 1–13, 1783–87; Pedro Pedesclaux, nos. 1–45, 1788–1803; Carlos Ximénez, no. 16 of Perdomo and nos. 1–19, 1790–1803; Francisco Broutin, no. 1 of Narciso Broutin and nos. 1–51, 1790–99; Narciso Broutin, nos. 1–61, 1799–1803; Esteban de Quiñones, nos. 1–9, 1778–1802; Court Proceedings of C. Ximénez, R. Perdomo, F. Broutin, and N. Broutin, 1784–1803.[41] In this work they are cited as a whole as the Notarial Records and individually as "Acts of" or "Court Proceedings of" the notary by last name, volume number, folio numbers, and date. Records that include libres or manumission of slaves begin in 1771; statistical analysis and case studies that derive from the notarial acts start from that date and are carried through 1803, the end of Spanish rule.

Disputed civil cases and criminal trials came under the jurisdiction of civil, military, and ecclesiastical tribunals, and notaries preserved the deliberations associated with these proceedings too. Parties brought civil and criminal disputes before *alcaldes* (judges elected by the *cabildo* or municipal council), the cabildo, or the governor, who also sat with the cabildo. An ecclesiastical court presided over cases to which clergy were party and over litigation involving marital disputes, permission to marry, and bigamy and other "moral" crimes. Military personnel protected by the *fuero militar* (military privileges) also came before the governor's tribunal, while the intendant adjudicated smuggling, customs, and treasury actions. All of these constitute the "Court Proceedings" arranged by notary at OPNA as well as the Spanish judicial records organized chronologically at the Louisiana State Museum's Historical Center (LHC). It is unclear why these records were divided and placed in two separate archives.

Also vital to this study are the sacramental records of St. Louis Parish, which encompassed New Orleans in the colonial era. These are the baptismal, marriage, and burial registers under the purview of the Archives of the Archdiocese of New Orleans and housed at the old Ursuline Convent in the French Quarter. Only in the past few years, under the able administration of Dr. Charles Nolan, have they been made available to scholars. These records mark the major rites of passage in the Catholic church, the only official religion in the Spanish empire, and are essential for reconstructing kinship and patronage networks. Through them, one can glimpse at the delicate relationships forged between and among libres, whites, and slaves, especially interracial unions and the reciprocal obligations of ritual or fictive kinship (*compadrazgo*), of which more will be said in chapter 3. Beginning in 1777 Spanish ecclesiastics separated the St. Louis Parish registers into white and nonwhite books for all three sacraments, with Native Americans appearing haphazardly in both sets of books. Most free blacks, along with slaves, are in the nonwhite books, although one can see evidence of some libres "passing" as white. Other types of documents identified them as of African descent, yet their families gradually moved from the nonwhite to the white sacramental registers.

Other primary sources utilized in this study were mainly generated by administrative bodies. On the local level they include the Records and Deliberations of the Cabildo (RDC) and the Petitions, Decrees, and Letters of the Cabildo (PDLC), both located at the New Orleans Public Library, Louisiana Division (NOPL). These encompass the minutes of weekly town council meetings and ancillary documents relevant to cabildo proceedings.

As a province, Louisiana was part of the captaincy general of Cuba within the Viceroyalty of New Spain and under the judicial jurisdiction of the *audiencia* (high court) of Santo Domingo. Thus primary materials from the Papeles Procedentes de la Isla de Cuba, Audiencia de Santo Domingo, and Estado sections of the Archivo General de Indias at Seville, Spain, and Guerra Moderna at the Archivo General de Simancas, also in Spain, proved invaluable to this study. Most useful were petitions, correspondence, censuses, militia rosters and regulations, and appellate cases.

One insight many of these documents reveal is that racial identity in New Orleans' hierarchical, patriarchal society was very malleable and subjective. A person's racial designation depended on who recorded it, what purpose it served, when it was recorded, and what physical characteristics were considered most relevant. For example, censuses taken during the era of French rule grouped New Orleanians into whites, blacks, and Indians, with no differentiation as to free or slave. When the Spanish took over, residents were now white, free pardo or moreno, and slave pardo or moreno. Where did all the Louisiana Indians go? They still lived in or around New Orleans,[42] but because Spanish officials outlawed Indian slavery, Native Americans most likely "became" (were reclassified as) persons of African descent. That way, they could still be slaves and would have to sue for their freedom on the basis of native ancestry in later decades. In addition, the terms used to designate phenotype were many and varied, as they were throughout the Spanish empire. People were not simply black or white by virtue of biology but rather fit into the racial hierarchy according to a complex formula that combined physical features, clothing style, language, religion, family reputation, occupation, and other factors and that differed depending on locality and time period.[43]

To simplify matters for the purposes of this study, I use the inclusive somatic terms "free black," "free person of color," and perhaps most preferably "libre" to designate anyone of African descent, be he or she pure African, part white, or part Native American. The exclusive terms pardo (light-skinned) and moreno (dark-skinned) — preferred by contemporary free blacks over *mulato* and *negro*[44] — are utilized to distinguish elements within the nonwhite population. In Spanish Louisiana notaries, parish priests, census takers, military officers, and libres themselves applied the term pardo to anyone who had at least half white ancestry and moreno to anyone with less than half white blood. Occasional references delineate further between *grifo* (in New Orleans the offspring of a pardo[a] and a morena[o] but in the countryside also meaning a mixture of black and native ancestry), *cuarterón* (offspring of a white and a pardo[a]), and *mestizo* (usually the offspring of a white and an *indio[a]* or Indian but in New Orleans sometimes referred to as the offspring of a black and an Indian). Some terms, like mulato mestizo, do not easily fit into this system, but in this case the person in question was placed in the pardo category.

With reference to additional terminology, because France held Louisiana before Spain did and most of the inhabitants spoke French and had French names, notaries and other officials spelled names a variety of ways. This is a study of *Spanish* New Orleans, however, so for consistency most first names are presented in their Spanish form and surnames the way individuals (or, if illiterate, their representatives) most frequently signed them.

The following pages begin with an analysis of the ways in which libres attained freedom, as well as other factors, such as immigration and natural increase, that contributed to the growth and concentration of a substantial free black population in New Orleans by the end of the Spanish era. As they multiplied, libres began to develop a sense of group identity that was further solidified by common experiences and activities: the occupations they pursued on the middle rungs of the economic ladder; the struggle to survive and possibly accumulate enough to improve the lives of their children; the consanguine, affinal, ritual, and *parentela* (patron-client) relations they constructed; the free pardo and moreno militia units with whom they weekly drilled, served in emergency situations, and paraded on feast days; the masses, processionals, baptisms, marriages, and funerals they celebrated in the St. Louis church; the dances and parties they held in places private and public. New Orleans libres forged kinship and patronage connections, attended church and religious ceremonies, and worked and played with whites and slaves, but increasingly did so with one another.

Chapter 1

AVENUES TO FREEDOM

Before free blacks could begin to develop a group consciousness, there had to be enough of them to make up a group, and it was during the late eighteenth and early nineteenth centuries that libres in New Orleans and other circum-Caribbean cities came to constitute a substantial segment of their populations. Evidence from Louisiana supports Arnold A. Sio's argument that "the development of group consciousness among the freedmen occurred in conjunction with an increase in population size and density and with the growth of social organization."[1] Although one must use census figures with caution, they do point to a growing libre presence within the populace over the era of Spanish rule: from 3.1 percent of New Orleanians in 1771 to 19.0 percent in 1805 (table 1.1). As important as size and density, however, was an increasing proportion of native-born blacks (creoles) among the libre population. These creoles were able to forge the kinship networks, join corporate entities like the militia and the church, accumulate the capital to invest in businesses, slaves, and other property, and in general develop the social organization needed to create libre cohesiveness and identity. Whereas a slave's legal status usually changed immediately once he or she became free, manumission did not entail a rapid, automatic alteration in condition (unless the ex-slave had support from other libres and whites) but rather was a process that could take generations to consolidate, with freeborn blacks benefiting from the struggles of their parents. And

TABLE 1.1   Proportion of Libres in the Total, Free,
and Nonwhite Populations, New Orleans, 1771–1805

Year	% of Total Population	N	% of Free Population	N	% of Nonwhite Population	N
1771	3.1	3,127	5.1	1,900	7.3	1,324
1777	9.8	3,202	15.4	2,051	21.5	1,466
1788	15.4	5,321	25.7	3,190	27.8	2,951
1791	17.1	5,037	26.5	3,248	32.5	2,651
1805	19.0	8,222	30.6	5,117	33.5	4,671

Sources: For 1771: Lawrence Kinnaird, *Spain in the Mississippi Valley, 1765–1794*, 4 vols. (Washington, D.C.: American Historical Association, 1946–49), 2:196; for 1777: "Padrón general de todos los individuos de la provincia de Luisiana," AGI PC 2351, 12 May 1777; for 1788: "Resumen general del padrón hecho en la provincia de la Luisiana, distrito de la Movila y plaza de Panzacola," AGI PC 1425, 1788; for 1791: Census of New Orleans, 6 November 1791, Louisiana Collection, NOPL; for 1805: Matthew Flannery, comp., *New Orleans in 1805: A Directory and a Census Together with Resolutions Authorizing Same Now Printed for the First Time* (New Orleans: Pelican Gallery, 1936).

even well-to-do second- and third-generation free blacks remained part of a subordinate group within New Orleans' hierarchical society.

Once libres reached a critical mass, however, which appears to have happened by the end of the Spanish period, they could begin to forge a group identity, a sense of distinctiveness, and exert some influence in the society. Demographic increase and the attainment of a critical mass among libres in New Orleans can be attributed primarily to manumission but also to natural increase and migration as well as escape and "passing" as free. Several factors contributed to the growth of the libre population in colonial New Orleans, among them the city's demographic profile, a demand for manual and skilled laborers, internal and external defensive needs, natural increase, and favorable legislation. The emergence of a free black group existing in an anomalous but constantly coalescing position between whites and slaves dated from the early years of European conquest and colonization of the Americas. The ease and frequency of this transition from bondage to freedom varied spatially and temporally. The Tannenbaum-Elkins school has argued that such institutions as the church and the state influenced slave treatment and access to freedom. Reality often did not match institutional ideals, but in general Tannenbaum correctly observed that the Spanish and Portuguese colonists most readily manumitted their slave property, with the French somewhere in the middle of the spectrum and the British and Dutch most reluctant to part with their bondmen.[2]

Although cultural attitudes influenced this trend, material factors, especially demographic patterns and economic trends, played a much more substantial role. The historian Eugene D. Genovese has labeled this debate as one between idealist and materialist approaches, and it underlies much of the scholarship on slavery and race relations conducted by North and South American, Caribbean, and European scholars.[3] A leading figure among the materialists is anthropologist Marvin Harris, who identified two key demographic variables: (1) the black-to-white ratio and (2) the sex ratio among whites.[4] Where white males heavily outnumbered white females, racial intermixture prevailed and white fathers tended to manumit their light-skinned offspring, and occasionally consorts, over other slaves. Societies that boasted a large black slave population and a small white planter group lacked persons who could perform the artisan, service, and transportation tasks of a middle sector. Both these demographic scenarios gave impetus to the creation of a free black and casta group, and these situations were found most commonly in areas held by Spain and Portugal.

Other materialists argue that market considerations rather than demographics or preexisting European racial attitudes most influenced an individual's or a society's propensity to manumit African slaves.[5] Slave treatment and manumission rates followed economic cycles. During boom periods of rising expectations and prosperity, planters worked their slaves intensively, the value of slaves escalated, and manumissions dropped off. Not only were masters reluctant to part with increasingly scarce labor, but also slaves found it difficult to raise the extra money required to purchase their freedom. On the downside of the economic cycle conditions for slaves could even worsen as slave owners struggled to return to the days of prosperity and worked their slaves harder still. At the very top and bottom of the cycle, however, manumission opportunities for slaves improved. Riding comfortable and secure at the peak of their material good fortune, masters could afford to part with bondmen, especially if slaves reimbursed their owners at inflated self-purchase prices. Inversely, slave owners strapped for cash during periods of extreme hardship also welcomed income from slave self-purchases, as well as release from the burden of caring for elderly or unproductive

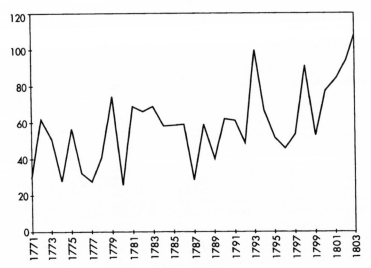

Figure 1.1 Number of manumissions per year, New Orleans.

charges. All too frequently masters reduced their costs by manumitting old, crippled, ill, or retarded slaves.

A combination of all the above—demographic, economic, legal, and cultural influences—as well as the special circumstances prevailing in a frontier society, contributed to the expansion of New Orleans' libre population during the Spanish era. Manumission in particular, along with natural increase and migration/immigration, boosted the number of free blacks and created what can be considered a critical mass. The average number of slave manumissions per year increased with each decade of the late eighteenth and early nineteenth centuries (figure 1.1).[6] In addition, the proportion of slaves obtaining liberty through their own or a third party's efforts with compensation to the master, rather than those given their freedom gratis (*graciosa*), rose from slightly less than half of all manumissions in the 1770s to more than two-thirds in the early 1800s (table 1.2). Along with the various legal avenues to freedom available to and pursued by persons of African descent were those methods deemed illegal and antisocial by the dominant white society: rebelling, running away, passing as free. They have been adequately investigated by other scholars[7] and will be referred to only occasionally in this work.

TABLE 1.2 Decade by Type of Manumission, New Orleans

Decade	Uncompensated	Compensated	Total	Average Number/Year
1771–1779	208 (52.0%)	192 (48.0%)	400	44.4
1780–1789	240 (45.2%)	290 (54.8%)	530	53.0
1790–1799	231 (36.7%)	397 (73.3%)	628	62.8
1800–1803	119 (32.7%)	244 (77.3%)	363	90.8
All years	798 (41.5%)	1,123 (58.4%)	1,921	58.2

Source: Notarial Records.

The Setting: Demographic, Economic, and Legal Conditions

At the time of Spain's acquisition, blacks outnumbered whites and white males outnumbered white females in most regions of Louisiana.[8] Thus there existed within the colony demographic elements favoring the growth of a free black population. In addition, Spanish administrators faced French merchants and planters who professed questionable loyalty and at times outright hostility toward Spain's rule in the colony. According to one author,

> the slaves were the wedge between countervailing French planter power and official Spanish authority, and the governors seem at times to have sought the approval of slaves in order to make them a counterpoise to the planters, whose allegiance to Spain was far from certain.[9]

Faced with a potentially restless multitude of African slaves and a small but vocal ensemble of resentful colonials, Spain courted the favor of any and all segments of Louisiana's society and encouraged the immigration of loyal subjects.[10]

Data presented in table 1.3 detail the city's demographic character over the period by status and sex. Although census figures conflict and provide only approximate accuracy, they can be used to study trends and as such reveal a growing population. During the Spanish period the white population of New Orleans almost doubled, while the slave population grew two and a half times. As a result of restrictions on slave importations, the num-

TABLE 1.3   New Orleans Population by Status and Sex, 1771–1805

Year	Whites				Free Blacks				Slaves			
	M	F	Total	Sex Ratio	M	F	Total	Sex Ratio	M	F	Total	Sex Ratio
1771	—	—	1,803	—	—	—	97	—	—	—	1,227	—
1777	1,104	632	1,736	175	101	214	315	47	518	633	1,151	82
1788	1,310	1,060	2,370	124	233	587	820	40	956	1,175	2,131	81
1791	1,474	912	2,386	162	324	538	862	60	871	918	1,789	95
1805	1,901	1,650	3,551	115	624	942	1,566	66	1,338	1,767	3,105	76

Sources: For 1771: Kinnaird, *Spain in the Mississippi Valley*, 2:196; for 1777: "Padrón general de todos los individuos de la provincia de Luisiana," AGI PC 2351, 12 May 1777; for 1788: "Resumen general del padrón hecho en la provincia de la Luisiana, distrito de la Movila y plaza de Panzacola," AGI PC 1425, 1788; for 1791: 1791 Census; for 1805: Flannery, *New Orleans in 1805*.

ber of slaves in New Orleans decreased in the 1790s but then multiplied in the early 1800s in response to the growing demand for slave labor and the lifting of import bans. The number of free blacks increased sixteenfold, and this group reportedly was undercounted throughout the period![11] By the end of the Spanish period libres made up almost one-fifth of the New Orleans populace (table 1.1).

As in many frontier regions, white males consistently outnumbered white females, with a sex ratio ranging from a high of 175 (175 males to every 100 females) in 1777 to a low of 115 in 1805 (table 1.3); the opposite held true for slaves and free blacks. Sex ratios among slaves were much more balanced than among libres and almost evened out in the early 1790s. In most urban centers like New Orleans, there were more slave females—mainly domestics—than males, in contrast to the countryside, where planters preferred men slaves to work the fields and perform skilled and managerial tasks.[12] Among libres, however, the disparity was much greater: females outnumbered males about two to one, primarily because about twice as many females as males acquired *cartas de libertad* (certificates of manumission) and because male libres tended to die at very young ages. For libres of childbearing age, sex ratios were even more unbalanced; the census of 1791, which categorized residents into three age groups (0–13, 14–49, 50+), shows that the sex ratio for those libres age fourteen through forty-nine was 39 (108 for ages 0–13 and 21 for 50+). High sex ratios among presumably non–sexually active children skewed the overall ratios upward and when factored out, reveal the very disproportionate numbers of adult libre females, who even if they had wanted to would have had difficulties finding a free black mate.

Such uneven sex ratios contributed to racial mixture in New Orleans and other American frontier territories, where white females were scarce and women of indigenous or African descent were plentiful. White conquerors, no matter what their nationality, believed that one of the rewards of conquest consisted of sexual favors from subordinated peoples, and thus there emerged a casta population. During the years of Spanish rule New Orleans became less of a frontier town and more of a cosmopolitan commercial city, and sex ratios reflect the transition. By the early nineteenth century, sex ratios for whites and free blacks had narrowed and more closely approached parity, thereby giving libres more opportunities to establish relationships with each other and promoting the emergence of a distinct free black community and identity. Indeed, marriages and consensual arrangements among free blacks, rather than between them and whites or slaves, increased toward the turn of the century (see chapter 3).

Offspring resulting from these interracial and intraracial unions often added to the free black populace. The percentage of libres increased not only in the total but also in the free and nonwhite populations over the period of Spanish rule (table 1.1). In fact, between 1788 and 1791 free blacks were the only group that grew. The percentage of libres expanded foremost among nonwhites, followed by free persons and then all persons. Primarily an urban phenomenon, the growth of a libre population in New Orleans was not replicated throughout Louisiana, where in rural areas free blacks remained small in both numbers and percentage of the populace, especially when compared to slaves.[13] In Louisiana, as throughout the American colonies, "all legal forms of manumission seem to have been more beneficent for the urban slave," who had closer relationships with the master (voluntary and involuntary), opportunities to learn skills, and easier access to borrowed credit sources and the judicial system.[14] Thus the libre population grew not only in size but also in density, concentrating more and more in New Orleans, a tendency that accelerated with the influx of Saint-Domingue refugees in 1809 and diminished only with increased repression after 1840.[15]

In Louisiana, as in many areas of Spanish America, the crown fostered the growth of a free black population in order to fill middle-sector occupations, defend the colony from external and internal foes, and give African and creole slaves an officially approved means to realize their desires for freedom. Colonial policymakers envisioned a society in which Africans would seek their freedom through legal channels, complete with compensation for their masters, rather than by running away or rising in revolt. In turn, slaves would look to the Spanish government to "rescatarnos de la esclavitud" (rescue/ransom us from slavery) and subsequently protect their rights and privileges as freedmen.[16]

With this vision in mind, Spain, upon acquiring Louisiana from France, made colonial laws conform to those prevailing throughout the empire. For the governing of slaves and free blacks, Spanish Louisiana codes (commonly referred to as "O'Reilly's Laws" for the early Spanish governor who proclaimed them) primarily drew upon provisions of Las Siete Partidas and the Recopilación de leyes de los reinos de las Indias (Compilation of the Laws of the Kingdoms of the Indies, which drew together diverse legislation applying to Spain's New World empire in 1681)[17] and also were influenced by the French Code noir (Black code) that had been issued for the French West Indies in 1685 and introduced in Louisiana in 1724. The Code noir imposed harsh penalties upon erring slaves and "proved to be one of the more oppressive slave codes in the Americas." It did, however, grant free blacks full legal rights to citizenship, even though this provision was inconsistent with preceding articles of the code that provided for unequal punishments and restricted their behavior.[18] In addition, local regulations frequently impinged on these rights, denying free blacks legal equality with white citizens.[19] When Spain took effective control of Louisiana in 1769, it imposed its laws on the colony, overriding the Code noir in the face of French planter resistance. By and large, Spanish officials enforced their government's laws, at least in the capital of New Orleans, where the bureaucratic and judicial structure was strongest. For example, even though the planter-dominated cabildo wrote and passed a much harsher slave code than the Spanish ones in 1778, the crown never approved it and judges continued to follow imperial law.[20]

Included in Spanish law emanating from Cuba and implemented in Louisiana was the codification of a customary practice known as *coartación,* the right of slaves "to purchase their freedom for a stipulated sum of money agreed upon by their masters or arbitrated in the courts."[21] Louisiana's Code noir had permitted masters over the age of twenty-five to manumit their slaves, with prior consent from the superior council (the French colonial governing body). Spanish regulations, however, did not require official permission for a master to free his or her slave and even allowed slaves to initiate manumission proceedings on their own behalf. The slave, a friend, or a relative could request a carta de libertad in front of the governor's tribunal. Two and sometimes three assessors declared the slave's monetary value, and upon receipt of that sum the tribunal issued the slave his or her carta. Under Spanish law a slave did not have to depend on the generosity of the master to attain freedom; rather, the slave relied on his or her own efforts and the aid of a favorable legal system. Louisiana slaves and parties arguing on their behalf recognized support from Spanish officials for "a cause so recommended by the law as that of liberty"[22] and began to realize that their "aspirations for liberty rested on the administration of justice by the Spanish in the colony." In addition, the institution of self-purchase "expressed the Spanish recognition (1) that slavery was not the natural condition of men; (2) that slaves had a right to aspire to freedom; and (3) that masters had a right to just return for their property."[23] It also recognized the slave's property rights (*peculium*).

Indeed, the text of several Spanish documents indicates that slaves and free persons acting in the interest of slaves were aware of and acted upon the privileges extended to them by Spain.[24] In all likelihood, as the Spanish period unfolded, New Orleans slaves and interests acting on their behalf gained greater experience, which allowed them to take advantage of the privileges Spain's judicial system offered. With the exception of the last decade, the number of cases brought before governors' and alcaldes' tribunals rose dramatically during the era under study. Like Africans in other colonial regions, slaves in New Orleans often had to struggle to secure their rights. Slave and master frequently haggled over the purchase price: in the absence of a written contract the slave encountered difficulties proving the existence of an agreement; sometimes courts denied slaves' petitions for freedom or set the purchase price prohibitively high; and if written in a will, provisions for self-purchase or gratis manumission could be—but rarely were— disputed by heirs.[25]

Nevertheless, in most cases coartación offered advantages to slaveholders, slaves, and the Spanish government alike. All three groups acted according to their best interests. The crown benefited from a growing libre population that tended to accept its middle status in a three-tiered society, aspired to attain the privileges of white subjects, and supplied the colony with skilled laborers and defensive forces. Coartación provided slave owners with incentives that encouraged slaves to work more productively, reduced their provisioning costs, and compensated them at the slaves' estimated fair values. Legal manumission also acted as an effective form of social control by holding out liberty to obedient bondpersons and denying it to rebellious ones. In turn, the system facilitated slaves' efforts to acquire the necessary cash or goods with which to purchase freedom independent of their masters' will.

Statistical Trends of Manumission

During the period when Spain ruled New Orleans, black slaves utilized both familiar and new, more effective methods guaranteed by Spanish law and practice to attain the status of libre. For the purposes of analysis, this study groups efforts to escape bondage through legal channels into two broad categories: (1) proceedings instituted voluntarily by the slave's master, who received no compensation (graciosa), and (2) those in which the slave or a third party took the initiative and the master was compensated in

TABLE 1.4 Phenotype and Sex of Slave by Type of
Manumission, New Orleans, 1771–1803

Phenotype and Sex		Gra-ciosa	Condi-tional	Self-Purchase	Third-Party Purchase	Tri-bunal	Total
Cuarterón	Female	35	4	7	25	3	74
	Male	17	0	1	23	0	41
Pardo	Female	180	23	49	91	30	373
	Male	148	8	26	93	16	291
Grifo	Female	9	0	9	15	2	35
	Male	6	0	1	8	0	15
Moreno	Female	260	25	242	104	55	686
	Male	86	6	116	56	34	298
Not given		57	6	1	30	14	108
Total		798	72	452	445	154	1,921

Source: Notarial Records.

the form of either money or additional service. The latter category is further differentiated according to who provided the compensation and whether the arrangement was agreed upon informally or the slave or an interested party had to take the master to court (conditional, self-purchase, third-party purchase, tribunal).

As noted previously, the overall number of manumissions, as well as the average per year, rose with each decade of Spanish rule, contributing to the libre population in substantial numbers (table 1.2). In addition, between 1771 (when notarial records begin registering manumissions) and 1803, an increasing percentage of slaves attained freedom by way of their own or a third party's initiative and with compensation to the slaveholder: 58.4 percent overall, rising from slightly less than half of all manumission cases in the 1770s to slightly more than three-quarters in the early 1800s. Concurrently, a declining proportion had to rely on their master's generosity (41.5 percent overall). Of compensated manumissions, about one out of seven was contested and involved bringing the owner or his or her guardian, executor, or legal representative before a tribunal to settle the dispute.[26]

A profile of the average slave who entered the libre population by way

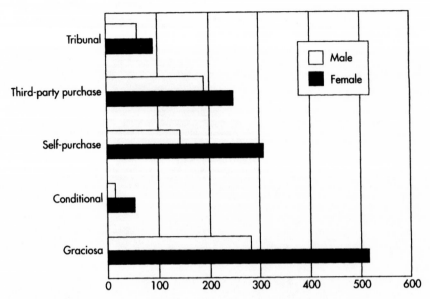

Figure 1.2 Type of manumission by sex, New Orleans, 1771–1803.

of legal manumission would depict a morena woman between the ages of fourteen and forty-nine who compensated her typically white male master with money or service provided by herself or a third party at an average cost of 347 pesos (the peso was equivalent to the dollar, which was based on the peso). Within almost every avenue to freedom females outnumbered males roughly two to one (table 1.4 and figure 1.2) for an overall sex ratio of 57. This ratio was comparable to that for manumitted populations in most American slave societies.[27] It also paralleled the sex ratio for New Orleans free blacks as a whole (an average of about 60) but was lower than that for the city's slaves, whose sex ratio hovered around 82 and rose to 95 in 1805. Thus, compared to their proportion of the total New Orleans slave population, bondwomen secured freedom more frequently than did bondmen. This trend can be attributed in part to the fact that female slaves could more readily acquire the necessary funds by selling services and goods and by begging. They were also frequently domestics involved in close relations with their masters and mistresses, who were more likely to free them gratis. In addition, less valuable females were able to collect their purchase prices more quickly, and masters were more willing to part with them than with male slaves, who were viewed as more uncontrollable and a greater threat to

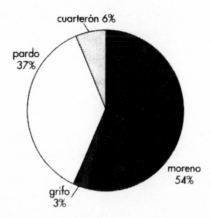

Figure 1.3 Phenotype of manumitted slaves, New Orleans, 1771–1803.

social order. Finally, female slaves outnumbered male slaves in urban areas like New Orleans, where self-purchase was more common.[28] The sex ratio was slightly higher among those slaves who compensated their owners (59) than those who did not (55), confirming a New World–wide finding that coartación tended to favor males and offer them more numerous opportunities to earn their freedom.[29] The difference, however, was negligible, and given that among slaves who purchased cartas themselves, the sex ratio was 47, it appears that in New Orleans at least coartación primarily benefited female slaves, whereas males more often obtained freedom through third-party purchase (table 1.4).

In terms of phenotype of the manumitted, New Orleans followed the pattern of most slave societies in the Americas, where gratis and third-party manumissions tended to favor pardos, especially children, and self-purchase offered morenos an equal or greater opportunity to achieve free status.[30] Overall, slaves with more than half African blood (morenos and grifos) made up 56.7 percent of those manumitted for whom race was clearly indicated ($N = 1,825$) and excluding thirteen indio and mestizo slaves (figure 1.3). Considering phenotype and age data together indicates that many of the slaves manumitted freely or with the assistance of a third party were the children of white males (table 1.5). Light-skinned slaves (pardos and cuarterones) obtained free status mainly as children and rarely as elderly persons; those of darker phenotype were manumitted overwhelmingly as adults or seniors who had to secure their own freedom without benefit from the lar-

TABLE 1.5   Age Category and Phenotype of Slave by Type of
Manumission, New Orleans, 1771–1803

Age Category and Phenotype		Gra- ciosa	Condi- tional	Self- Pur- chase	Third- Party Purchase	Tri- bunal	Total
Age 1	Pardo	245	18	1	190	17	471
(1–13)	Moreno	44	5	4	71	3	127
	Indio	3	1	0	0	0	4
	Not given	37	2	0	22	2	63
	Total	329	26	5	283	22	665
Age 2	Pardo	108	14	60	33	11	226
(14–49)	Moreno	176	19	210	69	23	497
	Indio	3	1	0	0	0	4
	Not given	4	1	0	2	0	7
	Total	291	35	270	104	34	734
Age 3	Pardo	4	0	6	0	0	10
(50+)	Moreno	87	4	103	19	7	220
	Indio	1	0	0	0	0	1
	Not given	0	0	0	0	0	0
	Total	92	4	109	19	7	231

Source: Notarial Records.

gess of others, be they parents, masters, friends, or relatives. For the manumitted population as a whole, 40.8 percent were under the age of fourteen,
45.0 percent were between the ages of fourteen and forty-nine, and 14.2 percent were fifty years of age or older ($N = 1,629$, those for whom an age was
given). This compared with the age distribution in 1791 for the entire libre
population (44.1, 46.2, and 9.5 percent respectively) and the entire slave
population (28.1, 68.7, and 3.1 percent respectively). It appears that masters
were manumitting a higher proportion of senior and junior slaves and fewer
prime-age slaves, confirming what scholars have found for other North and
South American slave societies.[31] Relatively larger numbers of manumitted
children and elderly expanded both ends of the age structure among free

TABLE 1.6 Average Price for Manumission (in Pesos Fuertes) by
Decade and Slave's Sex, New Orleans

Decade	Females	N	Males	N
1771–1779	254	97	270	57
1780–1789	419	166	507	101
1790–1799	355	244	328	136
1800–1803	359	131	385	101
All years	347	638	373	395

Source: Notarial Records.

blacks, although high death rates for young and old libres (discussed below)
modified their effect.

With each passing decade manumission of oneself or a slave relative or
friend required more resources (table 1.6). The price for a carta de libertad especially jumped in the 1780s—most likely on account of the increasing commercialization of agriculture and its concomitant demand for slave
labor[32]—fell back in the 1790s (but not to 1770s levels), and rose slightly in
the early 1800s. Yearly fluctuations were more volatile but also point to rising
costs (figure 1.4). Manumission for males was generally more expensive
than for females, except during the 1790s. Nevertheless, both sexes' prices
were fairly comparable, with an average difference of no more than thirty
pesos except in the 1780s, when, once again, male agricultural laborers were
especially valuable and not readily released from slavery. Whether one was
female or male, however, the purchase of a carta represented a major invest-
ment for the slave or a third party, be that party white, free black, or another
slave. In Louisiana the price of freedom rose even higher in the antebellum
era, as officials closed the foreign slave trade and restricted opportunities for
manumission. Many libres and poor whites labored long years and used the
bulk of their scarce resources to free themselves or friends and kin, indicating the premium they placed on freedom. Whether real or not in material
terms, there was at least a perceived difference between bondage and liberty.

An examination of masters who freed their slaves by one or another of
the various methods available reveals that all favored manumitting females,

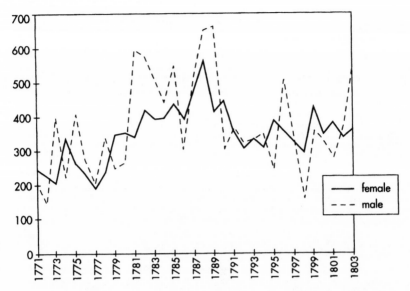

Figure 1.4 Average price (in pesos fuertes) paid for manumission by year and sex, New Orleans.

a tendency especially marked among light-skinned female (parda) and dark-skinned male (moreno) owners (tables 1.7 and 1.8). Given that the sex ratio for all slaves freed was 57, the manumission patterns for whites of both sexes and moreno and pardo males were fairly close to the norm, whereas pardas freed a higher proportion of female slaves and morenas more male slaves. In terms of type of manumission, about two-thirds (63.6 percent, or 133 masters) of the slaves owned by free blacks obtained freedom graciosa, compared with slightly less than two-fifths belonging to whites (39.0 percent, or 665 masters). A very small percentage of both white and libre owners requested additional service of their slaves (3.9 and 2.9 percent respectively). Of the remaining slaves belonging to libres, 37 (17.7 percent) purchased their freedom, 25 (12.0 percent) received funds from a third party, and 8 (3.8 percent) sought redress before a tribunal. Respective numbers for the slaves of white owners were 414 (24.3 percent), 417 (24.5 percent), and 143 (8.4 percent). Obviously, many libre masters were holding and then manumitting without compensation their slave kin, a topic discussed more fully in chapter 2.

A look at the masters themselves shows that nine out of ten were white and three out of four were male. Among both white and libre manumit-

TABLE I.7 Owner's Phenotype and Sex by Sex of Slave Manumitted, New Orleans, 1771–1803

Owner's Phenotype and Sex		Slave Female	Slave Male	Sex Ratio
White	Female	228	137	60
	Male	847	488	58
Pardo	Female	37	9	24
	Male	33	19	58
Moreno	Female	35	29	83
	Male	30	16	53

Source: Notarial Records.

ters, males outnumbered females by ratios much higher than those for their phenotypes as a whole (a ratio of 363 compared with 115 in 1805 for whites; 113 compared with 66 in 1805 for free blacks). This observation raises the likelihood that men owned—or at least had a controlling interest in—more slaves than did women and/or were more willing or financially able to manumit their slaves. The latter especially applies to libres, who were more likely to manumit slaves without compensation and thus would need greater financial resources.

TABLE I.8 Owner's Phenotype and Sex by Type of Manumission, New Orleans, 1771–1803

Owner's Phenotype and Sex		Gra-ciosa	Condi-tional	Self-Purchase	Third-Party Purchase	Tri-bunal	Total
White	Female	111	8	94	107	48	368
	Male	554	58	320	310	95	1,337
	Total	665	66	414	417	143	1,705
Libre	Female	61	0	29	18	3	111
	Male	72	6	8	7	5	98
	Total	133	6	37	25	8	209

Source: Notarial Records.

Types of Manumission Elucidated

Emancipation trends over the length of the Spanish period indicate that graciosa manumissions dropped off slightly in the 1790s; manumissions conditioned upon additional service rose in the 1770s to a high of twelve in 1779,
tapered off in the early 1780s, and disappeared almost entirely thereafter;
self-purchases rose after the 1770s, where they plateaued in the teens; third-
party purchases spiraled upward from the late 1780s onward; tribunal cases
also increased after the late 1780s but dropped off in the early 1800s.[33] It appears that as a percentage, fewer slaves were being given their freedom voluntarily and gratis and that more had to turn to a relative or friend or to the
courts for assistance. Nevertheless, overall the most common type of manumission remained the former, conferred during the master's lifetime (inter
vivos donation) or as a result of a testamentary behest; 798 (516 females and
282 males) of a total 1,921 slaves freed before a notary between 1771 and 1803
entered the libre population this way. In addition to manumitting slaves unconditionally during their lifetimes, slaveholders wrote provisions into their
wills for the eventual liberation of beloved servants. The time elapsed between the writing of the last testament and actual death, and thus freedom
for the designated slave, could amount to a few days or several years; indeed,
emancipation would not occur at all if the slave predeceased the master.[34]
Masters seldom granted cartas to all their slaves en masse. In their wills they
selectively conferred liberty gratis upon a favored few, allowed others to
purchase their freedom, and relegated the majority to continued bondage.

A greater proportion of libres than whites manumitted slaves without any
form of compensation, either by inter vivos donation or testamentary act
(table 1.8). One of them was the moreno libre Henrique Sambas, who issued
cartas to his morena slave and her daughter at the end of nine years of service.[35] In addition to holding slaves as investments and laborers, free blacks
purchased and freed parents, siblings, children, grandchildren, and godchildren. For elderly libres in particular the sums required to buy and manumit
slave kin took long years to accumulate. Often they could afford to invest
in little else.[36] In some instances free blacks had to purchase relatives and
friends on credit and could not free them until after repaying the debt. For
unexplained reasons, one pardo libre, Juan Medes, bought his grifo son Luis
but did not manumit him until twenty years later.[37]

Free blacks also wrote wills in which they freed slaves. Simón, a grifo libre, liberated his morena slave María, sixteen, whom he had raised in his house like a daughter, and appointed his grandfather, the moreno libre Alexandro, as her guardian. Simón also named María his only heir to property that included twelve cows, seven horses, and two arpents of land four leagues upriver from New Orleans in the district of Tchoupitoulas.[38] The morena libre Magdalena Naneta, alias Lecler, ordered her executor to free at her death two of her three slaves and to purchase the freedom of her slave husband at his estimated worth.[39]

In several instances white and libre slaveholders liberated without compensation an adult woman and her children, or even more complex kin units. In 1773 Don Juan Robin Sr. manumitted his morena slave María, age forty-eight, and three of María's children, all pardos born in Robin's house: Juan Luis (eighteen), María Juana (twenty-seven), and Isabel (twenty). In addition, Robin freed Isabel's two young daughters, Juana and Francisca. A few months later Robin voluntarily freed Catarina, an eighteen-year-old morena, and her four-year-old daughter, Holineta, also born in his house. Robin concurrently recorded his last will and testament in the notarial archives and passed away soon thereafter.[40] Almost two decades later the Anglo merchant brothers Evan and James Jones freed graciosa a morena slave, her parda daughter, and her cuarterón grandson, each successive generation a lighter phenotype. They manumitted the women for their long years of service and the eleven-month-old baby boy out of love and affection.[41] A few years earlier, Don Joseph Duval Demouy manumitted without additional compensation his forty-year-old morena slave, her nine pardo children ranging in age from twenty-four years to ten months, and her two parda granddaughters, ages two years and eight months.[42]

Slaveholders usually manumitted these female-headed families for good and loyal services and the love and care they had shown the master, without any allusion to informal sexual relationships or common-law unions. In some cases, however, these kinds of relationships can be deduced. For example, in 1773 Raymundo Gaillard manumitted his parda slave Marion, forty-seven years old, along with her six children, all cuarterones: Constanza (thirteen), Margarita (eleven), Adelaida (nine), Raymundo (at seven the oldest son, probably named after his father), Helena (five), and Basilio (eighteen months). In 1775 these same children received a donation of property from Gaillard, and according to the 1778 census of New Orleans, the parda libre Marion, her eight children, and one slave woman lived with

Gaillard, a cooper, on the left side of Ursulines Street. When she wrote her will and codicil in 1802, Marion Dubreuil identified herself as a native of New Orleans and the natural daughter of Juana, a deceased morena libre. She also listed her ten surviving natural children, five by Gaillard and five older ones by her first mate, the deceased moreno libre Bauptista. Among her belongings was a plot of land on the corner of Dumaine and Bourbon on which Don Raymundo had built her a house.[43]

Another man who emancipated and coresided with his parda mate and their offspring was Don Santiago Lemelle, a ship captain and native of New Orleans of French and German parentage. After holding her as a slave for ten years, Lemelle freed Jaquelina and her children Agata (twelve), Tonton (three), and Adelaida (one) in 1772. Shortly afterward, Jaquelina purchased cartas for her daughter María Juana and granddaughter Julia from Don Francisco Lemelle, brother of Santiago, for two hundred pesos. Don Francisco added the condition that Julia, who was four years old, serve him as his slave until she reached the age of twelve. According to the 1778 census, Santiago, Jaquelina, their four children, and one female slave lived on the left side of Ursulines Street, probably near the Gaillard family.[44] Lemelle died in 1784, and "although he did not admit paternity in his will, Santiago Lemelle named the free mulatress Jacquelina and her children, Agata, María Juana [alias Tonton], and Adelaida, his universal heirs."[45] Don Santiago specifically donated to all three some houses on Royal Street, to Jaquelina a morena slave named Francisca, and to her daughters a morena slave named Eulalia, two hundred pesos, and one-half his household goods. Jaquelina Lemelle also had a son named Luis Dusuau, a cuarterón libre, by Don Joseph Dusuau de la Croix.[46] Don Santiago and Jaquelina's daughter Adelaida Lemelle also maintained a long-term relationship with a white man, Don Luis Bruno Giradeau, and had at least nine children with him before he died in 1811.[47]

White and free black slaveholders who manumitted slave women and their children the same or the next day after purchasing them most likely were united in consensual unions. Take, for example, Juan Duriol and Juan Jason. In 1793 Duriol bought from Miguel Dapena a thirty-six-year-old morena slave and her three-year-old pardo son and freed them the next day graciosamente for services (of one day?!) and affection. One month earlier Jason, a moreno libre, purchased and liberated a morena slave, forty-two years of age, and her eighteen-month-old daughter. No other reason than love motivated Jason's act.[48] That same year strong feelings of affection moved

Don Luis Hazeur Delorme, a cavalryman in the Royal Military Order of St. Louis and former captain-commander of the Guadeloupe Regiment, to manumit graciosa his three-month-old cuarterona slave Helena. His mother had donated Helena to him that very day. In addition, Don Luis paid his mother six hundred pesos to free Helena's mother, the parda Feliciana Dreux Hazeur. The couple had three additional children prior to the end of the Spanish period, all born free because their mother was now free.[49]

Indeed, when a slave owner freed the very young pardo children of a morena slave, the stock term "for services rendered" can be doubted and a closer relationship than master-slave postulated. In 1776 Don Alejandro Chauvin de la Frenière voluntarily emancipated María Serafina, three years old, and Rosa, eighteen months old, parda daughters of his morena slave Carlota. He freed them out of great love for their mother and "other particulars that moved him."[50] Don René Huchet de Kernion manumitted the young pardo sons of the morena slave Susana: Francisco, Jácobo, and Junón, whom he had inherited from his father.[51] In these cases and many others white and libre male slaveholders owned or purchased and then freed only their offspring, leaving the mothers and presumed consorts in slavery. With consanguine ties stronger than affinal ones, these men obviously did not value their concubines as much as their children. But at least they manumitted their offspring; many more men never did so.

Occasionally slaveholders officially admitted paternity when freeing their slaves graciosa. When Carlos Begin manumitted the pardito Carlos in October 1793, he recognized the slave as his natural son by the morena María, also his slave. The eight-month-old Carlos was baptized one day later. Begin died intestate the following May, and Carlos Jr.'s guardian had to sue the succession to claim the child's inheritance. An inventory of Begin's property placed its value at 646 pesos 3 reales (including a plantation downriver from New Orleans and a slave, the child's own mother; there were eight reales to the peso), which young Carlos benefited from for only a short time, because he died at age seven in 1800. His mother María then petitioned to inherit her son's estate and purchase her own freedom (valued at 225 pesos) with the proceeds. She ended up with her carta but had to give the senior Begin's sister three hundred pesos, about half the value of young Carlos's estate. Court costs of about sixty-nine pesos consumed most of María's remaining share. The Begin case reiterates the concern some masters showed their natural offspring but not the enslaved mother.[52]

Other examples of masters admitting their fatherhood include the moreno libre Francisco Montreuil, alias Dedé, who freed his two slave sons when they were adults: Luis, about thirty-four years old, and Basilio, about twenty-three years old.[53] In 1802 Don Juan Bautista Nicollet denied paternity of one person of color while acknowledging fatherhood of another. In his will Nicollet emphatically revoked, denied, and declared null and void a note written in Spanish that he was forced to sign on his deathbed in which he recognized Magdalena Chauvin as his natural daughter. He claimed that the note was signed under duress and totally false. Nicollet, however, *did* recognize as his natural child his slave named Luis Nicollet, provided for his son's manumission, and gave him two thousand pesos. Nicollet ordered his testamentary executor to administer the donated money until Luis reached majority age and also to care for and educate Luis. In other articles Nicollet issued a carta for his slave Magdalena and gave her two thousand pesos and donated smaller sums to his slaves who remained in bondage, including one of his slave godchildren.[54]

In one strange and complicated case a half brother and sister—the moreno libre Luis Maxent and the parda libre Margarita Duplanty, wife of a white man, Don Roque Fantoni—agreed to manumit a slave they had both inherited from their mother, a morena libre. The slave was Luis Maxent's three-and-a-half-year-old son by another of his mother's slaves, the morena Mariana. In addition, Maxent conceded to sell his interest in the slave Mariana to his sister. Mariana went to Havana where Duplanty and her husband resided, while the young child stayed in New Orleans with his father.[55] Like many whites and libres noted above, Maxent cared about his child but showed no interest, except monetary, in the mother.

Special relationships of many other kinds also prompted graciosa manumissions. The New Orleans merchant Don Claudio Francisco Girod freed his pardita slave Francisca, the six-year-old daughter of his morena slave María Roseta, because she was his goddaughter.[56] In 1781 Don Francisco Broutin manumitted freely his morena slave Carlota, forty-five years old, for nursing his two youngest children.[57] One white man freed his loyal, responsible slave overseer, while another slaveholder granted a carta to his pardo slave for twenty-three years of service.[58] Juan, the pardo slave of Colonel Gilberto Antonio de St. Maxent, earned his carta through combat when he accompanied his master in the Spanish rout of the British at Pensacola in 1781. Unfortunately for Juan, he had to fight for freedom twice, once on the battlefield and once in the courtroom. Apparently St. Maxent failed to keep his promise to manumit the slave, because Juan had to bring St. Maxent's widow before a tribunal *eighteen years later*—and after he had been sold to someone else—to secure his hard-won freedom.[59]

Although not as frequently as children, elderly slaves were also manumitted voluntarily without conditions. When liberating older slaves, few slaveholders provided for their future care, or at least the records do not indicate so. Some donated items to them at a later date, and masters who liberated slaves in their wills also tended to bequeath them goods, although not exclusively or even primarily to elderly bondpersons. A typical inter vivos case was that of the emancipation of Catin, an eighty-year-old morena whom Don Pedro Deverges and his wife, Doña Catalina Dupard, manumitted without any allowance for her impending needs.[60] A slave for her entire life, Catin—and other elderly freedpersons like her—at age eighty could not hope to provide for herself other than by begging, stealing, or relying on friends and relatives.

New Orleans slaveholders also voluntarily liberated elderly slave couples, which might have reduced the ex-slaves' economic hardships and concurrently increased their support mechanisms. Once manumitted, these elderly black couples could enjoy their freedom together, even though they probably would not live long. Without children or kin to help them, however, senior slave couples could also double the burdens they placed on one another. Either way, slaveholders made few economic sacrifices by freeing any bondperson over fifty years of age; indeed, through manumission, masters often avoided the expense of caring for an infirm slave.[61] Though slightly better off than those elderly slaves who had to pay for their freedom, freely manumitted seniors nevertheless were usually bondpersons discarded and abandoned by their masters once their productive years had passed.[62]

Occasionally slaveholders guaranteed liberty to slaves only after their spouses' death. Don Antonio Felipe Marigny de Mandeville's will provided that the pardo slave Pablo be freed only on the death of Marigny's wife; in the meantime Marigny donated to Pablo all his "gross," or coarse, clothing.[63] One unusual testament combined provisions for a slave's welfare and paid labor along with compensation for the heirs. On 11 June 1776 Francisco Gauvin composed a will in which he specified that his heirs were to pay his morena slave Rosa, eighteen years of age, seventeen reales per month and supply her with food and clothing for a period of ten years. The heirs were to free her at the end of the ten years in exchange for her accumulated wages. Gauvin died two days after making out this will.[64]

There are a few cases from the Spanish era in which masters liberated their slaves graciosa only to have the former slaves turn around and obligate themselves to serve their former owners for an additional period of time. Apparently some slaves did not welcome the uncertainties of freedom, preferring the security of familiar surroundings and relationships. On 16 July 1778 Doña Elizabeth de Montault Dauterive unconditionally manumitted her nineteen-year-old cuarterona Felicidad, the daughter of Dauterive's other slave, Margarita, a mestíza. Moved by this generous act, the next day Felicidad voluntarily signed a note of obligation to Dauterive that stated she would labor for four more years.[65] In a similar case in 1772 Luisa, a twenty-one-year-old morena libre, obligated herself to serve her former master, the wholesale merchant Don Gerónimo La Chiapella, who had freed her two months earlier. Luisa stated that she acted voluntarily in recognition of the great benefits her former master had given her by freeing her graciosa and that she gave him, or his widow if he should die, complete dominion over her as if she were a slave. Although the obligation was to last four years, La Chiapella canceled it one year later.[66] Perhaps these newly freed women truly wanted to remunerate their former owners for generous acts, lacked the resources, skills, and kin networks needed to survive as free persons, or wished to retain benefits stemming from ties of patronage to influential whites.[67] Many ex-slaves, domestics in particular, continued to serve former masters, but few labored without monetary compensation.

Falling somewhere in between voluntary and slave- or third-party-initiated manumission was emancipation conditioned upon continued service to the former master or heirs over a number of years or the remainder of the master's lifetime (one finds a total of seventy-two such cases, seventeen males, fifty-four females, and one sex not given, between 1771 and 1803). Because such acts did involve compensation to the master, they are included in that category of manumission. Instead of paying for their freedom directly with hard currency, such slaves paid with unremunerated additional service. While working for their masters, former slaves in some instances were treated as free persons, able to sue and be sued, buy and sell property, and make contracts. At other times masters stipulated that these nominally free persons continue to serve them as slaves, and if they did not, the promise of freedom could be revoked. Such arrangements worked to the advantage of the master, who could manipulate the semislave's behavior and ensure docility and deference. For example, Don Cecilio Odoardo, lawyer of the royal audiencia of Santo Domingo and lieutenant governor of Louisiana, manumitted the two parda daughters of his parda slave Margarita—Feliciana, seven, and Margarita, five—on the condition that for the rest of his days they remain in his house and labor for his family and accompany him on journeys when his duty to the king called. In addition, if the slave Margarita caused Odoardo any problems, the act of manumission for her daughters was to be declared null and void.[68] A more generous master was Don Pedro Rousseau, a royal naval officer, captain and commander of the Spanish ship *Galveston*. In October 1782 he manumitted his twenty-four-year-old parda slave named Pelagia in return for six years further service, but one year later he canceled that obligation and ratified Pelagia's free status.[69]

Occasionally slaveholders freed their slaves with conditions but also furnished them with goods or property to make the transition to freedom smoother. Such benefits especially helped young or dependent slaves, who might have suffered in a free world with no one to provide for them. When liberating her eighteen-year-old parda slave, one white woman stipulated that the slave labor four more years but donated to her ten arpents of land and ten cows with their calves.[70] The sisters of the Ursuline Convent freed their fifty-five-year-old moreno, Joseph Leveillé, a servant in their convent since his youth. They did so with the condition that Joseph continue his services and conduct the convent's business dealings as he had done for many years. In turn they gave Joseph the meals he needed so that he could carry out these services. Apparently the Ursulines considered Joseph a free person, because he was designated as such when one year later he sold the sisters two moreno slaves.[71] When Juan Arnaldo Valentino Bobé left Louisiana in 1772, he instructed the person to whom he gave power of attorney to issue a carta for his slave María, then fifteen years old, after three years of additional service. Bobé vowed to reimburse her three years of labor with two arpents of land, two huts, and two cows. María, however, chose to exchange the promised property for her freedom and did so in 1773.[72]

At the other extreme was the master who combined conditional voluntary manumission with self-purchase in freeing a slave, thus placing a double burden on the freedperson. For a sum of three hundred pesos Don Juan Duclos liberated Cupidón, a thirty-year-old moreno creole. Duclos added the condition that his former slave serve him for four more years as Cupidón had done when he was a slave.[73] Fray Bernabé manumitted two of his slaves: María, about forty years old, who had labored for him since 1751, and her daughter Carlota, two years of age. Bernabé gave them their freedom for three hundred pesos—the amount he had paid for María—and the promise of service the rest of his days on earth.[74] The morena libre Catalina Vallière ordered a carta for her only slave, also named Catalina, but then added the note to her testament that the slave was to rent herself out and turn over her wages to Vallière's executor until a one-hundred-peso debt that Vallière owed had been satisfied.[75]

Although graciosa manumissions remained the largest single category, a rising proportion of slaves in New Orleans acquired liberty through purchase, which included those paid for by oneself or a third party, in the form of money or service, with the consent of the master or the aid of the judicial system (in the case of a reluctant master). Together these compensated manumissions constituted a majority of the total number for the Spanish period (table 1.2). Requests brought before a tribunal numbered 154 (61 males, 92 females, and 1 sex not given), third-party purchases 445 (192 males, 249 females, and 4 sex not given), and self-purchases 452 (144 males and 308 females), which made up the most frequent type of compensated manumission.

Cases from the New Orleans notarial records reveal that officials acting for Spain implemented, adjudicated, and enforced the right of slaves to self-purchase through gradual payment (coartación). Just as they did in Cuba, where the practice was legal as well as customary, slaves bought their liberty in large or small increments. Most slaveholders required complete restitution before issuing a carta. Don Fernando Alzar manumitted his morena slave Julia, age thirty-eight, whom he had purchased as a "coartada" three and a half years earlier, when she compensated him the sum he had paid for her.[76] One testamentary executor registered her promise to free Clemencia, a twenty-six-year-old morena from Guinea, if she paid four hundred pesos over a three-year period.[77] Other masters granted cartas to slaves who had remitted only part of their purchase price, with a promise to complete the transaction. In 1791 a white couple manumitted their moreno slave Michaut for one thousand pesos. At the time Michaut had already deposited installments of five hundred and one hundred pesos with his owners, and he swore to pay the remaining four hundred pesos at a rate of five pesos per month.[78]

As revealed by the above cases, Spanish law in Louisiana, as in Cuba, guaranteed and enforced the slave's right to transfer to a new master a promise of freedom and sums paid toward that end upon purchase by another person or on the death of the original master. In 1802 José Montegut sold his forty-year-old male slave, an accomplished shoemaker, to the pardo libre Agustín Bins, also a shoemaker. Montegut had promised the slave his freedom for seven hundred pesos, and the slave had already contributed 350 pesos. Thus when Montegut sold the slave to Bins, he did so for 350 pesos and on condition that Bins free the slave upon payment of that amount. Another white man affirmed his coartado slave's right to self-purchase in his will. Don Nicolás Redon Delille stipulated "es mi voluntad que el mulato Agustín mi esclavo que de coartado en 600 pesos y que entregando esta suma se le autoricé la correspondiente Escritura de libertad" (it is my wish that my mulato slave Agustín, who is purchasing himself for 600 pesos, be issued the corresponding manumission papers upon delivering this sum).[79]

Most slaves, however, bought their cartas with a one-time payment. Upon request, masters commonly allowed slaves to purchase themselves and sometimes even an entire slave family. María Luisa, the thirty-two-year-old parda slave of a white army officer, requested her carta and that of her four children: Noël (seven), Joseph (five), Miguel (two and a half), and Francisca (three months). She paid five hundred pesos for their freedom.[80] In this case and many others like it, María Luisa purchased herself and then acted as a third party to buy the cartas of her children. A more complex kin-group purchase involved the fifty-three-year-old morena Magdalena, who bought her own liberty for 350 pesos and within the next few days purchased cartas for her twenty-year-old son Francisco (300 pesos), twenty-three-year-old daughter Lileta (350 pesos), and Lileta's two young sons Francisco and Carlos (150 pesos each).[81]

Several slaves fifty years of age and older had to pay for liberty, making self-purchase the category with the highest proportion of elderly slaves (table 1.5). The sums senior slaves paid were usually nominal, but they nevertheless attested to years of sacrifice and toil. Their resources and physical strength expended for the gain of their owners, elderly libres faced a dismal future, unless they had kin or patrons to assist them. One of the oldest slaves to purchase her freedom was the morena Magnón. She was ninety-six years old when she paid thirty pesos to Nicolás Sampana to liberate her.[82] In 1777 the free morena Juana liberated her seventy-year-old moreno slave named Hipolito of the Fond nation when he paid her twenty pesos.

Don Carlos Tarascón freed Agustín, a seventy-eight-year-old moreno, for the rather high price of one hundred pesos.[83]

Fortunately, more generous slaveholders and residents abounded, freeing their slaves at the actual price they paid for them (and presumably at fair market value) or loaning money to slaves so that they could "retirar de la esclavitud" (withdraw from slavery). For example, the merchant Don Antonio Ramis loaned Santiago, alias Apolón, 240 of the eight hundred pesos needed to buy his freedom from Juan Raymundo Escot. And the morena libre Cecilia signed a note of obligation to work for Luis Patus at a salary of six pesos per month until she repaid the 325 pesos 5 reales borrowed to purchase her liberty.[84] In 1782 the free moreno Luis borrowed five hundred pesos, guaranteed with some of his real property. Luis in turn loaned the money to his legitimate sister María so that Father Antonio de Sedella, commissioner of the Inquisition in Louisiana, would issue her a carta.[85]

In one unusual case a slave gave her master another slave in exchange for her own freedom. Doña Luisa Dutisne manumitted Carlota, a sixty-year-old morena, when Carlota presented Dutisne a young moreno slave named Telemaco, ten or eleven years of age.[86] Although the practice of substituting one slave for another in order to obtain freedom was rare in New Orleans, it was customary in Rio de Janeiro, Brazil, and occasionally found in other American slave societies. During the first half of the nineteenth century supplies of slaves were plentiful and prices low in Rio, and slaves frequently owned other slaves. Slave artisans or retailers in particular possessed the means to purchase freshly arrived Africans, teach these *bozales* their craft, and acculturate newcomers in the process. Skilled slaves then exchanged the newly trained slaves for their own freedom. Masters, in turn, received young, skilled *ladino* (an African who had been "seasoned") slaves to replace older bondpersons.[87] The New Orleans slave Carlota probably engaged in much the same process.

At times masters or their heirs reneged on promises of freedom, either claiming that the slave had not paid them sums deposited over a period of several years or denying that they had purchased the slave coartado.[88] Because in colonial Louisiana there were no banking institutions as we know them today, slaves who were purchasing their freedom had to hide their savings "under a mattress," loan the money to others and collect the debt when ready to present the entire sum for a carta, or entrust their earnings to their masters and hope they would honor what was usually a verbal agreement.[89] Acts of deceit on the part of some masters warned other slaves to exercise greater caution. In March 1777 the morena Carlota requested that her master, Carlos Philibot, formally register in front of a notary his intent to free her upon payment of 283 pesos. Carlota had already given him fifty pesos; thirty-three pesos were due within one month, and the two hundred pesos remaining were to be paid by the end of December 1777. Until Carlota remitted the entire purchase price, she had to serve her master. Philibot appeared before the same notary in April 1778 to report that Carlota, thirty years old, had presented him the agreed-upon sum and that he wished to issue her carta de libertad.[90] In 1795 Antonio, a moreno slave of Don Juan Pedro Decuir, presented evidence to show that he had deposited sums with the free moreno Juan Bautista in an account to purchase his freedom. He wanted to make sure that more than just the parties involved were aware of this arrangement.[91]

In addition to slaves purchasing cartas for themselves, a relative or friend often paid the price of a slave's freedom, and because some documents did not specifically state the source of funds, financial aid from kin and acquaintances was probably more common than the numbers in table 1.4 indicate. The following data from the notarial records include interested parties who either purchased cartas directly from the master or sought mediation from the judicial system. In those cases where a relationship was indicated (430 out of 530), the vast majority of third-party purchasers were parents of the enslaved (315, 73.3 percent), followed by grandparents (30), siblings (29), spouses or consorts (25), children (12), aunts, uncles, or cousins (11), and godparents (8). Among carta purchasers for whom the record gave race and status ($N = 522$), 276 (52.9 percent) were libres, 148 (28.4 percent) whites, and 98 (18.8 percent) slaves.[92] Many of these slaves were mothers who saved in order to liberate their children rather than or before themselves.

Thus in more than one-fourth of all manumissions, a third party—white, libre, or slave, relative or not—requested masters to free certain bondpersons and supplied the money to pay for their release. One of them was Nicolás de Allo, who demanded and paid 250 pesos to the wholesale merchant Don Claudio Francisco Girod for the carta de libertad of José, the six-month-old pardito son of Girod's morena slave Teresa. Although he did not state it publicly, Allo most likely was José's father.[93] White fathers who did admit their paternity included Don Honorato Orao, *padre natural* (illegitimate but acknowledged father) of the pardito Martín, eight years old and the son of a morena slave named Adelaida. Orao paid four hundred pesos for Martín's carta. One month earlier Francisco Prera gave Don Luis Dupin 150 pesos for the carta of an unnamed nineteen-day-old cuarteroncita, the daughter of Prera and Dupin's parda slave Catiche. According to the terms of the contract, Prera allowed the baby to stay with Catiche for one year and paid all expenses arising from its care and upkeep.[94]

Children were much less expensive to manumit before, rather than after, they were born. A father who purchased the carta of an unborn slave paid the going price of only twenty-five pesos, and several white men risked that sum in order to take advantage of a bargain. Such a venture entailed some gambling because the child could be stillborn or die soon after birth. One white man, José Gilly, attempted to reduce elements of risk by paying the expenses of a midwife and renting the pregnant slave, Leonor, at ten pesos per month until she delivered the baby. Gilly, however, assured Leonor's owner, the parda libre Francisca Robert, that Leonor could continue to serve Robert as long as she did not overwork her.[95]

When prominent white men did not want their names associated with the carta purchase of a slave child, they used agents. In 1793 Don Joseph Xavier de Pontalba, a lieutenant colonel of the royal army and commandant of the German Coast (upriver from New Orleans), issued a carta for his ten-year-old pardita slave Eugenia, daughter of his morena slave Mariana, in exchange for the three hundred pesos Don Juan Bautista Beauregard gave him. Beauregard was commissioned for this task by a Señor Frachinet ("encargado para este efecto del Sr. Frachinet"), most likely the child's father.[96]

Free blacks also purchased cartas for slave kin. After soliciting Don Joseph Villar on many occasions, the parda libre Marion finally convinced him to liberate her son Janvier, a nineteen-year-old creole pardo, for four hundred pesos and her daughter Luisa, alias Mimi, a creole grifa about twenty years of age, for two hundred pesos.[97] In 1782 the free pardo Petit Baptista paid Doña Elizabeth Larroche the exorbitant sum of four hundred pesos to free his nine-year-old parda daughter. Three months later Petit Baptista also purchased from Larroche the carta of his younger daughter, a six- or seven-year-old parda.[98] In addition to paying with cash, libres also exchanged their services for the freedom of a loved one. The free pardo Esteban contracted with Don Francisco Langlois in 1792 to serve for five years in whatever capacity Langlois desired. In return Langlois granted Esteban the favor of freeing his mother, the parda Tonton, valued at four hundred pesos. Langlois also promised to maintain, feed, and care for Esteban if he became ill.[99] One military officer and his wife manumitted their creole morena slave for 350 pesos, an amount that just happened to equal the salaries they owed the slave's mate, the free pardo Francisco Dubreuil, for the time he had worked on their *habitación* (plantation).[100]

Like whites and free blacks, slaves paid masters to issue cartas for friends and relatives, but most likely such purchases entailed much greater personal and material sacrifices. When slaves used scarce resources to manumit others, they placed a desire to liberate fellow bondpersons above their own freedom in true acts of compassion, consideration, and selflessness. Most cases involved parents paying for their children's cartas, which were generally cheaper than their own. Examples include the parda slave Margarita, who gave her owner two hundred pesos to manumit her cuarterón son Pedro, two years of age, and Constanza, a morena slave who paid her white master one hundred pesos to emancipate her one-month-old daughter.[101] Don Carlos Delachaise's moreno slave Francisco requested the carta of his eighteen-month-old morena daughter, who along with the child's mother was also a slave of Delachaise. Francisco gave Delachaise one hundred pesos.[102] When the pardo slave Noël purchased his one-year-old son's freedom from Don Gilberto Leonard, a representative of the royal treasury, he promised to let the boy stay with his mother, also a royal slave, until able to support himself as an adult.[103]

This last case and others indicate that white, libre, and slave fathers frequently purchased cartas for their children while leaving the mother in bondage, just as they did when manumitting slaves by way of a will or inter vivos donation. Such fathers evidenced greater concern for their offspring than for their enslaved consorts. One possible explanation might have been that the mother was in a relatively good, stable slave situation, whereas what the child would later face was much more uncertain, and again, the cartas of children were generally less expensive than those of adults. Even the occasional grandparent bypassed a slave mother in favor of freeing her offspring. In one such case Don Pedro Lartigue manumitted his two pardito slaves, Eduardo (two and a half years) and Augusto (three months), whose parents were Lartigue's parda slave María and the cuarterón libre Eduardo Jenkin. Jenkin's mother, the parda libre Margarita Senette, paid three hundred pesos for her grandsons' liberty.[104]

Other free blacks stipulated in their testaments that funds from their estates be used to purchase cartas for slave relatives and friends. Before sailing for Havana, the parda libre Margarita wrote her will; she requested that her executor sell her house and land on Royal Street and use the proceeds to purchase the freedom of her mother, Genoveva, a morena slave. If Genoveva died before the will was executed, Margarita instructed her executor instead to purchase the carta of her brother Luis, also a moreno slave. What money remained was to be given to either Genoveva or Luis for their daily expenses.[105] When the parda libre María Francisca Riche wrote her will in 1791, she listed among her possessions a house also on Royal Street, one slave, and various household effects. She ordered her executor to take proceeds from the sale of some of her goods and purchase cartas for her brother Pedro and her sister María Luisa, both slaves of the same master. In turn, these siblings were to use what funds remained to free María Luisa's two slave daughters. Two and a half years later Pedro purchased his freedom for 550 pesos and María Luisa hers for one hundred pesos; both went before a tribunal to force their master to free them.[106] Why the above parties chose not to utilize their resources to purchase kin and friends while still alive is not clear.

According to Spanish law and practice, heroic service in the name of the crown could earn a slave his or her freedom, and in these cases the Spanish government acted as the third-party purchaser. This largess was very rare and usually applied to units of slaves who performed some military exploit, such as fighting against a European rival or hostile native group or capturing runaway slaves. Two such cases found for Louisiana during the Spanish period entailed individual acts and provided for government compensation to the master(s) for the slave's freedom. In 1784 Spanish administrators paid one thousand pesos to Don Carlos Honorato Olivier for the carta of his twenty-eight-year-old moreno slave Sebastian, who had earned his freedom "como gratificación echa al dicho mi esclavo por haver auxiliado las expediciones contra los Negros cimarrones" (as a reward made to my slave for having aided the expeditions against the runaway slaves).[107] Sebastian had served with Colonel Francisco Bouligny in taking the famous San Maló band.[108] One year later the Spanish governor Esteban Miró declared free a grifo slave of the Tallapoosa Indians named Tany. The Tallapoosas, along with Abehkas and Alibamons, formed a group known as the Upper Creeks, which inhabited the region north of Pensacola along the Coosa and Tallapoosa Rivers. Born in the English colonies but for the past four years a slave of the Tallapoosas, Tany had served as an interpreter at conferences held in Mobile between Spain, Great Britain, and the Tallapoosas during the United States War of Independence (Spain declared war on England in that struggle and captured British-held Baton Rouge, Mobile, and Pensacola). The notarial document stated that Tany's service had been extremely valuable, because few people were conversant with both the British and the Tallapoosas.[109]

When a master refused offers of money in exchange for freedom, the slave, a relative, or a friend could demand that a tribunal issue a carta de libertad at the slave's estimated worth. Knowledgeable slave appraisers (*tasadores*) took into consideration circumstances of the times when making their assessments.[110] Although most tasadores were fair and could agree on one value, occasionally the slave-appointed appraiser came up with a low figure, while the master's representative estimated high. In these cases a third, court-appointed tasador usually settled the dispute with an evaluation somewhere in the middle of the two extremes.

Most third parties who petitioned tribunals for a slave's freedom were free blacks, many of them parents, siblings, children, and other relatives of the enslaved. The pardo libre Joseph Casenave brought Don Alexandro Boré before the tribunal and requested that he manumit Casenave's consort, the morena Magdalena, and their pardo son named Joseph, both slaves of the estate of Boré's wife, Doña María Eva Labranche. Casenave wanted the slaves freed for the amount declared as their value in the estate's inventory. The court issued their cartas for 590 pesos, an amount Casenave agreed to pay Boré within three months.[111] When the moreno libre Juan Bautista convinced a tribunal to manumit his sister Constanza, he agreed that both he and Constanza would support and feed her two-year-old son Francisco, who remained a slave.[112] Another libre, the cuarterón Juan Bautista Cholán, asked a tribunal to free his natural daughter María. Both María and her morena mother belonged to the estate of Don Francisco Chauvin Delery. Because María was now over three years old, Cholán argued that she could live apart from her mother, and the court agreed. It granted María's carta for 200 pesos, 119 pesos 2 reales of which the estate already owed Cholán for wood. Again, like many males, Cholán made no attempt to free his slave consort.[113]

One white person who pleaded for a slave's manumission was Matheo Platella. He supplied the 425 pesos that bought a carta for Ignés, the morena slave of Madame Arand, after a lengthy dispute in which the estimated price ranged between five and six hundred pesos.[114] In 1781 Francisco Boyard borrowed five hundred pesos from Don Andrés Jung in order to pay for a carta he had secured before a tribunal. Boyard successfully sued for the manumission of Carlota, a former morena slave of Santiago Tarascón.[115] Another white man loaned money to and stood as guarantor for the parda libre Juana so that she could purchase her daughter's carta before a tribunal. In turn, the daughter agreed to serve her white benefactor until Juana repaid the debt.[116]

Some slaves took it upon themselves to petition the Spanish judiciary for a just appraisal. They included a parda named Catalina, thirty-three, who in June 1773 requested that the tribunal issue cartas for her and her daughter Felicidad, five years old, for their price of estimation. Catalina and Felicidad, along with Catalina's other two young children, were slaves of the estate of Don Juan Bautista Destrehan. After five months of disputed appraisals, the parties involved finally agreed on a price of 320 pesos for both Catalina and her daughter.[117] Insufficient funds also delayed settlement of petitions for manumission. The morena slave Francisca requested her freedom from the "tribunal de la Real Justicia" in June 1791. Appraised at 550 pesos, Francisca could not pay that amount. More than two years later she again appeared before the tribunal with the required money, demanding to purchase her carta.[118]

Some slaveholders or their representatives promised freedom but then rescinded their offers, thereby prompting slaves to seek redress through the judicial system. Pupona Eulalia, twenty-seven years old, and Eugenia, eighteen, both morena slaves of Don Pedro Dupain, brought their master before a tribunal in 1792 to demand freedom. After promising to issue their cartas upon payment of 350 pesos each, Dupain had mortgaged them. Like real property, mortgaged slaves could not be sold, transferred, or manumitted. The court sided with Pupona Eulalia and Eugenia.[119] Apparently Mauricio Meillon's executor was reluctant to free three of the estate's slaves, because they had to petition to obtain their cartas. In his will Meillon had granted liberty to Francisco (fifteen), Victoria (nine), and Luisa (two) Moris and donated all his clothes, a bed, and four horses to them. The court ordered cartas issued for the three "en virtud de la que serán habidos y reputados por libres" (according to which they will be held to be and respected as free persons).[120]

Even slaves of the king petitioned for cartas. In 1776 the morena Juliana approached Don Miguel Almonari for her freedom. Juliana was a slave of the royal hospital her master directed and thus belonged to the Spanish crown. She and Almonari went before a tribunal to request the governor's permission to allow Almonari to issue a carta at the price of 280 pesos.[121] The slave Agustín brought his overseer, in this case Intendant Martín Navarro, before a tribunal in order to secure official approval of manumission. Agustín formerly belonged to Mr. Bienville, who had participated in Jean-Baptiste Noyan's rebellion against the Spanish government in 1768. Upon asserting control over Louisiana in 1769, royal officials seized control of the rebel leaders' goods, including slaves. Twelve years later Agustín requested and a tribunal granted his freedom for the sum of 550 pesos.[122]

Natural Increase and Immigration

With the passing of each year over the era of Spanish rule, more and more slaves entered the libre population, but obviously not at a rate that could entirely account for the marked expansion of New Orleans' free black citizenry.[123] Natural increase and immigration/migration also contributed to this growth, though both are more difficult to measure than manumission. Given the port city's large transient population, it is more than likely that libres entered New Orleans—or left the city—for days, months, and years from—or for—both the countryside and other countries or colonies. Many documents attest to the mobility of people in the circum-Caribbean region of which New Orleans was a part, as well as up and down the Mississippi River. Sacramental records in particular identify the many varied countries of origin among those who became New Orleanians.[124] María Juana Prudhome, a free parda, and her cuarterona daughter Margarita Castanedo moved to New Orleans from Havana, as did the free parda María Teresa Cheval. The free pardo militia officer Antonio Joseph Bogarin was a native of Caracas, Venezuela, who wed New Orleans–born María de Flores in 1784 and produced four creole children before the end of the Spanish period. His fellow militia officer Francisco Dorville hailed from Mobile. Even before the mass influx of refugees in 1809, several free blacks from Saint-Domingue called New Orleans home, among them Juan Silvano Daquin, a free pardo who in 1807 married into the prominent free moreno Carrière family.

Enlarged by immigration and manumission, this libre population gave birth to free children and thereby further augmented its numbers through natural growth. One rough measure of natural increase can be gained by comparing the number of baptisms with the number of funerals for each

TABLE 1.9   Libre Baptisms and Burials, New Orleans, 1787–1799

Year	Number of Baptisms	Number of Burials	Ratio of Baptisms to Burials
1787	72	38	1.9
1788	55	40	1.4
1789	74	21	3.5
1790	79	32	2.5
1791	87	51	1.7
1792	79	38	2.1
1793	98	60	1.6
1794	72	46	1.6
1795	94	44	2.1
1796	102	47	2.2
1797	102	48	2.1
1798	101	51	2.0
1799	108	66	1.6
Total	1,123	582	1.9

Sources: Nonwhite Baptisms, books 4a, 5a, and 6a, 1787–99; Nonwhite Burials, books 1, 2, and 3, 1787–99.

year (table 1.9).[125] Although the ratio varied annually, the baptism-to-burial rate was almost two to one over the thirteen-year period from 1787 to 1799, pointing to a natural increase among the libre population. Light-skinned libres primarily benefited from this increase: of free blacks baptized over the eleven years between 1787 and 1797 where race was identified, 82.8 percent (738) were pardos and a mere 17.2 percent (153) were morenos. About an equal number of females as males were baptized, with males favored slightly (sex ratio of 104). Natural increase was most likely due to the high fertility rates of libre women, because the death rate was high and the median age at death was low among free blacks. The crude death rate based on the number of burials was 59 per 1,000 in 1791, and this was not a year in which a smallpox or yellow fever epidemic struck. The median age at death for libre females was 30.3 years and for males an unexplainable, extremely low *8.1 years;* the figures for whites were slightly less dismal, although reversed by sex, with a median age at death for white males of 30.6 years and 18.1 years for white females.[126] In some cases, at least half the children of libre parents died before they reached adulthood, among them two of the four cuarterón offspring of Carlos Decoudreaux and Margarita Castanedo (from Havana, mentioned above), who died at ages one day and seventeen months respectively. The free morenos Rafael Bernabé and Francisca Malbroux lost three of their six children before they reached two years of age, and another died in his youth.[127]

Given New Orleans' unhealthy semitropical climate and low-lying, mosquito-infested terrain, it is not surprising that inhabitants died frequently and at tender ages. Children in particular were subject to the ravages of smallpox, yellow fever, influenza, and malaria, women to the tortures of childbirth, and men to the uncertainties of warfare. During the Spanish regime the two most serious epidemic diseases were smallpox and yellow fever, with recent arrivals to the colony and those living in densely populated areas like New Orleans—in addition to children—the most susceptible. Early in the nineteenth century one observer complained that exaggerated accounts continue to "lead thousands into this country in search of a paradise, and they find a grave." Furthermore, "on an average nine strangers [foreigners] die out of ten, shortly after their arrival in the city [of New Orleans], and those who survive are of shattered constitution and debilitated frame."[128] It did little good to seek the assistance of a physician, because as in most regions of the eighteenth-century Western world, atmospheric theories of disease prevailed in Louisiana. As one surgeon wrote in 1804:

> If New Orleans is not at all healthful and the bad air that its inhabitants breathe occasions fatal diseases, the reason is due in part . . . to the abundance of stagnant water, which for lack of proper drainage lies the whole year round in the cypress groves surrounding the city.[129]

New Orleans was especially pernicious because it lay below sea level, reeked of garbage and dead animals rotting in the streets, and suffered from dogs digging up the remains of non-Catholics who had not received proper burial! The city's *procurador general* (roughly equivalent to an attorney general) summed up its lamentable conditions in a report dated January 1800:

> the part called the batture of the city fronting on the quarter from which the filth and rubbish collected is thrown out . . . causes a con-

tinual infection, both disagreeable and unhealthy, making the principal promenades of the city odious as well as unsanitary. The stenches and corruption of the said filth is particularly bad in warm weather.[130]

The fact that over the era of Spanish rule libres survived, increased in number, and contributed to what would be the antebellum South's largest urban free black population is indeed an amazing feat.

Conclusion

Through natural increase, immigration, and manumission—as well as escaping, revolting, and "passing" as free—libres in New Orleans reached a critical mass of population size and density by the end of the Spanish period. As in Cuba, Brazil, and other American colonies, free blacks in New Orleans grew in numbers and status during Iberian rule in response both to laws and cultural attitudes and to such material factors as demographics and economic activities. Slaves increasingly sought freedom through their own devices, encouraged by favorable Spanish legislation and in more and more cases with the help of funds provided by friends and relatives. Although free and freedpersons of color consistently faced exploitation and prejudice in a hierarchical society such as prevailed in New Orleans, the continuous, intensifying, and expensive struggles undertaken by many slaves to attain freedom attested to their appreciation of liberty as a desirable goal. Of course, not all slaves aspired to free status or viewed such status as advantageous. In an urban setting such as New Orleans, slave artisans and traders in particular moved about, transacted business, and socialized much the same as libres. Their ability to do so, however, could be taken away from them at any time at the whim of their owners.

Persons legally manumitted at least exercised a modicum of control over their lives. One aspect of this control was the ability to provide for themselves and improve their own and their children's life chances, although most of the jobs libres could get did not generate great wealth. The work free blacks did brought them together with slaves and whites, as well as with each other, and helped consolidate their place in the middle stratum of the social hierarchy.

Chapter 2

WORK AND PROPERTY

ACCUMULATION

Once manumitted, newly freed blacks often continued to practice the trades and toil at the jobs that had allowed them to purchase their cartas de libertad. They and other free blacks who had been born free or who had had the additional advantage of inheriting property spent the better part of their days at some form of gainful employment in order to survive, save, and sometimes flourish. Over time there emerged in New Orleans what might be considered a free black "elite," although not on the scale of the *gens de couleur* of Saint-Domingue in the same period or of the large free black property holders that made Louisiana distinctive in the antebellum United States South. During the Spanish period, however, elite status was defined not only by wealth but also by family connections and ties to the free pardo and moreno militias. These factors were often interrelated. Leading libres generally associated with the free black militia and were linked to prosperous, powerful free black and white families.

Few libres were able to lead a life of idle luxury. Even those who were fortunate enough to acquire estates by inheriting them had to work to preserve them intact and pass them on to the next generation. A careful survey of free black economic activities discounts the contemporary view of travelers and residents popular throughout the Americas that libres were by nature "idle, debauched, drunken, liars, ridiculously vain, insolent, and cowardly."[1] On the contrary, free blacks astutely availed themselves of legal, demographic, economic, and political conditions in Spanish New Orleans to attain economic stability—even prosperity—and advance their own and future generations' social standing.

Under the French and Spanish regimes libres ideally had legal rights and privileges equal to those of white citizens. Local regulations and customs occasionally curtailed their efficacy, but in general free blacks "were guaranteed equal property rights and full rights to make contracts and engage in all business transactions."[2] Unlike the French Code noir, Spanish law also permitted Louisiana's libres and slaves to accept donations of realty and personalty, including slave property, from whites and other free blacks. During the Spanish period "the free colored class was economically active and enjoyed full freedom to arrange contracts, own and transfer property, and bring suit, even if it involved civil litigation against whites."[3]

The busy commercial, agricultural, and service center of New Orleans relied on free blacks to provide transportation, distribution, provisions, skilled labor, and a variety of other services. As one scholar points out, "however zealous [Louisiana] society was to maintain the European conventions and barriers, mutual interdependence tended to weaken class differences."[4] Like libres in other American urban areas, those in New Orleans labored at middle- and lower-sector tasks in which they sometimes competed with lower-status whites and slaves but offered little threat to prominent whites. Policy and practice excluded them from the professions, clergy, and government positions, and relegated most of them to manual or skilled labor. Throughout the colonies competition and hostility flared between unpropertied whites and free people of color, most frequently manifested in attempts to limit free black participation in certain trades. Although craft guilds—modeled on the elaborate, centuries-old guilds of Europe—developed in some parts of the Americas, a general lack of trade restrictions characterized colonial New Orleans.[5] In the city demand for labor consistently surpassed supply, a situation that reduced competition and augmented chances for nonwhites to acquire skills. Especially during the rapid economic growth of the late eighteenth and early nineteenth centuries, opportunities for free labor multiplied. Excepting the United States South, where white workers were plentiful, in all American slave societies, including colonial Louisiana, "the free coloureds helped supply the need for a middle stratum between the slaves and the white proprietary/professional class."[6]

The tasks free blacks performed helped shape their identity yet paradoxically at the same time reinforced their ambivalent position in the community. New Orleans "society consisted of a small and exclusive aristocracy of higher officials, successful merchants, and prosperous planters" and

a larger middle-class grading from petty officials and small tradesmen and planters to a group which tended to merge itself with the free people of color, while these, in turn, drifted farther away from the ever increasing slave group without, however, becoming a recognized part of the other white castes.[7]

Although increasingly creating a separate identity from whites and slaves by the end of the Spanish period, free people of color still did not constitute a uniform group whose interests and character were one. Persistent dependency and even downward mobility plagued newly freed blacks, who often expended all their resources to gain liberty and then had to toil at the same tasks they had undertaken as slaves. Many performed the unskilled manual work that made it hard to distinguish their labor from that of slaves. Blacks manumitted long ago or born free, by contrast, frequently attained economic independence as smallholding farmers, slave owners, traders, and businesspersons. Economically successful libres usually endeavored to distance themselves from their slave past and identify with values espoused by hegemonic whites.[8] In a small-scale society such as New Orleans, however, racial and economic groups relied on each other to achieve peace and prosperity.

The 1791 and 1795 censuses furnish partial glimpses of the kind of work libres did in the public, service, manufacturing, or commerce sector.[9] A summation of numbers and percentages by sector is given in table 2.1.[10] Percentages for 1795 probably more closely mirrored reality, because census takers were more diligent in recording occupations for female and free black heads of household. In 1791 a preponderance of data for whites and a lack of it for libres distorted percentages in the public sector (where the figures are too high) and service sector (where they are too low).

Table 2.2 disaggregates data on the type of occupation by sex and age group solely for free black heads of household in 1795. Especially numerous were free black carpenters, shoemakers, seamstresses, laundresses, and retailers.[11] Scanty data from the 1791 census of New Orleans further indicate the frequency of certain occupations among free black male household heads: seven carpenters, five shoemakers, three tailors, one blacksmith, one hunter, one cooper, one wigmaker, and one gunsmith. A 1798 census of household

TABLE 2.1   Occupations of Heads of Household by Sector and
Phenotype, New Orleans, 1791 and 1795

	1791				1795			
Sector	Whites	Libres	Total	%	Whites	Libres	Total	%
Public	119	0	119	24.2	93	1	94	15.4
Service	164	5	169	34.3	175	83	258	42.2
Manufac- turing	83	15	98	19.9	64	46	110	18.0
Com- merce	106	0	106	21.5	121	29	150	24.5
Total	472	20	492	99.9	453	159	612	100.1

Sources: 1791 Census and 1795 Census.

heads in the suburb of St. Mary (Faubourg Ste. Marie) recorded three male
wood dealers, two male carpenters, one male carter, one male gardener, two
female settlers, one female tavernkeeper, and one female washer out of a
total free black population of ninety-six.[12]

Most likely, free blacks pursued those vocations in which they had been
trained as slaves, there was less competition from white workers, and/or demand exceeded supply. Although few written regulations restricted access
to jobs by race, custom and practice all too frequently relegated libres to
positions with low prestige, responsibility, and pay. One contemporary observer commented on the lucrative trades of baker and butcher, occupations
in which there appeared to have been few free blacks. He also noted that
among tailors the "competition of colored men practicing this trade does
not noticeably cut down the profit of Europeans, who are assumed to be
better acquainted with fashions."[13] Nevertheless, when given the chance in
New Orleans and elsewhere, libres dodged the menial manual tasks associated with slavery and aspired to managerial or skilled work.

As in most colonial societies, sex, as well as race, in large part defined
occupation.[14] With few exceptions, free black females and males in New
Orleans performed separate tasks, a practice reinforced by both African
and European traditions. Men functioned as artisans and laborers, whereas
women commanded retail activity, running small commercial establish-

TABLE 2.2 Occupations of Free Black Heads of Household by Sex and Age, New Orleans, 1795

Occupation	Females			Males		
	14–49	50+	Not Given	14–49	50+	Not Given
Public Sector						
Military				1		
Service Sector						
Midwife		1				
Tailor				3		
Seamstress	25	1	3			
Baker	1					
Pastry cook						1
Butcher	1			1	1	1
Blacksmith				2		
Tavernkeeper	1		1			
Laundress	25	4	3			
Hunter				4	2	
Manufacturing Sector						
Cooper				2		
Joiner				5		
Carpenter				17	4	1
Mason				1		
Shoemaker				9		1
Silversmith				2		
Gunsmith				1		
Mattress maker	1					
Commerce Sector						
Wholesaler				1		
Shopkeeper	11					
Retail dealer	9	5	3			
Agrarian Sector						
Farmer	1	—	—	1	—	—
Total	75	11	10	50	7	4

Source: 1795 Census.
Note: There were no free black heads of household in age category 1 (0–13). Returns for the fourth quarter are missing.

ments—such as shops and stalls—and peddling their wares on the streets. Women monopolized such gender-specific occupational titles as seamstress and laundress, while male tailors supplied and repaired men's clothing. Interestingly, tavernkeepers among the white population were most commonly males, whereas among free blacks they were females. In 1787 the city licensed sixty-three white male, two white female, two free black male, and six free black female tavernkeepers. These figures probably concealed male-female partnerships in which the man obtained the license but operated the business jointly with his female consort. For example, upon being imprisoned for debt, the free moreno Francisco Barba begged the court for leniency; he and his wife ran a tavern and boarded soldiers of the Mexican fixed regiment, and his wife faced difficulties managing the service by herself.[15]

Material from notarial registers and court cases, like the example above, adds color to the census's sketch. One visitor to New Orleans, Claude C. Robin, remarked that "almost all . . . have callings" and that the variety was astounding. He further observed that "in the New World, the cities still have few of those useless families who boast of the crime of doing nothing."[16] Constant labor shortages kept all hands busy and reduced competition. In New Orleans free morenos and pardos pursued numerous trades. Dispelling the myth of the lazy, idle free person of color was the traveler Pierre-Louis Berquin-Duvallon's observation that

a great number [of free blacks], men, women, and children, crowded together in the city, are busied some in the mechanical arts, for which they have great aptitude and little attachment, or in some little retail trade, and the others in the chase, the produce of which they bring into the city where they sell it.[17]

One of the most famous libres to emerge from the Spanish period was Santiago Derom (James Durham), the former slave of the Scottish doctor Roberto Dow and himself a skilled *médico*. Born in Philadelphia in 1762, Derom acquired his medical talents from one of his masters, Doctor John Kearsley, who was an authority on sore throat distempers. Doctor Dow of New Orleans subsequently purchased Derom. Derom in turn purchased his freedom in 1783 for five hundred pesos, and by 1788 the free moreno, "then 26 years of age, and speaking French, Spanish, and English fluently, had become the most distinguished physician in New Orleans, with a large practice among both races." Few physicians earned the designation "distinguished" in the eighteenth century, particularly a free black in a racially stratified society, but Derom did practice his craft with skill. These accomplishments, however, did not exempt him from financial difficulties, as a 1791 civil case shows. Derom successfully sued Doña Isabel Destrehan to collect a debt of one hundred pesos owed him from 1788, when he provided treatment and medicine to slaves on her plantation. An 1801 ruling from the cabildo limited Derom's practice to the treatment of throat ailments, his specialty. He was one of the few free black physicians in colonial Louisiana and the earliest known licensed African American physician in what became the United States.[18]

Other libres and slaves—both men and women—cured New Orleanians with less formal credentials using folk medicine they brought with them or learned from newly arrived Africans or local Louisiana Indians. As scholar Gwendolyn Midlo Hall points out, "African religious beliefs, including knowledge of herbs, poisons, and the creation of charms and amulets of support or power, came to Louisiana with the earliest contingents of slaves."[19] Their influence continued through the colonial period and persists in Louisiana today. When José Joffry Verbois, a free black native of the Guinea Coast, died in 1799, he noted in his testament that several persons owed him for his services as a healer. He primarily treated free blacks and slaves belonging to whites, although what types of medicine he used are not indicated.[20]

Libre men also often served as agricultural laborers, overseers, and managers; some even operated their own farms and plantations. One French planter from Saint-Domingue noted that "part of them [libres] who live in the country cultivate food products, especially rice, and some small fields of cotton."[21] In 1777 a white couple paid the free pardo Pedro 530 pesos for serving as an overseer on their plantation.[22] The document did not indicate how long Pedro worked to earn this amount. An annual salary of 530 pesos, however, would have been quite substantial in light of the discussion of wages below. Henrique Francisco, a pardo libre, herded forty head of livestock for Bautista Trenier on Isla Mon Luis.[23] Carlos, also a free pardo, operated a dairy farm belonging to Don Luis Allard, whose plantation now forms part of City Park in New Orleans. According to the terms of the three-year contract, Allard supplied a moreno slave to assist the free black, and Carlos earned one-fourth the newborn calves and half the milk produced.[24] In addition to owning a large plantation twelve leagues above

Figure 2.1 Glapion Armoire, c. 1800, Courtesy of the Louisiana State Museum. Like many libre men, Celestin Glapion was a carpenter and furniture maker by trade. This armoire is a rare signed piece. New Orleanians treasured their armoires and in their testaments frequently willed specific pieces to close relatives and friends.

New Orleans, the free pardo Simón Calpha commanded the free pardo and moreno militia and was awarded an annual pension of 240 pesos in 1782 for his heroic leadership in the campaigns of Baton Rouge, Mobile, and Pensacola.[25] A 1796 census of Metairie, a farming community situated just outside New Orleans, listed seven free black families who in total possessed thirty-four slaves and land measuring forty-two by forty *arpents* (in linear measure one arpent is about equivalent to 190 feet).[26] The area's three white families owned fifty slaves and twenty-four by forty arpents of land.

Free black males worked most often in the construction and shipbuilding industries.[27] They labored as skilled carpenters, joiners, masons, and caulkers. In 1791 Adelaida Raquet, a cuarterona libre, paid the free pardo carpenter, Pablo Mandeville 903 pesos for building her a house fifty-five by nineteen feet with a gallery of four feet. The house probably replaced the one for which Raquet claimed a loss of 1,500 pesos in the great fire of 1788. By 1801 Mandeville was forty-four years old and a first corporal in the first militia company of free pardos.[28] The last will and testament of Andrés Cheval, a pardo libre and the natural son of a morena libre, stated that three white persons and one free black man owed him money for his work as a carpenter. Cheval owned a young slave whom he ordered exchanged for the freedom of his legitimate daughter by his slave wife. He also provided funds to purchase the freedom of his legitimate son but not his wife. Apparently

Cheval survived his illness; although the will was dated 1790, in 1801 at age forty-six he held the position of second corporal in the pardo militia.[29]

Rafael Bernabé was another free black carpenter, more specifically a joiner, who served in the militia. In 1801 he was a forty-four-year-old first sergeant in the first moreno company. Freed graciosa by Father Pedro Bernabé in 1775, Rafael earned respect for his competency and loyalty. In 1797 Don Andrés Almonester y Roxas, the philanthropist who built the St. Louis Cathedral, the Cabildo, and other landmarks in New Orleans, commissioned Bernabé to craft all the doors, windows, staircases, and other woodwork in the Casa de Cabildo. Almonester y Roxas paid Bernabé 550 pesos up front, but the free moreno had to guarantee his work with the value of two houses he owned.[30] The work of Bernabé and other free black carpenters disproved the popular contemporary notion that the "carpentry of the colored people is always defective."[31]

Free black women also pursued a variety of trades and business enterprises. Several operated small stores or peddled goods that they had made themselves or had purchased wholesale from another merchant or producer through the streets of the city and along roads leading into New Orleans. Ethnohistorian Daniel H. Usner Jr. emphasizes the important contribution of women to food marketing and the frontier exchange economy:

> Women in general played a prominent role in town markets, but African-American women became perhaps the most influential buyers and sellers of food in New Orleans. Women from Indian villages and colonial households actively participated in all forms of petty exchange, placing themselves in an intermediary role between cultures.[32]

Colonial observers and officals corroborate his statement. City treasurer Pedro Pizanie collected eighty-one pesos from "las negras y otros individuos que venden en la Conga del mercado" in 1787.[33] Early in the nineteenth century traveler Thomas Ashe remarked that "people of color, and free negroes [along with Spaniards], also keep inferior shops, and sell goods and fruits."[34] According to the 1795 census of New Orleans (table 2.2), seventeen free black female household heads were *revendeuses* (secondhand dealers) and eleven were *marchandes* (shopkeepers). One retail dealer, the morena libre Margarita Trudeau, saved enough money to purchase the freedom of her forty-year-old son for eight hundred pesos from the widow Trudeau, also Margarita's former owner.[35]

In response to increasing numbers of retailers and complaints that street vendors posed unfair competition, the cabildo in 1784 resolved to construct a central, permanent market near the levee. Cabildo members in part created this marketplace in order to tax and regulate New Orleans' thriving commerce. Such an arrangement benefited several interested parties. The cabildo would receive rents from the stalls. The shopkeepers could reduce their prices and costs and face less competition, because their overhead expenses would now more closely equal those of stall renters. Finally, the general public could purchase officially regulated products in a central location. Although the fire of 1788 consumed this marketplace, the cabildo authorized construction of a replacement in the mid-1790s.[36]

Few libre women chose to or were allowed to rent stalls directly from the city council. Of the thirty-three persons licensed to vend goods from stalls on the levee in 1795, only two were free blacks, both males.[37] Apparently, however, license holders rarely actually sold items from these stalls but rather sublet them to free women of color and slave women. In 1797 Manuel de Guerra conferred a power of attorney upon Perina Armesto, a free morena, to sell goods from his "tienda" on the levee at prices that would bring him the greatest advantage.[38] Describing the market that "adjoins the levée at the lower end of the Town," the New York merchant John Pintard wrote in 1801:

> Market hours commense at 6 & are mostly over by 8   Very few people
> go to the market in person   All is brought by domestics   especially
> the females   who seem to be the chief buyers & sellers of the place
> One meets with wenches with large flat baskets containing all kinds of
> goods with a measure in her hand traversing the streets & country in
> all directions   they are experts in selling   wait upon the ladies with
> their wares and are very honest & faithful to their employers[39]

Judging from the account above and the following case, it appears that hawkers, most of them women, continued to roam city streets long after the establishment of a marketplace. In 1797 Don Fernando Alzar and Co. together with fifty other *mercaderes* (shopkeepers, retail merchants) asked the town council to prohibit the activities of increasing numbers of women —slave as well as free black—who daily sold merchandise on the streets and in other parts of New Orleans and even on plantations in the countryside. Lamenting that such practices detracted from their livelihood, the supplicants appealed to the mercy of the cabildo: they had to pay exorbitant rents for their shops and at the same time try to feed their families.[40]

Several libre women operated taverns and boarding houses, most of them located on streets lining the levee, to which sailors, soldiers, and travelers could gain ready access upon disembarking from their boats or leaving the barracks. Like other port cities in the Americas, New Orleans catered to the needs of a large transient population that kept the numerous tavernkeepers, innkeepers, and billiard hall owners in business. In fact, New Orleans probably had more publicans per capita than any other city in North America in the late eighteenth century: Boston had one tavernkeeper for every 694 residents and Philadelphia one for every 429 inhabitants, while New Orleans could boast one tavernkeeper for every *71 residents!*[41] Colonial governments taxed and regulated these institutions, which relieved the thirst of travelers and residents alike. Local authorities tried to protect the public from adulterated or sour alcohol, keep spirits out of the hands of Indians and Africans, and at the same time raise revenues from licensing fees.[42] As noted above, only six of the seventy-three persons in 1787 and six or seven of the sixty-six persons in 1800 licensed by the cabildo to operate a cabaret were free women of color, but, as in the case of free black retailers, others probably ran taverns whose licenses were in another person's name.

According to the 1795 census, the morena libre Carlota Derneville was one such tavernkeeper; she also owned several rental houses, despite losing two thousand pesos worth of property in the 1788 fire. Both as a slave and as a free person Carlota had labored diligently and saved her earnings. At age thirty-seven she purchased her freedom from Don Pedro Henrique Derneville, her father, for four hundred pesos. Two years later in 1775 she agreed to serve Santiago Landreau without running away as long as the court ordered, if he would free her twenty-one-year-old son Carlos. Carlota was among those persons who paid a thirty-peso licensing fee to operate a cabaret for the year 1787 and a forty-peso fee in 1799 and 1800. When she wrote her testament in 1801, Carlota possessed a house and one slave, to whom she granted a carta de libertad. She had outlived her son and named as her heir her niece, Carlota Wiltz, the free parda consort of Don Pedro Cázelar.[43]

Many New Orleans free black women labored as seamstresses and, like their counterparts throughout the Americas, "sewed dresses and made lace in the households and dressmaking establishments of the period."[44] The free morena seamstress Prudencia Cheval, "de nación Pular" (a native of the

African Pular nation), was given her freedom, along with that of her two pardo children, at age seventeen by Don Francisco Cheval. In his will dated three years later, Don Francisco designated Prudencia and her children his only and universal heirs. The inheritance included a two-story house, and Prudencia soon leased the top floor to a prominent white Spaniard at the monthly rate of six pesos for the first eighteen months and eight pesos for the second eighteen months. Boarders and renters often provided libres like Prudencia Cheval and Carlota Derneville with supplemental income.[45]

Some free black women were skilled at several tasks. The cuarterona Magdalena brought her master Pedro María Cabaret de Trepi before the governor's tribunal in 1793 to obtain manumission at the price of her estimation. In determining her worth, Cabaret de Trepi emphasized that she had mastered various domestic chores: cooking, sewing, washing, ironing, and candy and pastry making. Magdalena, by contrast, claimed that she was old, ill, had given birth to many children, and could not work much. Nevertheless, both appraisers valued her at seven hundred pesos, two hundred of which she had to borrow to obtain her carta de libertad.[46] Upon the death of Don Santiago Constant, the parda libre Mariana San Juan sued his estate for 1,344 pesos, the equivalent of what she considered a less than just salary of eight pesos per month for fourteen years. During this time Mariana had served as Don Santiago's companion, cook, and laundress and had sold goods from his store throughout the streets of the city. In addition, she had taken care of, directed, and managed the personal business of Constant's houses as a faithful servant and his best confidant. The court awarded her remuneration of five pesos per month for three years, for a miserly total of 180 pesos.[47]

In general, the wages libres earned varied by skill, competence, labor demand, and individual whim. Tasks women carried out usually commanded lower wages, although those involved in trade probably could earn as much or more than their male counterparts. A few examples will highlight the range of pay rates. The first Spanish governor, Don Antonio de Ulloa, imported skilled laborers, including libres, from Cuba and stipulated that they were to earn wages equivalent to those prevailing on the island. Monthly wages for master craftsmen ran sixty pesos for caulkers, coopers, and joiners; fifty pesos for masons and carpenters; thirty-six pesos for blacksmiths; and thirty pesos for stonecutters, in addition to provisions. Monthly wages for journeymen and apprentices in the respective occupational categories were sixty (with fewer provisions) and twenty-four pesos; thirty and twelve; twenty-seven and twelve; and twenty-seven (there were no apprentice stone-cutters). Of the sixty-nine craftsmen whom Ulloa commissioned, twenty-two (31.9 percent) were free blacks: one apprentice caulker; two master, three journeyman, and four apprentice masons; two master, three journeyman, and three apprentice carpenters; one master and one journeyman blacksmith; and two master stonecutters. Many of these skilled workers returned to Cuba in 1768 and 1769 following Ulloa's forced departure from Louisiana.[48]

Cuban wages were higher than those prevailing in New Orleans in the late eighteenth century. In 1782 Marion Gayarré and Batista, both pardos libres and coopers, agreed to work for Don Luis Boisdore at a rate of four hundred pesos per year (about thirty pesos monthly).[49] When the moreno libre Carlos Meunier appeared in court on charges of failing to pay his debts, the court ruled that as a carpenter he should be able to earn at least thirty pesos per month and ordered him to pay one-third of that amount to his creditors.[50] Juan Bruno, a moreno libre, worked as a ship's cook at twelve pesos per month and traveled to London and Trinidad.[51]

The government often hired slaves and libres to perform manual labor at low wages. When local officials called upon emergency workers to repair frequent breaks in the levee or simply to maintain it, they paid slaves and free blacks the same daily wage. Unskilled laborers working on the levee garnered three or four reales in *jornales* (daily wages), or nine to twelve pesos monthly.[52] Between 2 and 19 August 1791 the governor and intendant paid thirty "negros, libres y esclavos" four reales a day to unload cargo from the seized frigate *San Juan Bautista;* they obviously valued manual, unskilled black laborers—whether slave or free—the same. Officials paid whites two reales more per day for doing the same work.[53]

It seems that militia personnel were also regarded as unskilled laborers. According to the complaint of one free pardo officer, Pedro Bailly, on average the government reimbursed militia members at two reales per day, or seven and a half pesos per month. Bailly claimed that this wage was much lower than what most of them made at their trades. In addition, military authorities frequently employed members of the free black militia units in repairing fortifications, fighting fires, and patrolling the city's streets. Militiamen disdained these manual labor assignments, which they associated with slavery, especially when promised training for active combat.[54]

Proud of their free status, many libres like Bailly resented toiling alongside slaves and suffering equally abusive treatment and low economic returns. They occasionally vented their frustrations upon employers of mixed work-forces. In 1791 the pardo libre Juan Weit assailed Constancio Tardif, who had hired him to repair the levee that fronted his farm five leagues outside New Orleans. Tardif claimed that Weit had hidden in a distant field until his employer came along unaccompanied, jumped out, seized him by his hair, beat him, and knocked him down. Tardif was aware of no other motive than that Weit had complained about working with some slaves hired from another white man. Fortunately for Tardif, a second free black, Juan Grande, halted the attack. Documents for the case were incomplete, but Weit likely spent some time in jail.[55]

Domestic service, primarily employing women, paid even lower wages. A court gave the above-mentioned Mariana San Juan a monthly salary of only five pesos, despite the many services she provided her white consort. In order to reimburse her self-purchase price, the morena libre Cecilia contracted with her former master Luis Patus to serve him as a domestic at a monthly rate of six pesos.[56] Ursula Guillermo, a parda libre, also earned six pesos monthly as a laundress and found the work hazardous only when her employer occasionally attacked her.[57] All the above wages were substantially lower than the two-thousand-peso annual income some observers thought necessary for a family in Louisiana to subsist,[58] but most free blacks did not have to support (or did not have the luxury of supporting) a spouse, numerous children, and servants on their income alone. They probably would have put their children to work and hired out their slaves.

Like most white persons and slaves, libres acquired their skills by observation and apprenticeship. Excepting the Ursuline school for girls, the royal Spanish school, and some private classes given by "qualified" individuals, few institutions in New Orleans offered a formal education. Wealthy colonists sent their children to schools in Europe, but the majority relied on private libraries and the expertise of master tradespersons.[59] When free blacks could afford and had the opportunity to do so, they eagerly sought a classical education. Included in an accounting of expenses for the estate of Don Francisco Emanuel Dusuau Demasilière were twelve pesos per month for the schooling of his two natural sons, the free pardos Pedro Baltazar and Pedro Augusto. The latter did not benefit from his education because he died as a teenager, but Pedro Baltazar rose to prominence in the free black community: he married the natural daughter of a white Spanish officer, became an officer himself in the free black militia, and inherited an estate from his father valued at almost seven thousand pesos.[60]

Most young libres, however, acquired training through apprenticeships, because there was a demand for such skills, and because they were excluded from most professions that required formal learning. According to temporary resident Paul Alliot,

> there are many workmen of all kinds at New Orleans. All the men of color or free negroes make their sons learn a trade, and give a special education to their daughters.[61]

For example, Luison Santilly, a parda libre, apprenticed her son to José Joaquín Fernández, a master carpenter, for five years. During that time Santilly agreed to feed, care for, and provide medical expenses for the eleven-year-old Miguel.[62] Juan Bautista Hugón, captain of the free pardo militia, also wanted his son to learn the craft of carpentry. Hugón apprenticed seventeen-year-old Enrique to Luis Dufiliau, a free pardo master carpenter and fellow militiaman, for three years, at the end of which Enrique was to work for Dufiliau for one year without pay.[63]

Skilled free blacks like Dufiliau trained other libres and slaves. The free moreno carpenter Pedro Laviolet contracted with María Josefa Roy to teach his craft to her moreno slave Alexandro Josef, ten years old. According to the terms of the contract, Roy agreed to lodge, maintain, and dress the slave during the first four years of the deal, and Laviolet did the same during the final two years. Over the full six years Roy paid for the slave's medical care and reimbursed Laviolet for any time lost to illness or running away. Laviolet was only to work Alexandro Josef half a day, and on days that the slave was not needed by Laviolet he could work for Roy.[64]

Females and males involved in the service sector most likely obtained their talents less formally than artisans or managers did. They watched other slaves and free persons sewing, hunting, washing, cleaning, and vending and imitated their actions. On 21 May 1803 Don Antonio Jung manumitted graciosa his pardita slave María Clara, the seven-year-old daughter of his former parda slave Francisca. That same day Doña Margarita Landreau, widow of Don Julian Vienne, registered a note of obligation assuming responsibility for the education of María Clara. In exchange for the pardita's labor over a twelve-year period, Landreau agreed to teach her the arts of cooking, washing, and everything else necessary to manage a house. One day before he manumitted María Clara, Jung also freed María Clara's sister Virginia, a three-year-old pardita. In this case, the free morena Venus, who had purchased her carta de libertad from Jung at the same time, promised to educate and sustain Virginia until she could do so for herself. Virginia brought to the household all her clothes and fifty pesos to help Venus with food and clothing, but according to Venus's statement, love was the primary motivation of her action.[65]

Although most libres exhausted their incomes on daily necessities, some were able to save a portion of what they earned and accumulate property holdings, occasionally large estates. They invested in jewelry and other personal goods, real estate, and slaves. A few libres were also the beneficiaries of donations of these types of goods, either inter vivos or by testament. Free blacks expended some of these resources to free themselves or to purchase and then manumit or keep slave relatives and friends. However, they also owned slaves for purposes of service and speculation, just as their white neighbors did, although compared with whites, libres were less likely to own slaves and held fewer slaves per owner. The holding of African slave property by libres was customary throughout the Americas, and most colonial governments guaranteed the property rights of their free black citizens. Ownership of black slaves fostered free black identification with white society and thus dissipated white fears of racial collusion. The pattern of free black ownership of slaves in Spanish Louisiana closely resembled that of other Spanish, Portuguese, and French American colonial regions, where there were few legal restrictions on manumission. In these areas free blacks owned slaves primarily to help them in their trades in both cities and fields. As long as slave prices remained low, free people of color who could afford bondpersons used them. In addition, as noted above, free blacks often could afford to purchase their slave relatives and free them with few constraints and thus did not need to hold them as slaves.[66]

These characteristics of free black slave ownership did not remain static over time or place. White residents of American slave societies gradually tightened manumission requirements as the free black population grew in size and economic importance to a point at which whites deemed the situation intolerable. This trend toward restrictive manumission occurred primarily in the late eighteenth and nineteenth centuries in the French, British, and former British colonies. In Saint-Domingue, where during the 1700s a considerable number of large land- and slave owners emerged from the gens de couleur, a 1775 royal ordinance "imposed a heavy tax upon emancipations: at least 1,000 livres for each male, and 2,000 livres for each female under the age of forty."[67] The French Antilles, Barbados, and Jamaica likewise imposed extreme emancipation fees that most free black masters could not afford and that most white masters refused to pay. Under these conditions more and more free blacks owned slaves who were relatives rather than mere chattel, especially in the case of lower-class free blacks. In the French Antilles small slave owners "held their fathers, mothers, concubines, children, and other relatives in an official state of slavery because they were unable to pay the emancipation tax."[68]

In North America, too, laws making manumission difficult and expensive compelled free blacks to purchase and hold slave kin. The case of Virginia was typical. During the colonial period and into the early 1800s free blacks owned slaves as sources of labor and wealth and could purchase their still enslaved relatives and then immediately manumit them. An 1806 law required any slave manumitted after that date to leave the state, however. As a result, free blacks devised the strategy of buying their kin and friends; these slaves were free in most respects and could reside near their loved ones.[69] In the nineteenth-century United States South as a whole, free blacks owned slaves "as a way of circumventing laws against manumission."[70] Two states proved the exception: Louisiana and Alabama, which under French and Spanish colonial rule constituted one area. Practices instituted by the Spanish in Louisiana and Alabama accounted for their uniqueness in the antebellum period.

In Spanish New Orleans libres purchased rising numbers of slave laborers into the 1790s, with a slight dip in the 1800s as prices rose. A comparison of free black purchases of slave nonkin with those of kin reveals the prevalence of the former, a trend that increased over time. Analysis of a sample of the notarial records also indicates that almost two-thirds of the slaves free blacks acquired were females. In addition, the gap between the sex ratios in the free black population and those of free black purchasers closed until the ratios were almost at parity. Initially, a disproportionately large percentage of slave buyers were free morenas and pardas, but with each decade the percentage of female purchasers declined while that of males increased, until by the early 1800s the percentage of purchasers by sex almost mirrored sex ratios among free blacks. Census and purchasing data show that in 1777 females made up 67.9 percent of the free black population in New Orleans but purchased 77.8 percent of the slaves bought by libres from 1771 through 1773. Respective proportions for the 1780s were 71.6 and 75.8 percent; for the 1790s 62.4 and 64.8 percent; and for the 1800s 60.2 and 60.4 percent. The proportion of males in the free black population in 1777 (32.1 percent) and in the universe of free black buyers 1771–73 (22.2 percent) rose to 39.8 and 39.6 percent respectively in the first years of the nineteenth century. Why female purchasers were so prevalent in the early years of Spanish rule is not clear; perhaps they had access to greater cash or credit resources than males did.[71]

Given the total available slaves purchased and free black buyers by sex and phenotype, it appears that free morenas and pardas purchased greater numbers of female and fewer male slaves than would be expected, whereas free morenos and pardos preferred male slaves. Most likely, the gender-based use for which a slave was intended, along with higher prices for male slaves, influenced this pattern. Free black women used slaves to perform domestic chores and peddle their trade goods; free black men were more likely to buy slaves who could assist them in their trades and care for their houses. Both men and women augmented their income by hiring out skilled slaves, and they bought and sold slaves for speculative purposes. As an example, take María Teresa Cheval, a free parda tavernkeeper: she purchased a morena bozal from one man for ninety pesos and sold her the next day to another man for three hundred pesos![72] Another libre woman repurchased a slave from a white man who could not satisfy the debt and promptly sold the slave to a free black man at a price fifty pesos higher (a ten-percent increase over the five-hundred-peso original price of the slave). For some unknown reason, he then sold the slave two days later at a twenty-five-peso loss.[73]

In addition to procuring bondpersons through purchase, libres acquired slave and other types of property by way of testamentary and inter vivos acts. Heirs rarely contested these generous bequests to free blacks, and Spanish colonial courts usually upheld the deceased's wishes as long as there existed a written, witnessed last will and testament. According to the December 1779 will of Henrique Mentzinger, who was a sergeant in the white militia, the two-year-old free pardito Juan Baptista was to receive Mentzinger's twenty-six-year-old morena slave named Fatima. In addition, Mentzinger left to the parda libre Luison, eight years of age, his eight-year-old moreno slave named Manuel. Both Juan Baptista and Luison were the

children of the free morena Gabriela, Mentzinger's former slave and probable common-law mate, to whom he willed two hundred pesos.[74]

Doña Magdalena Brazilier's will stipulated that María Luisa, a free parda
about seven or eight years old, was to receive two slaves—Batista (twenty
years old) and Luisa (eighteen years old)—along with Brazilier's residence in
New Orleans and all her clothes, jewelry, household goods, kitchen utensils,
and furniture. María Luisa was the daughter of Brazilier's "mulata mestiza"
slave named Maneta. In the will Brazilier freed seven of her slaves, many
of them other children of Maneta, but she did not manumit Maneta. The
transition of Maneta's children to free status was probably made smoother
with this gift of property and the assistance of their brother Poiquon, a free
pardo whom Brazilier had manumitted prior to making out her will.[75]

Upon his death in 1791 Don Marcos de Olivares, a native of Coruña in
Spain, bestowed upon his natural daughter, the free parda María Josepha de
los Dolores, ownership of a morena slave and her two children, along with
another morena slave. Olivares also willed her two thousand pesos, two
houses, furniture, clothing, silver, and various household effects. Thirteen
years earlier Olivares had given his then four-year-old daughter perhaps the
most precious gift: her freedom. In his testament Don Marcos donated to
María Josepha's mother, the free morena Mariana Voisín, a morena slave,
a small house and land, and one thousand pesos and instructed her to administer their daughter's inheritance until she reached majority. Other free
blacks, including María Josepha's grandmother, also benefited from Olivares's generosity.[76]

Libres, as well as whites, donated slave property to friends and kin in their
wills. Near death in 1793, the fifty-six-year-old free morena criolla Mariana
Meuillon designated her natural son as her only heir. Bautista Meuillon, a
twenty-five-year-old free pardo, thus acquired his mother's silverware, two
lots and houses in New Orleans, a large tract of land upriver from the city,
and a morena bozal named Mariana. The last two possessions Mariana had
received from Don Luis Meuillon, her likely consort, who had freed her and
Bautista without conditions in 1777. Several people owed Mariana money,
including one white woman, four free black women, and one free black
man.[77] Unmarried and without heirs, the morena libre Margarita Momplessir stated in her testament that she owned thirteen "piezas de esclavos": the
morena Juli, her nine children (ages eight months to twenty-two years), and

the three children of Juli's oldest daughter, Clarisa (one to six years of age). Momplessir distributed this slave family to free and slave female friends and relatives: Clarisa to Catalina, a morena slave belonging to the estate of Don Francisco Momplessir; one of Clarisa's daughters to a pardita libre named Eufrosina Dimitry, the daughter of Don Andrias Dimitry; and the remaining slaves to the free cuarterona Francisca Momplessir. She also donated one hundred pesos to each of the three children of another free black woman.[78]

Though not as common as testamentary bequests, inter vivos donations of slaves to libres occasionally appear in the notarial registers. Among living benefactors was Don Francisco Raquet, who in 1782 donated two young morena slaves and two pieces of land to Adelaida, a free cuarterona, daughter of the free parda Francisca Lecler, alias Raquet. In his will dated twenty years later Don Francisco recognized the now twenty-four-year-old Adelaida as his natural daughter; donated three thousand pesos to her, four hundred pesos to her mother Francisca, and one thousand pesos to each of Adelaida's two sons; and named as heir to his plantation and twelve slaves Adelaida's daughter named Adelaida Dupry.[79] Apparently Don Francisco preferred his granddaughter to his grandsons. His generosity improved the material well-being of three generations of free black women.

In addition to acts of purchase, sale, and donation, some of the most valuable information on free black slave ownership can be found in wills and marriage contracts made by libres, transactions in which free blacks used their slave property as collateral, and tax lists. For example, sometime during the late 1790s or early 1800s Spanish administrators compiled a list of persons owning land along the levee near New Orleans. This list recorded the extent of land and number of slaves each individual possessed, most likely for purposes of taxation.[80] Whites on these properties held over four times as many slaves as did libre landowners. In all, 52 landowners held 562 slaves, an average of 10.8 slaves per proprietor. Of the 52 owners 46 were white, and they held 540 slaves for an average of 11.7. The 6 remaining free black owners possessed 22 slaves, or an average of 3.7. Pedro Demouy and Antonio Conway, both free pardos, owned eight slaves each, but the morena libre Agnes (Inés) Mathieu and the parda libre Feliciana Forneret owned only two slaves each, and the pardo libre Joseph and the morena libre Fanchon (Francisca) Carrière (Montreuil) owned only one slave each, although Carrière also owned land and slaves in the city. White slaveholdings ranged from a low of one to a high of forty.

Free blacks, like white persons, frequently mortgaged their slave property in order to obtain cash loans or purchase slaves and real estate on credit. The parda libre Genoveva Simón mortgaged her morena slave María, a native of the Guinea Coast, in order to secure a one-hundred-peso loan from Francisco Chávez.[81] In January 1803 the free morena María Rosa Tisoneau borrowed 150 pesos payable by the end of the year from the free cuarterón Luis Dusuau, offering as collateral her ten-year-old pardo slave. A notary's margin scribbling indicates that Tisoneau's debt was not canceled until March 1806.[82] The morena libre Magdalena Paquet demanded that María Paquet, another free morena and possible relative, guarantee an eight-hundred-peso loan with three slaves: a mother and her two children.[83]

During the Spanish period thirty-one of the sixty-nine libres who recorded testaments listed slaves as part of their estates.[84] These thirty-one individuals possessed a total of 102.3 slaves (one testator owned a slave jointly with his two brothers), for an average of 3.3 slaves per testator. The number of slaves belonging to any one person ranged from one to thirteen, with half the owners holding only one or two slaves. Three-fifths of the slaves owned were females; slightly fewer than two-thirds of the owners were female, and they owned slightly more than two-thirds of the slaves. These percentages generally agree with data on slave purchases mentioned earlier: free black women owned more slaves than free black males did and libres owned more female than male slaves, as did the population as a whole. When he wrote his will in 1802, Pedro Demouy claimed ownership of only four of the eight slaves declared on the above-mentioned levee landowners' tax list; the other four—along with half the remainder of his property— belonged to his common-law wife Juana, with whom he had "trabajado en comunidad" (worked jointly or in partnership) since 1779. He named as heirs to his half of the couple's communal property their five natural children. By marrying Juana that same day and legitimating their children, Demouy made their claims as his heirs even stronger, stabilized their position in society, and, in his own words, lifted them from "la vida viciosa" (depraved way of life) they had led up to this point.[85] Although legally married to a free morena named María, Henrique Sambas, a native of Senegal, had produced four children out of wedlock. María Luisa (about twenty-three years old, slave), Naneta (about twenty, free), Enrique (seven, free), and Pedro (about four, free) together inherited Sambas's land in the suburb of St. Mary, three horses, two mules, about forty head of cattle, and three slaves. Sambas also held as a slave his brother Francisco but instructed his executor to manumit Francisco upon Sambas's death.[86]

Between 1771 and 1803 notaries recorded ten marriage contracts in which both partners were libres. Of these twenty persons, nine made known the slave property they were bringing into the marriage; in the remaining eleven cases, it was not clear whether the parties did not own slaves or had grouped them with other property in a declaration of their general worth. The nine who explicitly listed slave property owned a total of eighteen and one-third slaves (one bride had a one-third interest in a slave) for an average of about two slaves per owner. The number of slaves owned by any one party ranged from one to five. These numbers were lower than those for testators, but they represented an earlier stage in the life cycle, at which persons generally had not accumulated as much property. The free pardos Joseph Cabaret and María Juana Prudhome entered into one of these prenuptial contracts. Cabaret brought to the marriage land, three cabins, a garden, a canal, eight cows, and four slaves, all located on the Camino del Bayou San Juan between New Orleans and Lake Pontchartrain. A forty-year-old militia officer and recent widower, Cabaret also introduced two children from his previous marriage, one of whom died a few months after his father's second wedding; three others had already died. In turn, Prudhome contributed to the union two houses in New Orleans, one slave, and three children from previous relationships (another had died shortly after birth). She also possessed 325 pesos that her former white consort, Don Juan Antonio Lugar, had given her; upon her death the money was to go to her two natural daughters fathered by Lugar, Rita and Petrona.[87]

Although free black ownership of slaves was common throughout the Americas, slaves rarely owned other slaves. One exception was early-nineteenth-century Rio de Janeiro. During this period supplies of slaves were plentiful and prices low. Masters of trusted skilled and managerial slaves "permitted them to acquire property for their own use, including land and other slaves, and eventually to earn their freedom by buying themselves." In fact, "the success of the slave tended to increase the slaveowner's status and position in society, since command over people was a function of high status in the society."[88] A few cases from the notarial records indicate that slaves owned and purchased other slaves in Spanish New Orleans too. As seen in chapter 1, one slave paid for her manumission by giving her master another slave. Whites and free blacks occasionally donated slave property to favored bondpersons. Another example was Fabre, the morena slave of Andrés Boret, who owned a parda slave of no given name. In 1777 Boret willed Fabre, her three children, and Fabre's slave to the free morena Luisa. Luisa was forty-one years old and the former slave of Boret, whom he had freed one year earlier.[89]

Overall, slave values were high in the early 1780s, depreciated in the early 1790s, and rose even higher in the early 1800s (table 2.3). As with most commodities, prices for slaves, who in the preindustrial era represented both capital and labor, fluctuated in response to supply and demand. In the late 1770s and early 1780s supplies of slaves were low and demand high because of restrictive Spanish commercial regulations and wartime dislocations. Acquiescing to colonial demands, the Spanish crown issued a royal cédula in 1782 that opened New Orleans to legal trade with any French port where a Spanish consul had resided for at least ten years. African slaves routed through the French West Indies poured into Louisiana. By the early 1790s this influx of slaves during the 1780s, combined with an agricultural slump and slaveholders' fears of massive numbers of "infected" slaves coming into Louisiana from rebellious French islands, contributed to depressed slave prices. A nervous governor and cabildo prohibited the introduction of slaves first from the islands and then from Africa, a ban that held until 1800. Even then, Louisianians could import only bozales, or slaves direct from Africa. Planters cried out for additional labor sources to produce increasingly profitable sugar and cotton crops.[90] Thus by the early 1800s supplies of slaves were low and demand—as well as prices—higher than ever before.

A comparison of trends in slave prices and in slave transactions involving libres during the Spanish period reveals some interesting patterns. In order to maximize scant resources, libres had to make choices, and as a group they usually made intelligent ones. When slaves cost less (the early 1790s), free blacks bought more of them, especially cheaper adult females. As the value of bondpersons escalated in the opening years of the nineteenth century, free black owners purchased fewer and sold greater numbers of them. Interestingly, rising slave prices and a widening gap between the value of male and female slaves accompanied an increase in the percentage of males purchasing and being purchased. Whites donated fewer slaves to free blacks when value and demand for labor was high in the early 1800s, but gifts of slave property from one libre to another increased at the same time. Kin purchases rose each decade until the 1800s, when there were none, but

TABLE 2.3 Mean Value (in Pesos Fuertes) of Slaves Purchased, Sold, Manumitted, and Owned by Libres, by Age Cohort of the Slave, New Orleans, 1771–1803

Years	0–9	10–19	20–29	30–39	40–49	50–59	60–69	Not Given
1771–1773								
Females	123 (N = 3)	195 (N = 2)	—	—	400 (N = 1)	—	—	—
Males	—	—	345 (N = 2)	200 (N = 1)	—	—	100 (N = 1)	—
1781–1783								
Females	295 (N = 2)	415 (N = 13)	403 (N = 10)	372 (N = 7)	400 (N = 3)	250 (N = 4)	—	395 (N = 2)
Males	176 (N = 5)	400 (N = 6)	771 (N = 7)	—	350 (N = 2)	500 (N = 1)	—	—
1791–1793								
Females	172 (N = 11)	296 (N = 23)	388 (N = 18)	302 (N = 9)	384 (N = 5)	175 (N = 2)	—	244 (N = 31)
Males	160 (N = 5)	293 (N = 10)	436 (N = 15)	468 (N = 6)	450 (N = 2)	—	155 (N = 2)	387 (N = 8)
1801–1803								
Females	158 (N = 15)	479 (N = 21)	615 (N = 16)	468 (N = 10)	403 (N = 10)	398 (N = 6)	75 (N = 2)	383 (N = 10)
Males	146 (N = 11)	663 (N = 8)	770 (N = 12)	710 (N = 11)	551 (N = 16)	469 (N = 6)	225 (N = 2)	497 (N = 7)

Source: Notarial Records.

concurrently there was a dramatic expansion in the number of libres contributing monies so that their kin could obtain cartas de libertad, primarily
through third-party purchase (as discussed in chapter 1). In the early years
of the 1800s it appears that free blacks used their resources to liberate enslaved relatives and friends rather than to acquire slave property.

Free people of African descent in colonial New Orleans acquired slave,
real, and personal property by working for wages, operating successful business enterprises, and receiving inheritances or donations from whites, slaves,
and other libres. Within their own lifetimes or over generations some free
blacks amassed sizable estates, although they were generally much smaller
than those recorded for wealthy white New Orleanians. No matter how
much or what they owned, however, most libres actively endeavored to protect and expand their resources in order to improve their own material conditions and social standing and those of their kin and friends.[91] Many court
cases attest to their struggle to protect their rights within a society that exploited them as nonwhites but also gave them some advantages over slaves.

Although libres generally acted upon every opportunity presented them,
several factors influenced their capacity to acquire enough goods to provide
economic security for themselves and their families, or in other words to
accumulate wealth that was then passed on to their descendants. These factors also aided in the coalescence of what can be called a free black "elite."[92]
First, free blacks who acquired marketable skills either before or after being
freed tended to prosper. Throughout the Americas skilled blacks found it
easier to purchase freedom and to continue to earn a living as a free person.[93] The free morena Helena poignantly revealed the impact that possess-
ing a skill high in demand could have on attaining and retaining free status.
Helena tried to convince the court that appraisals of her slave son were ex-
cessive because he knew no trade and his master had readily admitted that
the slave was a thief and drunkard. In her plea Helena provided several examples of skilled slaves who had purchased their freedom for the amount
at which her son was appraised and pointed out that an unskilled moreno
slave could never earn such exorbitant sums.[94]

A libre's ties to and reputation in the white community constituted
a second factor in the success or failure equation. Much of the wealth
that free blacks in Spanish Louisiana possessed was passed on to them by
whites and other free blacks through intricate kinship and friendship networks.[95] Associations with whites—whether sexual, familial, friendship, or

business—benefited free blacks, women in particular. In New Orleans' corporate society, advantages accrued to those libres who were linked by kin
and patronage to leading white families. The importance of such connections can be demonstrated by an example of what could happen when they
were threatened. As the free pardo Pedro Bailly quickly discovered, alienat-
ing influential whites could damage one's status. When a prominent white
man, Don Luis de Lalande Daprémont, brought charges of criminal activity against Bailly, he threatened the livelihood of Bailly and his family.
Bailly claimed that the charges were false and entered out of spite; Daprémont had just recently lost a suit that Bailly had brought against him for
collection of a debt. Bailly also stated that the mistrust engendered by these
charges had seriously affected his retail business, because white patrons from
whom Bailly had borrowed funds and goods were beginning to harass him
for payment and refused to extend him additional credit. A militia officer
and loyal servant of the king, Bailly had earned the distinction of a *buen
vasallo* (good subject) meriting the favor of local *jefes* (leaders). The court
eventually dropped Daprémont's charges against Bailly, thereby restoring
his favorable reputation, at least for the moment.[96]

Whites occasionally formed business partnerships with libres. Pedro Viejo
jointly owned a small dry goods store with the morena libre Juana. A native
of Guinea, Juana was a former slave of Luis Poirson and the legitimate
daughter of two slaves. Half of the enterprise belonged to her, and she designated Viejo as her only heir.[97] Antonio Sánchez and María Juana Ester,
a free cuarterona, were partners in another retail business. Born in New
Orleans to a parda libre and an unknown father, María Juana had one natural daughter, also a free cuarterona. In her will María Juana entrusted
Sánchez with selling her share of the partnership's goods and placing its
proceeds in her daughter's possession. Included in the estate inventory were
farm and carpentry implements, wagons, ox teams, cows, horses, lumber, a
canoe, slaves, and two farms.[98]

Kinship ties to white persons as well as patronage gave some libres added
economic leverage. Occasionally white fathers publicly acknowledged their
free black consorts and offspring and donated personal and real property to
them, and other examples confirm the benefits accruing to libres with influential white relatives. In his will dated 1794 Don Pedro Aubry declared
that he was single but that he had two natural children—Pedro Esteban and
María Genoveva—by the morena libre María Emilia Aubry, all his former

slaves. As his only heirs, the children received a farm seven leagues from New Orleans, two slaves, livestock, furniture, and household goods.[99] An ancestor of the famous Civil War general P. G. T. Beauregard—Don Bartolomé Toutant Beauregard—had four natural daughters by the free morena Margarita Leveillé Toutant, upon whom he bestowed two houses, furniture, two slaves, and currency during his lifetime and in his testament. With this property the Toutant women were able to secure advantageous marriages with men who were leading members of the free black community and militia.[100]

In some cases, however, patronage placed free blacks in positions of dependency much like slavery. Mary C. Karasch found that in early-nineteenth-century Rio de Janeiro "since so many freedpersons were women, many continued to work as servants for their previous owners and to maintain old patterns of dependency." Other scholars note that throughout the New World "newly 'freed' persons were typically enveloped in conditions of lingering servitude resulting from provisos in their manumission papers or from debts incurred in self-purchase."[101] Such a continuing dependent relationship involving a benefactor and a recently manumitted slave existed in New Orleans between Angélica and Don Antonio Pascual y de Regas. Pedro Visoso manumitted his morena slave Angélica, about thirty years old, for four hundred pesos paid by Don Antonio. Angélica in turn contracted with Don Antonio to serve him the rest of his life and travel with him wherever he should go, but she retained all the rights of a free person.[102] These arrangements, while exploitative, also offered a newly manumitted person who had few skills or assets protection from the many uncertainties and possible downward mobility freedom could entail.

A third factor that could help a libre succeed materially was that of being born a free person or having free kin. Free blacks passed their goods to lineal and lateral kin and to friends, thereby contributing to the well-being of others. Both the Spanish and French practiced partible inheritance, whereby children received at least somewhat equitable portions of their parents' estates. Even illegitimate children could inherit up to one-third and consorts up to one-fifth of the estate, although parties often left larger shares without having their testaments contested by other heirs.[103] Second- or third-generation free blacks usually inherited the accumulated riches, no matter how meager, of past generations, and slaves who had well-established free black friends or relatives stood a better chance of being "rescued" from slavery than those with no ties to the libre population. In 1775 the thirty-nine-year-old morena Francisca Montreuil reimbursed her master, Don Roberto Montreuil, eight hundred pesos for her freedom and that of her parda daughter Naneta, more commonly known in later documents as Ana Cadis. A *panadera* (baker) by trade, Francisca also registered her obligation to pay Montreuil an additional three hundred pesos within one year; he canceled the note one year and two days later. By 1777 the morena libre Francisca Montreuil had accumulated the three hundred pesos needed to purchase from her former master the carta of her son Carlos, a twenty-year-old pardo blacksmith.[104]

When Francisca died in 1803, she possessed an estate valued at 10,459 pesos, which when debts of 3,157 pesos 3 reales were subtracted left 7,301 pesos 5 reales to be divided in four parts among her three living children (Carlos, María Genoveva, and Agata) and her three living grandchildren by her deceased daughter Naneta. A native of Louisiana and the natural daughter of Francisco Rancontre and Susana, Francisca was about seventy years old when she died. Included in her substantial estate were five slaves worth 2,650 pesos, one slave who was promised his freedom, a house and lot in New Orleans worth 2,825 pesos, two plantations along Bayou Road worth 1,735 pesos, livestock, furniture, and household goods. Not listed were sums distributed during her lifetime, which included one-thousand-peso donations to two of her grandsons (who were also her godsons) and dowries worth 390 pesos and 450 pesos to her daughters Naneta and María Genoveva.[105]

Naneta died three years before Francisca, in 1800 at the age of forty-one, and, like her mother, left a large estate acquired during her quarter century of freedom. Naneta had married Pedro Bailly, also a recently freed pardo, in 1778 and brought the aforementioned dowry of 350 pesos in silver and four cows worth forty pesos. Naneta's father was a white man, Don Pedro Cadis. She gave birth to five legitimate children, two of whom died before they reached the age of ten, and all of whom had leading white citizens and officials as their godparents. Naneta was left to care for her family, properties, and slaves while her husband spent over two years in prison in Cuba, convicted of espousing radical French ideals and of conspiring to overthrow the Spanish government in 1794. Pleading for the welfare of her children, Naneta successfully petitioned the Spanish crown to release her husband in 1796. These children, second-generation free blacks, benefited greatly from the business acumen of their mother and grandmother when they inherited their estates in the early 1800s.[106]

Testaments and estate inventories like Montreuil's and Cadis's illuminate the extent of property free blacks could accumulate during their lifetimes and bestow upon relatives and friends when they died. They also reveal intricate kinship and patronage ties among free blacks, whites, and slaves. The childless parda libre María Francisca Riche distributed her estate among her closest kin and longtime friends, as well as the poor. A natural daughter of the free morena Carlota Riche, a native of Pointe Coupée, and a resident of New Orleans, Riche donated ten pesos to indigent patients at Charity Hospital and one hundred pesos and a harness decorated with silver to Doña Julia Bauvais of Pointe Coupée (Riche had served as Bauvais's nurse when Bauvais was a child). She ordered her executor to sell her household goods and a morena slave and spend the proceeds to liberate her brother and sister, Pedro and María Luisa. In turn, the siblings were to use what funds remained to purchase the cartas of María Luisa's two daughters, and these nieces were to inherit Riche's estate.[107]

Unlike Riche, the free morenas Janeton Laliberté and María Belair had living children, and their estates can be traced down through at least two generations during the Spanish period. A native of Senegal, Laliberté wrote her will in 1771 and noted that thirty years earlier she had been married to a moreno named Gran Jacot (also known as Luis) and that they had had a daughter named María Juana. She later married another free moreno, but this union produced no children. Laliberté willed to her daughter her half lot in New Orleans, a plantation downriver from the city at English Turn located adjacent to lands of Pedro Tomás, her son-in-law, and four cows with their calves. Thirty years later María Juana Tomás wrote her will. Her marriage to Pedro Tomás had produced eight children, six of whom were still living, the oldest forty-four years old and the youngest twenty-five. Tomás's only property consisted of the half lot and house inherited from her mother, and she left this to her children and the one son of one of her dead children.[108]

Prior to her marriage to the pardo libre Luis Daunoy, María Belair had two natural daughters, Carlota and Martona, to each of whom she willed one-fifth of her estate when she died in 1794. The rest of her estate she left to her and Daunoy's legitimate son, also named Luis. María's property consisted of her dowry (500 pesos) and half the goods communally owned with her husband, which included a half lot and cabin in New Orleans. Martona Belair followed her mother to the grave one year later and left her one-fifth share of María's estate to her six natural children, ranging in age from thirteen years to twenty months. Martona made her living as a dry goods retailer and during her lifetime had acquired much more property than her mother. Appraisers valued her estate—furniture, household goods, personal clothing, a half lot and house in New Orleans, a promissory note, and dry goods for her business—at 1,572.5 pesos. Martona owed one white woman and eight white men (most of them wholesale merchants) 553 pesos, thus leaving 1,019.5 pesos for her six children. In addition, Martona held as guardian one female slave (valued at 400 pesos) for two of her minor children and another female slave (valued at 350 pesos) for one of her other minor children. Two white men, probably the respective fathers, had donated the slaves to the children.[109]

Marriage contracts that specify dowries hint at the material well-being of free blacks earlier in their life cycles than do wills and estate inventories.[110] On 10 January 1779 Pedro Langlois wed Carlota Adelaida, both pardos libres, and thirteen days later they entered into a marriage contract. Langlois declared his possessions as three slaves and cash totaling 1,800 pesos. A widow with a young child, Carlota Adelaida declared both the property she brought from her former marriage and her daughter's inheritance. This included land, slaves, and debts worth a net total of 1,350 pesos. While Langlois administered his new wife's and stepdaughter's possessions, he could not alienate them without their consent.[111]

In a second example the husband, cuarterón libre Francisco Alexandro Colombé, was marrying for the second time and made clear in the prenuptial agreement that half of his goods—valued at 3,000 pesos—belonged to the three children from his previous marriage. His new wife, the parda libre Henriqueta Toutant, also carefully delineated the possessions her family—in particular her wealthy white father Don Bartolomé Toutant Beauregard—had bestowed on her. Hard currency, jewelry, clothes, furniture, and household utensils valued at 1,200 pesos constituted Toutant's dowry.[112] The cuarterona libre María Constancia's dowry was also appraised at 1,200 pesos and included 540 pesos' worth of stamped silver (which she had acquired "through personal work in an honest manner"), 360 pesos' worth of clothes and furniture, and a young female slave valued at 300 pesos. She entered into a marriage contract with Carlos Lavibarière, a free pardo, but their marriage is not recorded in the sacramental records for St. Louis Parish.[113] When Agustín Malet, the natural son of Mr. Rocheblave and the morena libre Juana Malet, wed Jacinta Demasilière, the natural daughter of Don Joseph Wiltz and the morena libre Teresa Dufaut, in 1785, he brought 1,400 pesos in cash and a half lot in New Orleans worth 300 pesos. Demasilière's dowry consisted of 1,100 pesos in cash given her by her mother. Fifteen years later Malet, an officer in the free pardo militia and a wood dealer, wrote his will. He and Demasilière had produced three offspring, ages fourteen, eight, and seven, whom Malet named as his heirs. A fourth son, who would have been ten years old, must have died in the interim. Malet's goods included slaves, lands, houses, furniture, and personal effects, which the three children named in the will and at least one sister born after the will was written shared equally.[114]

Although many libres increased their material worth between the time of their marriage and that of their death, some experienced a decline in wealth and status. Among them was Luison Brouner (Mandeville), a parda libre who in many documents is recorded as a mestiza. Brouner was freed in 1770 at age twenty-three. Into her marriage to pardo libre Francisco Durand in 1785 Brouner brought a plot of land and a house with a separate kitchen in New Orleans, much furniture, personal clothing, and five slaves. Brouner was the natural daughter of Mr. Mandeville and María Juana, an "india mestiza libre," and had had a common-law relationship with Don José López de la Peña, which had produced four natural daughters, before marrying Durand. Brouner and Durand had no children. When she wrote her will in 1794, Brouner's holdings had been reduced to one slave plus a half interest in a slave and plantation near Baton Rouge that her godmother, the parda libre Naneta Chabert, had donated to Brouner and Durand. Brouner owed her former white consort four hundred pesos, an amount somewhat off-set by the two hundred pesos that one of her daughters owed her.[115] Most likely, Brouner had dispersed the majority of her properties over her lifetime or had faced some misfortune, thus indicating that wills made near the end of a lifetime were sometimes not representative of one's maximum material value. Brouner's luck changed again, however. She benefited somewhat from the donation of a plantation made her by her white son-in-law, Don Luis Declouet, in 1802. The land was located one-quarter league below New

Orleans, where Declouet was captain of the royal army and commander of militia volunteers for the lower coast. Brouner merely had usufruct of the plantation; at her death it was to go to her daughter and grandchildren.[116]

A list of losses incurred in the first great fire to sweep colonial New Orleans (March 1788) is another useful source for estimating at least the real and personal property holdings of the city's free blacks and for comparing them with those of white men and women. In September 1788 a list of 496 claims for damage to buildings and interior furnishings (plus ten claims on state and church property) totaling more than 2.5 million pesos was submitted to the Spanish crown. Fifty-one of the claimants were free black women, and their average estimated loss to real and personal property was 1,814 pesos. Free black men made up only twenty-one of the claimants, with an average loss of 1,700 pesos. Another sixty-seven of the claimants were white women (average loss of 2,880 pesos), almost half of them widows, and the remaining 357 claims were made by white men. The white male average claim of 6,090 pesos was more than double that of white females and about three and a half times greater than that of free black women or men.[117] Clearly, white men possessed the vast majority of material wealth in late-eighteenth-century New Orleans. More free black women held property than free black men (which one would expect given the demographic makeup of the city), and they possessed more valuable or larger amounts of property. The colony's patriarchal social structure ordered by race, class, and gender hampered free black efforts to achieve the status of upper-sector whites; law and custom excluded them from high-paying, prestigious positions in the bureaucracy, professions, and commercial and landholding aristocracy.

Nevertheless, an examination of the work New Orleans' libres engaged in and the property they accumulated reveals the germination of a free black "elite" based on wealth and kinship and militia ties. Many of those who made up antebellum New Orleans' famous free Creole of Color elite could trace their ancestry and the foundations for their prosperity back to free blacks living in the Spanish colonial era. During this period free people of color used patronage and kinship networks, inherited property, and individual talent to improve their economic and social standing in the community, or at least that of their children. They acquired marketable skills and forged favorable relationships with influential whites and free blacks. Inheritance from propertied white and free black *vecinos* (residents), in particular, augmented one's material standard of living. Even with the advantage of inheritance, though, privileged free people of color had to employ all their energy, skills, and business acumen in order to maintain and increase their property holdings. Efforts to free friends and family members from bondage, along with race and gender discrimination on the part of many whites, placed additional constraints on the ability of free blacks to prosper, despite their utmost attempts.

The successes and failures of individual libres and their families and the emergence of a free black "elite" led to further social and economic differentiation among New Orleans' free population of color, while at the same time fostering a stronger group identity. At no time in their history did all free blacks have identical goals and concerns, but members of the emerging elite began to assume control of at least defining the group's public interests. They became the "voice" of the libre community, especially through such influential Spanish institutions as the family, the church, the military, and the judicial system.

Chapter 3

"FAMILY VALUES"

AND KINSHIP STRATEGIES

In Louisiana and other colonial regions, family, business, and honor were closely interrelated. Through a variety of kinship strategies free blacks, especially the emerging "elite," used consanguine, affinal, and fictive kin to enhance their economic and social standing. Iberian society, of which New Orleans was a part, was both patriarchal and corporatist, characteristics that made the family much more important than the individual. Like white inhabitants, libres used many devices to construct family networks that would strengthen their position and that of their children within a social hierarchy ordered by race, class, legal status, and gender. In so doing, they also reinforced their intermediary position within that hierarchy and began to define a nascent group identity constructed around the ideals, values, and goals of the leading libre families.

Familial associations linked New Orleans free blacks to one another, slaves, and whites in ways that could benefit or antagonize, promote group and family cohesiveness or tear groups and families apart. As in most eighteenth-century urban centers of the semitropical and tropical circum-Caribbean, the death rate in New Orleans was high and life spans were short, trends exacerbated by a notoriously unhealthy climate. In most cases such precarious daily conditions drew family and friends together; people worked in tandem to survive in a hostile environment. Free black kin frequently pooled their resources to engage in business enterprises and purchase property and the cartas of enslaved relatives. In addition, fictive kin networks reinforced consanguine, affinal, and fraternal relationships among New Orleans' white and nonwhite populations, especially among officers and soldiers of the free pardo and moreno militias. Throughout the Latin world—past and present—compadrazgo has served to connect people both horizontally and vertically within a social hierarchy through a system of reciprocal obligation. Patronage, godparenthood, and family intertwined, crossing, uniting, and usually strengthening the social and racial order. Libres participated in this process of building community solidarity.

Associations among free black, slave, and white relatives and friends were by no means all rosy, however. Limited resources sometimes incited contests for control of family resources among heirs. Court cases indicate that parental favoritism strained sibling relationships and that tension and sometimes violence between couples erupted—and disrupted family ties. Libres in late-eighteenth-century New Orleans wove intricate family patterns and utilized complex kinship strategies to promote their own well-being and that of succeeding generations, the goal of most Spaniards in the Old and New Worlds. By its nature, a study such as this one emphasizes the activities of so-called "elite" members of free black society. After all, they were the ones concerned with finding spouses and godparents for their children who were persons of equal or higher status, with accumulating estates and passing them on to succeeding generations, with gaining acceptance in the white community and even "passing" into it.

Free blacks lived as husband and wife with other free blacks, whites, and slaves in sexual relationships that were either permanent or temporary, formal or informal, sanctioned or barely tolerated by church and state authorities. An official church wedding was definitely not the norm for persons of any race in late-eighteenth-century New Orleans, or in any other frontier region of the Spanish realm. People entered into matrimony mainly for economic reasons, most of them individuals of high social and economic standing who sought to protect and extend their families' estates and honor.[1] If one had no honor (which by definition of the dominant European society included all blacks, Indians, and persons of mixed race) and few resources to protect and pass on, marriage made little sense, especially considering the expensive fees one had to pay for the appropriate ceremony. In New Orleans, for example, a Catholic priest finally married José Fich and Moneta Arlu, both free pardos, in 1796. Fich and Arlu had been living in a state of public concubinage condemned by the church and wanted to marry,

TABLE 3.1 Marriages of Whites, Libres, and Slaves as a Percentage of
(1) Their Respective Population Groups and (2) All Marriages Performed
in That Year, New Orleans

Year		Whites	Libres	Slaves
1777	(1)	4.8% (84/1,736)	2.5% (8/315)	0.0% (0/1,151)
	(2)	91.3% (42/46)	8.7% (4/46)	—
1788	(1)	2.9% (68/2,370)	0.5% (4/820)	0.2% (4/2,131)
	(2)	89.5% (68/76)	5.3% (4/76)	5.3% (4/76)
1791	(1)	2.1% (50/2,386)	0.2% (2/862)	0.2% (4/1,789)
	(2)	89.3% (50/56)	3.6% (2/56)	7.1% (4/56)
1805	(1)	1.9% (68/3,551)	1.1% (17/1,566)	0.0% (1/3,105)
	(2)	79.1% (68/86)	19.8% (17/86)	1.2% (1/86)

Source: Nonwhite Marriages, book 1, 20 January 1777–29 July 1830.

but the expense of a wedding had detained them.[2] Several other free black
couples most likely faced the same dilemma, as did whites and slaves. The
problem became so acute by the end of the Spanish period as to prompt
New Orleans' attorney general to complain before the cabildo about the
high cost of marriages and funerals, of concern to the public as a whole
because the Capuchin fathers would not bury or marry anyone until paid
in full.[3]

Data presented in table 3.1, combined with demographic information
from tables 1.1 and 1.3, indicate the infrequency of official marriage for all
segments of the population. Between 1777, when the church began keeping
separate marriage (as well as baptismal and funeral) registers for whites and
nonwhites, and 1805, when a census was taken just shortly after Spain turned
Louisiana over to French and then U.S. officials, a maximum 4.8 percent of
whites, 2.5 percent of free blacks, and 0.2 percent of slaves married in any
given year for which census data were available. At the beginning and end
of the period, the percentage of marriages involving free blacks was about
equal to their percentage of the total population (8.7 compared with 9.8
percent in 1777; 19.8 compared with 19.0 percent in 1805). Of all persons
entering matrimony from 1777 to 1805, whites made up 88 percent, libres
8 percent, and slaves 3 percent (N = 2,636). Perhaps more appropriate is a

comparison of marriage rates involving only the free population, since slaves rarely had a choice in marrying and most slaves who married belonged to nuns, friars, and priests. In 1777 libres made up 15.4 percent of the free population and were partners in 8.7 percent of marriages for that year. The ratio had declined somewhat by 1805, when 30.6 percent of all free persons were of African descent and 19.8 percent of marriages involved this group. Clearly, whites dominated the marriage market when compared with free blacks and especially slaves, but even so, surprisingly few white New Orleanians married (an average of forty couples per year between 1777 and 1805).

Some marriages took place between libres, whites, and slaves, even though such marriages violated the intent of the Real Pragmática, or Royal Pragmatic, issued by the crown in 1776 and promulgated for the Viceroyalty of New Spain (of which Louisiana was a part) in 1778. Concerned with the effect that the "passions of youth" might have on the economic stability of aristocratic families, Spain required all persons under age twenty-five (the age of majority) to obtain parental permission to marry. The Pragmatic exempted castas and blacks, because it was assumed that they were illegitmate or did not know who or where their parents were. Of greater consequence, the Royal Pragmatic additionally gave parents the right to prevent the marriage of their offspring to someone of "substantial social inequality." Inequality was officially defined in racial terms but could also be interpreted in terms of wealth, occupation, and status disparities.[4]

Nevertheless, after receiving special permission and the consent of their families, a white and free black couple could marry in the Catholic Church in many colonial societies, including New Orleans.[5] Couples found obtaining waivers of parental permission especially easy in frontier regions, because often they had no idea where their parents were currently living or if they still lived at all. One scholar of Saint-Domingue notes that "even during the last few decades of the colony, marriage between . . . impecunious white Frenchmen and comfortably placed women of color were common enough to inspire bitter comment."[6] In New Spain as well marriages between whites and blacks, while generally tolerated in the sixteenth and seventeenth centuries, became an issue of contention in the eighteenth century, when "Spanish elites responded defensively to the efforts of increasingly well-to-do mulattoes to intermarry with their ranks."[7] Interracial marriage, however, was primarily of concern to status-conscious white aristocrats; few poor Spanish and wealthy mixed-race families objected to unions between their members and darker-skinned castas.

Although official unions between whites and libres were not common in New Orleans, they occurred frequently enough to cause Fray Firso de Peleagonzalo to assume that Don Juan Antonio Lugar and the free parda María Juana Prudhome (alias de Justis) were wed, when actually they had lived in a state of public concubinage for four years. A native of Havana, Prudhome was herself the natural daughter of Mr. Prudhome and Angélica Forest, a morena libre. After Prudhome bore Lugar a daughter in 1793, she presented herself to the priest in order to receive benediction. In his own words Peleagonzalo expressed his surprise: he "had not even suspected that [Prudhome] was not the legitimate wife of Lugar, *as there were in New Orleans other whites married to mulatas* [author's italics]."[8] Prudhome subsequently bore Lugar another daughter and then in 1801 wed a free pardo, the natural son of a free morena and white man and the father of four children by his first wife, another free parda. When Lugar died that same year, he named his two natural daughters as his heirs but also left half the value of his house to Prudhome's oldest daughter by another white man she had known in Havana before her involvement with Lugar.[9] One of the marriages between a free black and a white to which Father Peleagonzalo probably referred involved Bautista Rafael, a free moreno and the legitimate son of two other free morenos, and María Andrea Gitana, the white widow of Vilime Alemán. Church officials recorded their wedding date of 1 May 1779 in the nonwhite registers.[10]

Occasionally marriages between whites and free blacks appeared in the white registers, but only when the free person of color successfully "passed" into white society. They were usually very light-skinned and had strong ties to influential members of the white community. Such was the case of Doña Clara López de la Peña, a free cuarterona or mestiza, and Don Luis Declouet, a white officer in the Spanish regiment. Although they wed on 1 October 1797, it was not until 20 November 1801 that a priest entered their marriage into the white register and made a notation that the children already born to them (a total of six) were now legitimated, by decree of the vicar general. Two years earlier Clara had instituted proceedings before an ecclesiastical tribunal to prove her descent from Native Americans rather than Africans (obviously less of a stigma) and to have her oldest daughter Luisa's baptismal record transferred from the black to the white books.

Baptisms of the five other children, as well as Clara's baptism, were already recorded in the white registers. Clara most likely *was* of African descent, but even for persons of native descent, it was rare to pass as white and sport the title "Doña."[11] Even more remarkable was that the appointed godfather of Clara and Luis's son Luis (named after his older brother, who along with his twin had died just days before the second Luis's birth) was "St. Francis, our seraphic father because of special devotion to the holy patriarch!" Clara's mother Luison Brouner, a free mulata, cuarterona, or mestiza (depending on the document), stood as the baby's godmother, as she did for two of Doña Clara and Don Luis's other children.[12]

In Spanish New Orleans libres also interacted frequently with slaves—at work and at play, in the streets, markets, homes, and religious institutions of the city—and occasionally married them. Uneven sex ratios in the free black population prompted libre women to seek mates among slaves. Of the 136 marriages recorded in the black registers between 1777 and 1803, ten (7.4 percent) were between a libre and a slave, and in six of the ten cases the bride was the free partner.[13] Only two of the twenty partners were light-skinned, both of them free pardo men.

In addition, both freed men and freed women of color who had wed while in slavery continued their relationships with still-enslaved partners. For example, in 1803 the free morena Mannon Arnoult purchased the freedom of her forty-one-year-old slave husband, Santiago Arnoult, from the sisters of the Ursuline Convent. Three days later the sisters manumitted the moreno slave Antonio when his wife, the free morena Roseta, paid them four hundred pesos.[14] Indeed, most slave marriages were between slaves belonging to the religious orders or a clergy member, for whom marriage fees were waived.

Several free blacks acted in accordance with the rules of church and crown and married persons of the same race and status. These marriages between libres often linked kin and friends who belonged to the free pardo and moreno militias. Because female libres outnumbered males two to one, the latter were much sought after as marriage partners and occasionally provoked contests among free women of color. One such dispute, between María Luisa Venus Doriocour and Mariana Carrière, both free morenas, for the hand of the free moreno Antonio de Noyan, alias Conway, further reveals attitudes toward marriage and concubinage among free blacks and whites and the influence of families in marriage decisions.

On 22 September 1789 Conway and Carrière announced their intention to marry and presented the ecclesiastical tribunal with information and witnesses who confirmed that both parties were single and the legitimate children of free black parents who consented to the marriage. One week later Doriocour appeared before the court to assert that Conway had already given a promise of marriage to her and had lived with her for a long time. Although Conway concurred with Doriocour's statement, he claimed that when he had asked her to marry him two months earlier, she had refused him. Two libre women who were friends of Doriocour offered testimony in support of Conway. The couple had lived together as husband and wife for six or seven years, with Doriocour cleaning, ironing, and cooking for Conway, but she had turned down his proposal and told him to take another mate if he wanted to do so. During a conversation with one of the witnesses, Doriocour had indicated that she did not want to marry Conway because she had started a relationship with a white Spanish warrant officer who provided her with gifts and everything she needed in exchange for living with him illicitly. Doriocour apparently saw greater advantages in cohabitating with an influential, well-to-do white than in marrying a free black.

Additional testimony given by this same witness provides another perspective on the complex relationship, however. The witness stated that Doriocour had wanted to protest the marriage of Conway and Carrière to the bishop long before but feared the Carrière family, one of the leading clans in the free black community. Perhaps too late Doriocour regretted her decision to spurn Conway, or her estimation of him might have improved when he became the desired choice of the Carrière family. In either case, the court ruled against her; Conway and Carrière wed one month later.[15]

As was true for the above parties, free blacks usually married someone with similar skin coloring. Of the ninety-three marriages recorded in the black registers between 1777 and 1803 in which both partners were libres, seventy-one (over three-quarters) involved partners of the same phenotype; for the remaining cases, in thirteen the male was lighter and in nine the female was lighter. One of those nine united Catarina Labastille (also known as Lafrance), a cuarterona, and Bartolomé Bautista, a grifo, in 1788. Catarina had consented to marry Bartolomé, but her father, a white plantation owner named Pedro Pablo Labastille (Lafrance), objected to the marriage on grounds of "la desigualdad de los contrayentes respecto ser la dicha mi hija quarterona, y el subrodicho Bartolomé grifo" (inequality of the marriage partners because my daughter is a cuarterona and the above-mentioned Bartolomé is a grifo), all within his rights according to the Royal Pragmatic. Arrested and imprisoned, Bartolomé pleaded for justice before a civil court, claiming that he was not forcing Catarina to marry him against her will and requesting expediency with regard to the marriage ceremony because he needed to harvest his crops. When convinced by "sensible persons" that there was no "diversity of class" between the parties, Don Pedro Pablo finally relented and dropped his objections. The court referred the case to the commissioner of the Inquisition so that he could arrange for the wedding celebration, which took place the next day. In the marriage record, the priest recorded Catarina as the legitimate daughter of Pablo Lafrance and María Charles, the offspring of an official union between a white man and free woman of color.[16]

Although there is no record of how long Catarina and Bartolomé remained together, many unions between libres endured several years, indicating the value they placed on such family relationships. In her will the free morena Angélica stated that she had been married to Roberto Horry, a moreno libre, for thirty-five years and that they had had two children.[17] Horry's brother Juan Bautista, also a free moreno, married Carlota Adelaida, but he died shortly after the birth of their daughter. Carlota Adelaida soon remarried, this time to Pedro Langlois, a free pardo who was the legitimate son of a white man and a free morena.[18] When Juan Castelain, a free pardo, finally married the cuarterona Juana Nivete in 1811, their relationship had lasted at least twenty-five years already and produced ten children. Juan and his two sisters (who stood as witnesses to the marriage) were the natural children of a white man and free parda, as were Juana and her sister, María Francisca Nivete. María Francisca had married Bernardo Mayeaux, the free son of a parda slave and a white man, in 1794; they had two children during the Spanish period.[19]

Although Mayeaux, Castelain, and the Nivete sisters were the offspring of unwed mixed-race unions, they and their children chose to marry persons of the same phenotype and to legitimate their marriages in the Catholic Church. The recent research of Carl A. Brasseaux, Keith P. Fontenot, and Claude F. Oubre on Creoles of Color in the rural areas of southern Louisiana substantiates findings for New Orleans that second- and third-generation libres frequently married other libres rather than entered into less formal relationships with whites and slaves as their parents had done.

Endogamous marriage within the free black population further advanced a sense of group cohesiveness and became even more prevalent in the antebellum period, creating what one scholar terms a free black "caste."[20] The Decoudreaux siblings—Mariana, Catalina, Carlos, and María Francisca—and their mates further exemplify these tendencies. Three of Fanchoneta Decoudreaux's four cuarterón children, the natural offspring of her relationship with a white man, married cuarterón children of other mixed-race consensual unions. Carlos, his brothers-in-law, and some of his nephews enhanced their sense of comradery and corporate identity by serving in the free pardo militia. Fictive ties reinforced consanguine and affinal networks as grandmother, siblings, and in-laws were named godparents to the third generation of Decoudreaux children. The "black sheep" of the family was María Francisca, who had a long-standing relationship and several children with Don Luis Dauqueminil de Morant, a white man. Although not a relative by official marriage, Don Luis cemented his ties with the Decoudreaux family by acting as godparent to María Francisca's nieces and nephews and standing as guarantor for a loan her sister Mariana took out in order to support her business as a tavernkeeper.[21]

Although not typical for the Decoudreaux family, the consensual union between María Francisca and Don Luis was closer to the norm for most residents of colonial New Orleans, who usually did not marry before the church and lived together in what today would be considered common-law marriages. The data presented in table 3.1 substantiate the infrequency of marriage among all racial and status sectors of the population. Several of the informal marital arrangements of the period involved women of color and white men. Because white women were scarce and died young, white men often sought partners among the more numerous and longer-lived free black and slave women of New Orleans. Such unions—most of them unsanctioned by church and crown—produced mixed-race children and confounded official efforts to keep bloodlines "pure," marriages legitimate, and women subordinate to men.

The free black women who engaged in sexual relationships with white men, and even those who did not, were often condemned as "lewd," "lascivious," and "licentious," in New Orleans and throughout the Americas.[22] One late-eighteenth-century observer of New Orleans lifestyles, Claude C. Robin, denounced the many white men who were tempted to "form liaisons with these lascivious, coarse, and lavish [libre] women" and subsequently were "ruined."[23] He blamed the women for such sinful practices, however, as did physician Paul Alliot, who believed that free black women inspired "such lust through their bearing, their gestures, and their dress, that many quite well-to-do persons are ruined in pleasing them."[24] When accused of repossessing a slave he had donated to his former concubine (the free parda Magdalena Canelle, mother of his two cuarterona daughters), Don Luis Beaurepos dismissed Canelle's claims, alleging that her "only proof to ownership rests on the sworn word of some *mulatas,* libertines like herself."[25]

The objects of this derision did not perceive themselves in this way, however, and resisted efforts to denigrate them as women and nonwhites. Like all libres living in slave societies, free women of color operated from an undefined, anomalous position, the middle section of a three-tiered hierarchy in which they were not truly free or slave, often not pure black or white. Libre women were also trapped in a patriarchal society that valued males more than females but that did not afford them the paternal protection due the weaker sex, because they ostensibly did not possess honor and virtue, attributes accorded only to whites. In one unusual case a white man was actually prosecuted for living with a woman of color without benefit of marriage, but only because he stated as much at a trial concerning another matter, and he was not forced to marry her. Carlos Budé went to jail when evidence at a trial revealed that he was involved in an illicit affair with a parda slave. Ironically, Budé had instituted the initial proceedings against a free morena for striking and slandering him. He lost the case and was arrested.[26] Caught in between the interests of officials and residents, of white, libre, and slave men, free black women fought daily oppression and sought to assert their identity, in part by striving to attain what was important to them: freedom for themselves, friends, and relatives; stable, long-lasting unions that produced children and cemented kin networks; prosperity for themselves and future generations; and respect as hardworking, religious members of the community. In most cases, they faced an uphill battle.

Although concern for honor dissuaded most white males from seeking official church weddings with their libre consorts, some did acknowledge these partners and their natural children in wills, inter vivos donations, and sacramental records and revealed that the lengthy, solid relationships to which libre women aspired did exist, if not in official form, at least in fact. Don Pedro Darby and the morena libre Naneta represented a typical example. In his will dated 1803 Darby, a native of New Orleans and single, acknowledged his seven natural children by Naneta, ranging in age from thirty-three to ten years. The children's ages attest to an enduring relationship between the two consorts. Darby donated half his animals and a slave to Naneta, and left the rest of his estate (two plantations, furniture, and half the animals) to the children. He appointed his eldest son Francisco guardian of the minor children.[27]

Another white man who freely recognized his long-term union with a free woman of color was Don Pedro Cázelar. In his will dated June 1797 Cázelar—single, thirty-two years old, and a native of New Orleans—affirmed that he and the free cuarterona Carlota Wiltz had produced four daughters, all between the ages of five and ten. He left the mother and daughters a morena slave and her four children, furniture, household goods, one thousand pesos, and a farm located next to land owned by Don Joseph Dusuau. A sixth heir was added when Carlota bore Don Pedro a son in 1800.[28]

Several families exemplified mixed patterns, with some members maintaining long-term common-law relationships with one partner, as in the Cázelar-Wiltz case, others seeking legitimate marriages, and still others having relationships with many partners. The Hisnard-Grondel-Vidal-Dauphin kin group and its offshoots is one such family. A native New Orleans wholesale merchant, Don Francisco Hisnard lived with his consort, the free morena María or Mariana Grondel, for over a quarter of a century and raised three daughters: Clemencia, Eufrosina, and Mariana, commonly called Sofía. When Hisnard died eleven months after Grondel, his property was evaluated at much less than his free black consort's, which he held for their minor daughters.[29] The oldest, Clemencia, a tavernkeeper, had at least two children by unidentified fathers. Eufrosina had four children with the lieutenant governor of Louisiana, Don Nicolás María Vidal: three daughters and a son who died seven days after his birth. Following the cession of Louisiana to the United States, the family moved to Pensacola, Florida, where Vidal died in 1806. Prior to his relationship with Eufrosina, Vidal had produced two children by two other free black women, one in New Orleans and one in Cartagena, where he had served the Spanish crown before being appointed to office in Louisiana.[30] Hisnard and Grondel's youngest daughter Mariana wed Francisco Dauphin, a free pardo militiaman, in the St. Louis Cathedral of New Orleans when she was a mere fourteen years old.[31] Francisco was one of the eleven natural children born between 1775 and 1799 to Juan Pedro Dauphin, a white man, and Martona, a free grifa. In 1802 Francisco and his older brother Augusto donated to three of their younger brothers a large plot of land in Barataria (the haunting ground of privateer Jean Lafitte) that they had purchased a few weeks earlier.[32] Their father Juan Pedro also practiced brotherly love and utilized kin connections in business deals. He owned and operated a sawmill in partnership with his brother Joseph, who like Juan Pedro lived with a free black consort.[33] Their brother Santiago also had a free black consort, the parda María, and five cuarterón children. Santiago possessed a plantation and fifteen slaves, along with several animals owned jointly with his two brothers.[34]

Like the Dauphin clan, free black kin frequently pooled their resources to purchase property, and to ensure that these holdings remained in the family they appointed kin as guardians of their children or named them as heirs. In 1796 the free parda sisters Constanza and María Rosa Forneret sold a half plot of land they jointly owned to another free parda; the land abutted that of their other sister Feliciana. Two years later Feliciana died while only some twenty years old and appointed Constanza guardian of her three minor children. Constanza and another sister, Angélica, gave power of attorney to their brother Carlos Forneret to represent them in any challenges to Feliciana's will. When their natural father, Don Luis Forneret, traveled to the United States in 1799 on offical business as the Spanish government's interpreter to Native American nations, he also gave Carlos power of attorney to represent the family's interests during his absence. In addition to the five children named above, Don Luis and the free morena María had two daughters and two sons. The siblings frequently stood as godparents to each other's children.[35] After purchasing a half plot of land in New Orleans from her former mistress Doña María Luisa Darensbourg, the free morena Margarita Darensbourg donated it to her niece, Inés Boisclaire. Inés's mother and Margarita's sister Victoria was Doña María Luisa's slave. Margarita stated that she donated the property to Inés in gratitude for the many services Victoria had provided her.[36]

Not all such relationships between family members and sexual partners were so congenial, however. White, slave, and libre men abused and exploited women. They sometimes forced slave and free black women into intimate relations and brutalized their unwanted offspring. In addition, jealous wives—such as Doña María Luisa Allarie—unjustly vented their wrath on slave women, like Margarita, who were suspected of living in concubinage with their husbands. And they could do so without reprisal unless a concerned relative or friend had the courage to bring the culprit to trial. In Margarita's case, it was her Aunt Rosa, a free parda, who petitioned the court to find a new master for her niece, at the time very ill and almost dead from constant whippings. Rosa buttressed her appeal for Margarita's life with what was probably a greater concern to the court: the need to preserve a marriage between two leading white citizens.[37]

There was tension and occasional violence even between men and women who had chosen marriage and entered into it voluntarily, just as in today's society. Despite powerful social norms and the efforts made by couples and church authorities, some marriages between free persons of color experienced difficulties and failed. The moreno libre Joaquín, alias José Pueso, a native of Saint-Domingue, requested that his wife María Teresa, a morena libre, return to marital life with him. Joaquín stated that she had left him two years ago without cause or formal divorce to live with Antonio, a white man known as "el Gallego" (the Galician). María Teresa told quite a different story. Owing to his scandalous behavior, verbal and physical abuse, scorn, and neglect, Joaquín had made her life miserable. He worked from day to day as an unskilled laborer and had failed to provide her with the basic necessities. In addition, when María Teresa had the measles, Joaquín banished her to her father's house until she recovered four months later. To prevent any further abuse she fled and now requested separation or perpetual divorce. The court dropped the suit when the two parties appeared and stated that they had compromised and agreed to return to married life once more.[38] Lack of a better alternative most likely kept them together.

This and other cases indicate that free black, as well as white, males occasionally translated their personal frustrations into antisocial behavior directed toward women. In 1803 Josefina Malbroux, a thirty-two-year-old free morena, sued for divorce from her husband of three months, the moreno libre Juan Bautista Marigny. Apparently without any motive he suddenly disrupted their conjugal harmony by verbally abusing her and beating her with either a horsewhip or a stick, which left marks on her arms and face. These attacks culminated in a threat to kill her by strangling her with a rope. Only the interference of a neighbor halted the attack. After seeking refuge in her mother's house, Malbroux appeared before the court to request a divorce and return of her dowry, furniture, and clothes. The couple reconciled, but one month later Malbroux was back in court. An increasingly

violent Marigny had thrown her out of their house in front of all the neighbors, who supported Malbroux's claims. Witnesses stated that Marigny was
widely known as a thief and accomplice of runaway slaves. Confronted this
time with a man who posed a threat not only to an individual woman but
also to an "ordered" society, the court agreed that Marigny could not be
reformed and granted Malbroux a divorce.[39]

Like Malbroux and María Teresa, libre women who sought separation
were often counseled to reconcile differences with their husbands and return to "la vida maridable" (married life). Church and state officials endeavored to maintain the sacred union and rarely granted a separation, but they
also tried to protect injured parties, male and female. Exasperated by con-
tinual verbal and physical abuse, the free morena María Luisa knifed her
husband Nicolás, also a free moreno, who then brought her up on criminal
charges. According to the testimony of María Luisa, Nicolás, and his sister
Juana, who was outside the house at the time of the incident, María Luisa
had been slicing bread when Nicolás accused her of taking four pesos from
him and became so enraged that he hit her with a stick and a pestle. She
in turn stabbed him in the outer left thigh with the bread knife and fled
from the house but returned three days later when she heard Nicolás was ill.
She stayed there until she was arrested and placed in jail three weeks later.
The pharmacy assistant who treated Nicolás stated that the wound was not
serious and only slightly inflamed, requiring nothing more than a poultice.
What prompted Nicolás to accuse his wife of such a serious crime more
than three weeks after the incident is not clear.

María Luisa's view of the matter is recorded for posterity, however. Following a month of sitting in jail, she petitioned the court to release her
on the grounds that she had inflicted the wound on Nicolás accidentally
without intention and that her imprisonment was hampering her ability to
make a living as a hawkster. She appealed to the mercy of the court as "una
pobre mujer" (poor woman). Apparently the presiding judge, Governor
Carondelet, agreed with María Luisa's contention that the injury was not
grave and was merely the result of a marital dispute, the private concern of
a husband and wife. Two weeks later he released María Luisa with a warn-
ing to both partners to act with moderation and treat each other with the
respect that corresponded to their status. As punishment for his frivolous
suit, Nicolás had to pay all costs associated with the proceedings.[40]

Disputes also arose between parents and children or sisters and brothers that tore families apart. Limited resources sometimes incited contests among heirs for control of the family's property. Exemplifying the stereotypical discord between in-laws was one libre's efforts to have his free parda mother-in-law declared mentally incompetent and thus unable to care for her estate.[41] He undoubtedly hoped that the court would designate him guardian. Court records also indicate that parental favoritism strained sibling relationships. When the free moreno Santiago Coursiac wrote his will, he stated that he had given his natural son, the free moreno Carlos Meunier, a piece of land and that he, Coursiac, had stood as guarantor for a 250-peso loan Meunier had made. The will also stipulated that if Meunier did not repay the loan, the gift of land was to be returned to the estate as compensation. One year later Coursiac's executor sued Meunier for collection of the debt or return of the gift. In defense Meunier avowed that his father's will was unfair: Coursiac had given his legitimate son Esteban Peraux 860 pesos to purchase his freedom and had left the remainder of his estate to his enslaved grandson with instructions to purchase a carta de libertad.[42] Although generous, Coursiac failed to distribute his assets evenly among family members, thereby instigating dissension. The executor eventually dropped the case on account of rising court costs.

One unusually extreme example of sibling factionalism involved the natural children of Don Francisco Emanuel Demasilière and the morena libre María Bienvenu—Pedro Baltazar and Pedro Augusto—and Bienvenu's other children, one a free parda and the others moreno slaves owned by their pardo half brothers. The troubles were created in large part by Don Francisco and his legal representatives. In 1782 he manumitted gratis his morena slave María, age thirty-one, and her pardo son Pedro Baltazar, four months old. By the time Don Francisco wrote a will in 1787, he and María had produced another son, Pedro Augusto. In this testament Don Francisco stipulated that in remuneration for her services, his former slave María Bienvenu was to receive property and a sawmill outside the city, a house in New Orleans, money, housewares, livestock, and nine slaves, three of whom—Basilio, Rosalía, and Iris—were her children by a moreno man (an earlier testament had named one additional child, Henrique, who had evidently died). This property was Bienvenu's to use during her lifetime, but she could not sell it, and it was to go to the two Pedros when she died.[43]

Bienvenu died in 1791. She claimed to have six natural children: the three slaves, the two Pedros, and Rosalía Clemencia. Clemencia was a parda whose freedom her mother had purchased for fourteen hundred pesos in 1788 when the child was fifteen years old. She might have been Don Francisco's daughter (he had several mixed-race children by other libre women), because even though she was quite a bit older than the two Pedros and was not mentioned in his will, she took the Demasilière name. In addition to the usufruct of goods Don Francisco had left their two sons, Bienvenu possessed one slave, household goods, and clothing, which she donated to her mother, a free morena. Named as her executor was Agustín Malet, the free pardo husband of her relative Jacinta Demasilière.[44]

Three years later Clemencia Demasilière, a parda libre, appeared before the governor's tribunal to obtain the freedom of her half sister, the morena slave María Iris. The slave's owners were Pedro Baltazar and Pedro Augusto, the brothers or half brothers of Clemencia and the half brothers of María Iris. Clemencia paid 450 pesos to manumit María Iris. Another seven years passed before she was able to come up with the 400 pesos needed to purchase the freedom of her other half sister, Rosalía. Once again Clemencia had to bring her brothers, or rather their guardian, before a tribunal.[45]

Most likely the two Pedros were too young to comprehend the intricacies of the case; maybe until they were older they were not even aware that the slaves they owned were their half sisters and brother. Even though their guardian was acting on his charges' behalf, an amicable agreement on the purchase prices of María Iris and Rosalía probably could have been arranged without resorting to the deliberations of a tribunal. The bulk of the blame for tearing apart this family rested, however, on Don Francisco, the powerful white patron who manipulated his natural family's lives. One can only imagine the contradictory feelings María Bienvenu must have experienced; she owned her children as slaves, could not manumit them, and was forced to pass them on to her other children, all because the provisions of a white man's will decreed it so. And she probably wanted to free them, as evidenced by the rather exorbitant sum she paid for Clemencia's manumission. To her pardo son's credit, however, once Pedro Baltazar did reach majority age, he freed gratis his last remaining enslaved half sibling, Basilio, a skilled carpenter and moreno militiaman. Pedro Augusto had died one year earlier after a long illness, thus leaving his brother sole heir to their father's estate worth about seven thousand pesos.[46]

Fictive kinship sought to reinforce familial ties and sometimes replace linkages broken by the death of or squabbles between blood relatives. Schol-

TABLE 3.2   Phenotype and Status of Padrinos, New Orleans, 1787–1797

Phenotype of Baptized	Godfather				Godmother			
	White	Libre	Slave	Total	White	Libre	Slave	Total
Pardo	464	247	21	732	280	425	28	733
Moreno	36	90	26	152	18	107	27	152
Total	500	337	47	884	298	532	55	885

Sources: Nonwhite Baptisms, books 4a and 5a, 1787–1797.

ars have noted that "in use, godparenthood is joined to other kinds of ties, and this total complex of the sacred and the secular determines who is selected to enter the relationships."[47] Within a hierarchical society like that of Spanish New Orleans compadrazgo served to link persons of lower with those of higher status, slaves with free persons, nonwhites with whites, clients with patrons. The goal of most parents was to find godparents of equal or preferably higher status for their children and thereby gain privileges for those children. New Orleans society, like all Latin societies, was also patriarchal, and godfathers constituted the most important fictive connection. Libres most commonly selected white godfathers and free black godmothers for their offspring (table 3.2). Among free blacks baptized between January 1787 and December 1797 for whom the race of the child and the *padrinos* was identified, 56.6 percent had white godfathers, 38.1 percent free black godfathers, and a mere 5.3 percent slave godfathers. An almost reverse ratio prevailed among white and free black godmothers, with slaves still making up a small proportion: 33.7 percent, 60.1 percent, and 6.2 percent respectively.

When libres are further separated by phenotype, data reveal that pardos had a larger percentage of white godparents, a smaller percentage of free black godparents, and a much smaller percentage of slave godparents than morenos did. This tendency was to be expected in a hierarchical society where race as well as status was an important factor in making advantageous compadrazgo choices. However, for cases in which libres had other libres as godparents, they tended to select free blacks of the same phenotype: morenos had morenos and pardos had pardos. When looking at changes in godparent choice over time, one sees that for godmothers the choice of whites, libres, or slaves remained about the same proportionately. Although the selection of libre godfathers was also fairly constant, the percentage of white godfathers increased while slave godfathers decreased between 1787 and 1797 (for whites from 40.8 percent to 62.6 percent, with a high in 1794 of 68.1 percent; for slaves from 12.7 percent to 2.0 percent). Thus compadrazgo could strengthen both vertical and horizontal ties among racial and status groups in New Orleans society.

Libres benefited from associations with fictive kin, just as they did from those with family members related by blood or marriage. Masters frequently stood as godparents to their slaves and occasionally freed them; a few more padrinos acted as third parties in purchasing cartas for their *ahijados* (godchildren). Only three slave owners—two free black women and a white man—explicitly stated that the slave they were freeing was their godchild, although more might have freed godchildren without indicating the relationship. Two moreno padrinos and two cuarterona and four morena *madrinas* proffered funds to manumit their ahijados. Among them were the free parda Francisca Riche, who freed graciosa her seven-year-old cuarterona slave and ahijada Luisa Bataylle, the daughter of another free parda; María Foucher, a free cuarterona who paid Doña María Juana Broutin two hundred pesos to issue a carta for Foucher's godson Honorato, an eight-year-old moreno; and Pedro Claver, a free moreno militia sergeant who convinced the sisters of the Ursuline Convent to manumit his goddaughter María Angela for six hundred pesos.[48] Ahijados also inherited goods from their libre and white padrinos. In April 1786 Naneta Chabert, a free parda and native of New Orleans, died without marrying or producing children. Her will stipulated that her goddaughter Luison Mandeville (Brouner) and Luison's husband Francisco Durand, both free pardos, inherit Chabert's entire estate, including land near New Orleans and Baton Rouge, four slaves, and ten cartloads of rice. Chabert must have felt stronger ties to her goddaughter than to her mother, whom Chabert had purchased and freed in 1773 and who was still alive in Mobile. Chabert did stipulate, however, that one of her slaves was to remain in Mobile and care for her mother as long as she lived.[49] On a smaller scale, the free morena Angélica Pascal donated by testament one hundred pesos to her ahijado Narciso, a pardo libre. Pascal divided the remainder of her holdings among her nieces, nephews, and friends.[50]

As libres advanced in the social hierarchy, they often chose more prestigious individuals to stand as godparents for their children. Take, for example, the Bailly family, headed by the free pardo Pedro. A perusal of Pedro's personal, business, and military life during the Spanish period reveals an aggressive, ambitious man who utilized New Orleans' patrimonial, hierarchical social structure and legal system for his own and his family's benefit. He pursued every business opportunity, buying and selling real estate and slaves and borrowing and lending money. Manumitted gratis by Josef Bailly in 1776 at the age of twenty-five, Pedro immediately began accumulating property, including his mother, whom he immediately freed. He labored as a carter, blacksmith, wood dealer, and militia officer. Between 1779 and 1793 he advanced from corporal second class to first lieutenant in the free pardo militia and served with that unit in the Baton Rouge, Mobile, and Pensacola expeditions against the British during the American Revolution.[51] Bailly and his wife Naneta Cadis gave birth to five children between 1782 and 1797. The first, Pedro Jr., had as his godparents Francisco Brantan, a free moreno militia officer, and Francisca Montreuil, the child's maternal grandmother—in other words, two free blacks. Pedro and Naneta's second son, Joseph Pedro, had one white godparent, a captain in the Spanish fixed regiment, and one free black godparent, the captain's cuarterona daughter. For their third and fourth sons Bailly and Cadis chose white godfathers *and* white godmothers; both godfathers were officials in the Spanish government. Their fifth child—a daughter born after Bailly had served two years in a Cuban prison for espousing treasonous maxims in favor of the French and Haitian Revolutions—had a white godfather and free black godmother.[52] When Bailly finally did return from El Morro Castle in Havana, he resumed his business transactions with whites and libres, even though he never served in the militia again. Bailly probably called upon his connections of patronage with his children's godparents to restore his reputation as a buen vasallo. Both Bailly and his oldest son Pedro, who followed his father's lead in serving in the free pardo militia, signed an "Address from the Free People of Color" to the first U.S. governor of Louisiana, William C. C. Claiborne, on 17 January 1804.[53]

Although always a subordinate group within New Orleans' hierarchical society, the Bailly and other families of the emerging libre "elite" obviously identified more closely with and aspired to gain acceptance from dominant whites. Some, like Clara López de la Peña, eventually even "passed" and reclassified themselves as white. Most, however, had to be content with constructing consanguine, affinal, and fictive kinship networks to strengthen their relationships with white patrons and with each other. Nonetheless, many libres continued to associate with slaves on a casual basis in the workplace, on streets, in homes and places of recreation, in the markets and the church, and in more formal arrangements such as marriage and compadrazgo. Although few libres selected slaves as marriage partners (official and consensual) or as godparents for their children, slaves often named free blacks as godparents, thereby affirming a system of reciprocal, though unequal, obligation.

Such kinship strategies reinforced a colonial social and racial order that firmly placed libres in a middle stratum between whites and slaves, while at the same time they provided opportunities for movement within the echelons of free black society and occasional melding into white society. Even though they still occupied an amorphous, ambiguous position in the community, free blacks were beginning to forge their own identity and create an elite leadership based on wealth, kin connections, and militia service. In order to advance their status, they intertwined ties between such corporate entities as the family and the militia by naming militia members as godparents and guardians, marrying militiamen or female relations of military families, and entering into business deals with each other. Such alliances promoted group cohesiveness and identity among libres.

Chapter 4

A PRIVILEGE AND HONOR

TO SERVE

Free black militia units played a vital role in defending New Orleans and in promoting a sense of corporate identity among the city's libre population. Spain's primary interest in Louisiana was strategic. Throughout the French and Spanish colonial periods Louisiana's populace remained sparse, and both metropolitan governments were faced with little choice but to turn to libres for their defensive needs. Forming part of the strategic circum-Caribbean region, the colony lacked any realistic alternative to arming and organizing substantial numbers of free black males. Some colonial leaders even preferred free black militiamen to regular troops and white militias.[1] Spanish governors thus called upon the free pardo and moreno militias of New Orleans to serve in almost every military campaign, the most noteworthy ones being the North American War of Independence and threatened repercussions stemming from the French Revolution. City and provincial leaders also relied on the militia to chase cimarrones, repair breaks in the levee, fight fires, and patrol city streets at night.

Militia members in turn utilized their positions and consanguine, affinal, and fictive kin connections to advance within New Orleans society, as well as to promote group cohesiveness and identity among libres. Free black militiamen, most notably officers, married each other's daughters and sisters, acted as godparents for each other's children, stood as witnesses at each other's weddings, and loaned money, guaranteed loans, and provided other types of financial assistance to each other. They called on their titles, reputations as loyal, honorable vecinos, and patronage from leading whites, many of them military men themselves, to attain increased material and social influence. The four decades of Spanish rule witnessed an increase in the size and prominence of the free black militia. As can be ascertained from the constant struggle to maintain the militia's existence and integrity in the early years of United States rule, free militiamen of color in New Orleans viewed their organization as a corporate entity that allowed them to associate with whites on a theoretically equal basis and that bestowed upon them the honor and privileges that libres aspired to attain.

The character and purpose of New Orleans' free militia of color closely resembled those of other free pardo and moreno militias in the Spanish realm.[2] Demographic realities in most frontier or marginal regions necessitated the enlistment of free blacks in urban and provincial (or disciplined) militias, especially in the strategic circum-Caribbean, where fortifications were hard to defend and constantly under attack by foreign privateers and naval forces. In contrast to the situation in Anglo North America and central areas of Spanish America, there simply were not enough whites to fill the ranks, in particular during the last quarter of the eighteenth century, when Spain attempted to place the burden of defense on its colonies. In addition, most colonials actively endeavored to shirk their obligation as able-bodied royal subjects to train for and fight in what they considered to be metropolitan squabbles that were of little concern to them. Administrators thus drew upon the lower, often mixed-race, sectors of society, who were more cooperative because more easily coerced. In some areas, however, libres were the soldiers of choice. For instance, Leon G. Campbell found that in Peru "the best soldiers were the free Negroes and Indians, but the serious doubts which the Spanish held about their loyalty meant that they had to be carefully supervised."[3] The baron de Carondelet, governor-general of Louisiana from 1791 to 1797, considered militiamen—libre and white—superior to regular troops because they were familiar with the terrain and also less expensive.[4]

Militia duty offered libres several opportunities throughout Spanish America, where "the admission of colored castes into the newly reformed militia . . . opened yet another door for social acceptance of blacks within the empire."[5] By belonging to the corporate military body, free blacks had the potential to transcend at least some race and class barriers. In many respects, "the military minimized racial and social differences—both legally and in practice—in favor of corporate unity," although the militia, more so than the *fijo* regiments (fixed units raised and stationed permanently in the colonies), reflected the hierarchical Spanish social structure.[6] Eventually extended to libre as well as white militias, the fuero militar constituted a set of coveted military privileges, among them exemption from paying tribute, opportunities to receive retirement and death benefits, and the right to bear arms and wear uniforms, a distinction that separated libres from slaves and associated them with whites. The most important aspect of the fuero militar, however, was its system of judicial administration in which members of the military corporate body judged accused personnel. That is, according to provisions of the military reorganization of the 1760s, militia officers were tried by a military court rather than by an ordinary tribunal in all civil and criminal cases in which they were defendants. Enlisted personnel not on active duty were granted protection of the fuero solely in criminal cases, but when mobilized for active service, they, too, received the full fuero. Militiamen protected by the fuero militar also could be detained not in public jails but rather only in military structures.[7]

The expansion of militia units to include free blacks was part of the Bourbon monarchy's larger reorganization of the entire Spanish American military system, led by minister Juan de Villalba. In war-torn Cuba, where the supply of eligible whites was insufficient, General Alejandro O'Reilly, who spearheaded the reforms and later governed Louisiana, recruited many free pardos. Hoping to boost loyalty, performance, and morale among the large free black population, he extended the fuero to the free militia of color on the same basis as for the white. Viceroy marqués de Croix did the same for Mexico in 1767. Many colonial administrators, especially those outside the strategic Caribbean, balked at granting free black militiamen equal privileges, but most of them eventually complied with at least some of the reorganizational measures.[8] As one expert points out,

> the growing need to defend the empire, especially after the Seven Years' War which ended in 1763, precluded, to an extent, their [Spanish civil and military officials'] concerns as to whether former African slaves could be trusted in view of the moral deficiencies Europeans believed them to have.[9]

The fuero militar accorded free black militiamen, officers in particular, privileges many white persons and slaves were denied. A significant symbol of differentiation, the fuero "placed the holder above and apart from the rest of society and in effect constituted the militia as a social elite," and it "provided for free black militiamen to be distinguished from slaves."[10] Because libres coveted this distinctive badge and whites envied their having it, colonial administrators had to appease both groups cautiously: they relied on free blacks to defend their New World kingdoms but were reluctant to upset the traditional social order. Although the fuero and other privileges, such as pensions and exemption from taxes, helped foster corporate over class unity and brought black militiamen together as a group recognized by society, they did not dissolve the hierarchical social barriers that segmented colonial society by race and class.[11]

Indeed, the militias of New Orleans reflected strong racial and class divisions within the society. In its formation of the free black militia, New Orleans evidenced even greater concern with color distinctions than did many regions of the New World and even of Louisiana. Colonial administrators in many parts of Spanish America combined morenos, pardos, indios, and mestizos in free pardo units, and in New Granada these racial groups, along with whites, formed "all colors" integrated units.[12] In Opelousas and Natchitoches, Louisiana, free blacks served in white militias.[13] New Orleans, by contrast, created and sustained distinct free pardo and moreno militia companies throughout the Spanish period.

This organization based on strict racial differentiation is accounted for in part by simple imitation. Cuba had established the pattern for separate free pardo and moreno units and maintained them well into the nineteenth century, as did Mexico, Panama, Colombia, Venezuela, Santo Domingo, Puerto Rico, Florida, and other areas of the circum-Caribbean.[14] Louisiana came under the jurisdiction of Cuba, and New Orleans, as the administrative center of Louisiana, had the greatest contact with Havana. Another explanation might be that local authorities endeavored to divide and thus further control members of the proportionately large and growing free black population in New Orleans. Also, in New Orleans resided the greatest number of libres who could be organized into their own separate units; they formed a critical mass. But whether they were congregated into multiracial groups or separated into units according to phenotype, the free militias of color in each region received equal pay, provisions, and treatment. The distinctions made between pardos and morenos in Louisiana and Cuba did not materially affect free black soldiers.

Militia service was not without its drawbacks. It was compulsory for all able-bodied free black males, and white commanders often assigned free pardo and moreno companies the least desirable duties. Providing the first line of defense in battle, free blacks acted as scouts, flankers, and diversionary forces. In times of war they also replenished the fijo units. When the colony and metropolis were not embroiled in war, free black militia members labored on public works, acted as an urban nighttime police force, and rode in slave patrols. For the rank and file, militia service was especially toilsome: it involved frequent travel away from family and community, possible danger, and infrequent promotion. Enlisted men were often taken away from lucrative civilian jobs and pressed into lower-paying militia duty. They also faced prejudice and disdain from white militiamen, many of whom doubted their loyalty.[15]

Although free black militia officers also encountered social prejudice and discrimination, they reaped many more benefits than did enlisted personnel. They were more fully covered by the fuero militar and received higher pay and retirement benefits. Prestige accompanied military leadership; for outstanding feats of combat libre officers merited commendation in the form of praise, medals, and money. Militia officers commonly assumed positions of leadership within the larger society, where they were called upon to testify as character witnesses, stand as godparents, and cosign for loans. In addition, authorities frequently exempted officers from paying taxes, tribute, and licensing fees. When white officials threatened to disband free militias of color or replace their black officers with white ones, members voiced their opposition and struggled to maintain their status as influential participants in the society.[16]

During the Spanish period the free militia of color in New Orleans increased in size and concurrently in prestige, as did the libre population as a whole. Over a span of twenty-two years the number of free black forces in the city rose from 89 in 1779 to 469 in 1801, representing a fivefold increase and an approximate average annual growth rate of 17 percent.[17] This increase in the militia paralleled that of free black males in general and was slightly greater than that of all libres. Census data indicate that between 1778 and 1805 the number of free black males in New Orleans jumped from 121 to 624 and all free blacks from 353 to 1,566.[18]

Militia rolls provide substantial evidence of a much more numerous libre population than has formerly been acknowledged. H. E. Sterkx found that the free population of color numbered 165 for all Louisiana in 1769, with 99 libres residing in the capital,[19] and subsequent scholars have accepted Sterkx's figures. By contrast, rosters of free pardo and moreno males eligible for military service and living within four leagues (twelve land miles) of New Orleans listed 61 free pardos and 238 free morenos in 1770.[20] Obviously, the census taker undercounted pardos, but even so, the number of males between the ages of fifteen and forty-five far exceeded Sterkx's sum. When one takes into account that females usually outnumbered males two to one in the New Orleans libre population,[21] the extent of undercounting is even more astounding. As later censuses showed, not all these men actively served in the free black militia; nevertheless, Louisiana governors had vast reserves upon which to call if the need arose.

Officers compiled the next substantial set of militia rolls during the United States War of Independence, when the Spanish government formally created two companies of free black militia for the first time. These militia lists enumerated fifty-six pardos and thirty-three morenos, for a total of eighty-nine men, nine of whom were officers.[22] In attacks on several English forts on the Mississippi River in the fall of 1779, Governor Bernardo de Gálvez led 1,427 men, including 80 of the free morenos and pardos from New Orleans.[23] The numbers of free black troops embarking from New Orleans rose to 107 for the Mobile campaign and to 143 free pardos (5 officers, 24 noncoms, and 114 soldiers) joined by 128 free morenos (5 officers, 22 noncoms, and 101 soldiers) in the Pensacola attack.[24]

Following these battles colonial administrators in Spanish Louisiana did not compile any militia rosters until the early 1790s, when European warfare once again prompted defensive concerns to flare. By 1791 the size of the adult male free pardo population had grown large enough to warrant the formation of a second company, and on 3 July 1791 the recently appointed Governor Carondelet promoted several officers and noncommissioned officers from the original company to higher posts within the new company.[25] One of these promotions went to Francisco Dorville, who rose from lieutenant of the first company to captain of the second. Dorville had a long and illustrious service record, beginning with campaigns against the English at Baton Rouge, Mobile, and Pensacola. As a second lieutenant in the free pardo company, Dorville earned a distinctive medal of merit and monetary gratification from the king for his acts of bravery at Baton Rouge and an award of three hundred pesos for courage displayed at Mobile and Pensa-

TABLE 4.1   Organization of the Free Black Militias of New Orleans, 1793

Position	Free Pardos 1st Company	Free Pardos 2nd Company	Free Morenos
Captain	1	1	1
Assistant captain	—	—	1
Lieutenant	1	1	1
Second lieutenant	1	1	2
First sergeant	1	1	2
Second sergeant	2	2	2
First corporal	6	6	6
Second corporal	5	5	3
Soldiers	98	98	66
Total	115	115	84

Sources: AGI PC 191, 6 November 1793; AGI PC 159-B, 7 November 1793.

cola. By the end of the Spanish period Dorville had risen to the position of commander of the Battalion of Free Pardos of New Orleans, in which his son Narciso was a second lieutenant and son Esteban a second sergeant.[26]

During the 1790s free black militia numbers increased and organization became more complex. Table 4.1 details the size and structure of the free pardo and moreno companies in 1793, and table 4.2 does the same for 1801. In addition to the figures for 1801 presented in table 4.2, each pardo and moreno battalion had one commander of the respective phenotype; he was listed as part of the general command staff (*plana mayor*). During the 1790s the free pardo units grew much more rapidly than the moreno ones, probably paralleling a trend in population figures for all libres.[27]

One of the New Orleans militia rosters compiled on 1 May 1801 recorded information on age, height, and health. Although there were no data for militiamen dispatched to other areas of the province, absent, or incarcerated, information on a fairly representative sample is presented in table 4.3. Because most promotions were based on number of years of service, the positive linear correlation between an increase in age and an advancement in

TABLE 4.2   Organization of the Free Black Militias of New Orleans, 1801

Position	Battalion of Pardos			Battalion of Morenos		
	Grenadiers	Company 1	Company 2	Company 3	Grenadiers	Company 1
Captain	1	1	1	1	1	1
Lieutenant	1	1	1	1	1	1
Second lieutenant	1	1	1	1	1	1
First sergeant	1	1	1	1	1	1
Second sergeant	2	2	2	2	1	2
Drummer	—	—	—	—	1	—
First corporal	3	3	4	4	4	5
Second corporal	5	3	4	4	3	2
Soldiers	36	97	94	94	35	79
Total	46	106	105	105	45	89

Source: AGI PC 160-A, 1 May 1801.

TABLE 4.3   Age, Height, and Health of the
Free Black Militias, New Orleans, 1801

Rank	Average Age	N^a	Average Height[b]	N^c	Good Health	Average Health	Total[a]
Pardos							
Officers	42.3	13	5'4"3	13	1	3	4
Noncoms	31.6	30	5'3"3	30	16	6	22
Soldiers	23.1	151	5'3"3	84	137	32	169
Morenos							
Officers	44.4	7	5'5"2	7	1	2	3
Noncoms	38.5	18	5'2"5	18	15	—	15
Soldiers	33.8	59	5'3"3	49	53	12	65

Source: AGI PC 160-A, fols. 342–65, 1 May 1801.
   a. Did not include members stationed elsewhere, absent, or incarcerated, for whom no data were provided.
   b. Height measured in European feet, inches, and *líneas,* which were slightly larger than the English measure.
   c. Included militiamen age twenty and older; they most likely had reached their final height.

rank is expected. Height also tended to correspond to rank in a positive relationship. Free pardo and moreno militiamen seem to have been quite tall in comparison with their contemporaries. In his work on the Canary Islanders who immigrated to Louisiana, Gilbert C. Din provides evidence for his assertion that Spaniards, and Europeans in general, were short in stature. Officials hired persons to procure recruits and compensated them according to the height of the prospective soldier/immigrant: "15 *reales* for a recruit 5 feet ½ inch tall, 30 *reales* for a recruit 5 feet 2 inches tall, and 45 *reales* for one over 5 feet 3 inches tall. The height requirement was similar to the army's."[28]

   In addition to numbers, the New Orleans free pardo and moreno militias grew in importance over the Spanish period. As Roland C. McConnell aptly states, "black troops left an enduring legacy to Louisiana," and "in fighting for France, Spain, and the U.S.A., [they] were freedom fighters fighting for themselves."[29] This legacy originated in the French regime, when colonial leaders first formed and employed free black troops in the 1735 campaign against the Chickasaw. After organizing a company of forty-five free blacks and slaves with free black officers, Governor Jean Baptiste Lemoyne, sieur de Bienville led them into battle. French authorities subsequently created a company of fifty free black militiamen in 1739. This company battled Native Americans at Fort Assumption into the next year but then dissipated. From 1740 until 1779 free black troops were not employed in active combat.[30]

The Spaniards recognized the presence of a "ghost" free black militia, however. Following the Seven Years' War and the acquisition of Louisiana, the Spanish crown assigned Alejandro O'Reilly to the enormous task of re-organizing defenses in the New World. During the 1760s he "dictated the regulations which came to govern not only the Caribbean, but also Louisi-ana and the Floridas."[31] Of a total force of 2,056 accompanying O'Reilly on his journey to Louisiana, there were eighty each from the free pardo and free moreno militia units of Havana. Most of these forces returned to Cuba with O'Reilly in 1770.[32] Upon arriving in Louisiana O'Reilly demanded oaths of allegiance to His Catholic Majesty Carlos III from various cor-porate groups, one of which was "La Compagnie des Mulâtres et Nègres Libres de cette colonie de la Louisianne." Thirty-four men signed or placed their mark on this oath.[33] O'Reilly also compiled lists of free black males who could be called into military service, and he intended to create a com-pany of libres along with the four white militia units that he did form.

Some scholars claim that O'Reilly failed to organize free blacks because their numbers were too low, but the 1770 lists disprove this contention. Perhaps French colonials objected to organizing and arming libres—they had previously decried such efforts—and O'Reilly decided not to push his reforms too far and fast.[34] Nonetheless, O'Reilly appointed Pedro Simón, a free pardo of New Orleans, captain and commander of the free pardo and moreno militia from the Acadian Coast to Balize on 24 February 1770, just days before he returned to Cuba.[35] Like most colonial authorities in the New World, Spaniards were wary about arming free blacks, but the ex-panding role of Louisiana in confrontations with France, England, and the United States forced O'Reilly to this decision.[36]

The existence in the 1770s of at least an informal free black militia can be ascertained from various documents. The "Liste de la quantité des nai-gres libres de la Nouvelle Orléans, 1770" acknowledged Nicolás Bacus, a free moreno captain, as having compiled it.[37] On 2 November 1772 a notary recorded the emancipation of a black woman and her two-year-old son by Simón Calpha, identified as a pardo libre and commander of the free pardo and moreno militia.[38] Pedro Simón's official command of the free black militia obviously was not of long duration; most likely he had died. During the United States War of Independence and into the mid-1780s Calpha headed the companies of free pardos and morenos. A common peacetime responsibility for free black militias throughout Spanish America was the apprehension of runaway slaves. On 15 October 1773 the New Orleans cabildo paid eighteen free black men—and probable militiamen—two pesos each for chasing and capturing cimarrones. The cabildo paid this amount free and clear of rewards individual masters might offer successful libres.[39]

Governor Gálvez rejuvenated the free black militia in 1778 and dispatched it to battle the British at Baton Rouge (1779), Mobile (1780), and Pensacola (1781).[40] It is important to highlight free black participation in the American Revolution, because other than the occasional mention of Crispus Attucks and a few blacks who fought in the northern Anglo colonies, little attention has been accorded the service of African Americans in this historic episode.[41] Recent scholarship has sought to address this void and point to the role slaves and libres played, as well as the steps they took to free themselves in the southern colonies, in particular. As Peter Kolchin points out, the "destruction, confusion, and loss of authority that accompanied the war provided slaves with numerous opportunities to escape bondage. . . . Upon occasion the population of entire plantations . . . ran away."[42] Nevertheless, the contributions of Spanish-speaking blacks (and Spain in general) are still slighted.[43]

When Gálvez departed New Orleans on 27 August 1779 on his way up the Mississippi River to Manchac and Baton Rouge, he took with him 667 men, 89 of them from the free pardo and moreno militias. Along the way additional militiamen and Native American allies joined him to compose a total force of 1,427. Gálvez's army also included twelve civilian craftsmen; two of these were libres (Carlos, a free pardo carpenter, and Francisco Fortière, a free moreno gunsmith) and one was a black slave (Antonio, a blacksmith). At Baton Rouge the white and free black militias, along with Louisiana Indians, performed a feinting action and drew fire from the British batteries. This diversion allowed Gálvez to construct his own batteries. Within twenty-four hours the English had surrendered unconditionally, not only Baton Rouge but also Natchez and other river posts.[44]

Gálvez roundly praised his courageous troops, white and black. He submitted the following names to the crown for appropriate commendations:

Simón Calpha, captain of the free pardo and moreno militias,[45] Juan Bautista Hugón (Ogón), a pardo lieutenant, and Francisco Dorville, a pardo second lieutenant, all men of valor and good conduct; Felipe Rueben, a moreno lieutenant, and Manuel Noël Carrière, a moreno second lieutenant, for sufficient service; and Nicolás Bacus and Luis la Nuit, moreno assistant second lieutenants, both of whom had displayed much valor and activity. Gálvez asked that the crown bestow upon these men favors similar to those distributed to militia officers of the same phenotype in Havana and elsewhere. On 12 January 1780 the crown granted Gálvez's request, dispensing ten silver medals of honor to officers of the free black militia for their exemplary battle conduct in the Mississippi River campaigns. In addition, administrators promoted several free black officers.[46]

The New Orleans free black militiamen who accompanied Gálvez on his next expedition against Mobile numbered 107, plus officers. Although Simón Calpha was the free black commander and captain of the New Orleans forces, a white officer, Lieutenant Pedro de Marigny, held ultimate command power. Foul weather delayed the expedition, but finally by the end of February 1780 New Orleans forces joined Cuban reinforcements, several of them free blacks, outside Mobile. Once again Gálvez employed free black troops in a feinting action. This tactic eventually succeeded, but the siege was longer and casualties greater than at Baton Rouge. Among those injured was one free moreno.[47] The crown did not commend any free black militiamen for their actions at Mobile; however, it did issue statements of approbation for activities carried out at both Mobile and Pensacola.

Gálvez directed his third and final campaign against the English at Pensacola. He could not launch this expedition until 23 March 1781 because of a hurricane, but when he did leave New Orleans, he took 271 free black militiamen with him. Many of these free blacks belonged to Havana companies.[48] By 10 April 1781 the British surrendered West Florida to Spain, and Gálvez's troops returned victorious to New Orleans. Gálvez again requested, and the crown granted, rewards for officers of the free black militia. From Pensacola on 26 May 1781 Gálvez forwarded the names of Simón Calpha, who had commanded the Louisiana free black militias in all three expeditions and witnessed the death of one son and the wounding of another at Mobile, for a pension; Carlos Calpha, a pardo second lieutenant who had been injured while performing meritorious service at Mobile, for a medal; and Pedro Tomás, a moreno lieutenant who had displayed courage in the

Pensacola attack, for a medal. Eventually the crown conferred an annual pension of 240 pesos on Simón Calpha, which ceased at his death in 1786 and could not be granted to his successor. The king also awarded distinctive medals of honor to Carlos Calpha and Tomás, medals of honor and bonuses of 300 pesos each to moreno lieutenant Carrière and pardo lieutenants Hugón and Dorville, and a medal of honor and bonus of 250 pesos to pardo second lieutenant Nicolás Bacus Boisclair for their valiant conduct at Mobile and Pensacola.[49]

On 15 February 1781 Gálvez relinquished his position as colonel of the Fixed Infantry Regiment of Louisiana in order to seek promotion to field marshal of the royal armies. He concurrently was named captain-general of Louisiana and West Florida, and Louisiana was designated a government separate from Cuba. Gálvez served as governor of Cuba until 1785, when the crown appointed him viceroy of New Spain. He died on 30 November 1786 in Mexico City. In March 1787 the Militia Corps of Free Morenos and Pardos addressed a letter to José de Gálvez, uncle of Bernardo and minister of the Indies, expressing their concern and sympathy upon the death of their former leader. They proclaimed Gálvez their venerated protector and emphasized how deeply his sudden death pained them. According to the letter, nothing could equal the love and gratitude in their hearts that his beneficent leadership had nurtured.[50]

From 1782 to 1791 Esteban Miró governed Louisiana, and during that period the free black militia did not engage in active combat with a foreign enemy. It did, however, participate in expeditions against cimarrones, repair breaks in the levee, and fight the fires that plagued New Orleans, in particular the Great Conflagration of 1788. The lack of rosters for this decade probably indicates that the libre militia did not meet very regularly or in an organized form. Nevertheless, Miró promoted Don Juan Bautista Mentzinger, a white officer, to the post of Sargento Primero, Garzón de los Pardos y Morenos Libres in 1784, a position he held until 1789. Mentzinger was to instruct the free black militia in matters of discipline and military preparedness.[51] Because these militiamen were already organized for military duty, colonial administrators called on them in emergency situations.

In 1782 and 1784 Miró employed free black militia members to hunt runaway slaves in the swamps and bayous, a task for which he and Carondelet considered them well suited because of their familiarity with the terrain. The free moreno captain Carrière, along with his moreno lieutenant Tomás and pardo sergeant Juan Medes, led a detachment of seven free pardos and seven free morenos in search of cimarrones for two and a half days. The cabildo paid them thirty-five pesos five reales for their efforts. Apparently the cabildo surrendered these funds reluctantly; seven months after the first promise of funds, Carrière again appealed for payment.[52] For this expedition and the one in 1784 the governor combined free pardos and morenos in one unit, and interestingly appointed two free morenos to the highest positions, even though whites usually ranked light-skinned above dark-skinned blacks.

Lieutenant Colonel Francisco Bouligny commanded the 1784 expedition against the infamous San Maló band.[53] Cimarrón gangs consistently menaced Louisiana settlements, but the San Maló band's power posed a serious threat to racial control in the countryside and towns. In addition to veteran troops and white militias, Bouligny utilized one detachment of free pardo volunteers, a combined detachment of free pardos and black slaves, and three free black militia detachments led by Carrière, Dorville, and Bacus. According to the expedition's payroll, free black lieutenants earned eight reales per day, sergeants six reales, and soldiers and guides four reales. These daily rates were equal for pardo and moreno units; white soldiers earned the same pay, but white sergeants and officers were paid higher wages. Although Bouligny complained that his small force of free pardos and morenos offered a meager challenge to the growing numbers of cimarrones and that some of them engaged in commerce with the runaways, he and his men disrupted the band, captured fifty of its members, and brought to execution four of the ringleaders. Among the men Bouligny recommended for royal commendation was Juan Bautista Hugón, captain of the free pardos. Miró rejected many of the men Bouligny recommended, however, including Hugón, and did not forward his name to the crown.[54]

When natural disasters struck New Orleans, civil leaders called upon members of the free black militia for assistance. The fire that swept through most of the city on 21 March 1788 occasioned the use of all available men to rescue persons and property and bring the blaze under control. Once property damage was assessed, free blacks along with their white neighbors petitioned the crown for indemnification. Included among these petitioners were Josef Duplessis, Josef Favrot, and Carlos Brulé, free pardo militiamen who claimed 500, 307, and 2,850 pesos respectively in losses; the pardo sergeant Pedro Bailly, who lost 2,615 pesos in buildings and assets; and the officers Tomás, Carrière, and Dorville, who lost 500, 2,500, and 3,000 pesos worth of property respectively.[55]

Breaks in the levee also occurred frequently, and many libre militiamen worked to repair them. In the spring of 1790 the cabildo issued a proclamation announcing the demand for free black and slave workers to repair recent ruptures in the river banks that threatened New Orleans and surrounding plantations. The city council offered to pay free black laborers and to rent slaves at the daily wage of three reales. Owing to revenue shortfalls caused by the 1788 fire, hurricanes, and additional levee inundations, the cabildo implored city residents to contribute funds to pay the workers.[56] According to McConnell, "ninety-one free men of color—forty-two morenos, forty-five pardos, and four officers—responded for crevasse work," and "each group worked for a month or more."[57]

During the 1780s libre militiamen engaged in ransoming one of their members. The British had captured the free moreno soldier Juan Gros in the Mobile campaign of 1780, whereafter they sold him to a wealthy native named Enexaqui. The 1770 "Etat des mulâtres et nègres libres" identified Gros as being thirty-four years old and living below New Orleans at Tour des Anglois (English Turn); he most likely participated in the Mississippi River campaigns before fighting on the Gulf Coast. Enexaqui removed Gros to the village of Mecsuque outside of Mobile. Over a nine-year interval Enexaqui came to regard Gros with much affection and expressed reluctance to part with him. When solicited by officers of the free pardo and moreno militias of New Orleans, who stressed Gros's valor and service to the king, the Spanish government attempted to ransom Gros. After much wrangling, Enexaqui agreed to part with Gros for 177 pesos, payable in goods through the Panton and Leslie company store. Enexaqui subsequently withdrew his offer, but with additional convincing and the temptation of hard cash, he acquiesced.[58] Once again listed as a soldier in the 1793 roster of the company of free morenos, Gros did not appear in the 1801 rosters, whether on account of death or old age.[59]

When Carondelet replaced Miró as governor in 1791, one of his primary goals was to reorganize and strengthen Louisiana's defenses. In the early 1790s Spain found itself in the unenviable position of mediator between revolutionary France and monarchist England, and on 21 January 1793 Spain declared war on France in response to the execution of Louis XVI.[60] As a former French colony and a neighbor of the pro-Enlightenment, expansionist United States, Louisiana faced potential invasion by one or both powers, either by land or by sea. Impending war worried Spanish colonial administrators; Louisiana's primary role within the empire was as a defensive bulwark for New Spain. In addition, a combined French and United States invasionary force preaching liberty, equality, and fraternity stood a good chance of success in Louisiana owing to the pro-French sentiments espoused by many colonists and to the growing numbers of American immigrant settlers and merchants. Fear of internal insurrection also plagued Spanish leaders, once again because of favorable opinions of French and United States revolutionary ideals that were exacerbated by wartime economic disruptions.

According to Ernest R. Liljegren, most of the colony was ready and eager to rally behind the French republican flag. His account appears exaggerated, however.[61] Several colonists who settled during the French period naturally hoped to reunite Louisiana with the French empire; a change in government logically seemed to enhance that possibility. These individuals rarely, if ever, expressed a desire to create an independent republic, however. The prospect of a massive slave uprising modeled on that occurring in Saint-Domingue raised the apprehensions of white colonials in Louisiana and throughout the Americas, including the southern United States.[62] This dread discouraged much revolutionary activity. During the 1790s the actions of libres came under even closer scrutiny, as the racial warfare sweeping Saint-Domingue exacerbated always present anxieties about sympathetic collusion between slaves and free blacks.[63] Overall, colonists expressed discontent more with Spain's economic policies than with its philosophy of government. Even Liljegren admits that in New Orleans "most of the inhabitants were well disposed toward the government and took an active part in the preparations for its defense."[64]

One group in particular drilled regularly in order to defend New Orleans and Louisiana in the event of an invasion: the free black militia. Upon assuming the governorship, Carondelet vowed to increase military potential and at the same time decrease expenses. Not only were militias more economical, they were also more adept at traversing local terrain than were veteran troops. To this end Carondelet reorganized and expanded the militias, including those of free blacks. On 3 July 1791 Carondelet created a second company of free pardos and added to the number of corporals in each company. During the 1790s promotions occurred rapidly, enhancing the loyalty of free black militiamen to the Spanish government. Carondelet stationed free black troops at the recently erected fortifications surrounding New Orleans. Late in 1793 he also dispatched members of the free pardo and moreno militias downriver to reinforce Fort San Felipe de Placaminas, where they guarded the colony against an anticipated French invasion from the Gulf of Mexico.[65]

Most members of the free black militia remained loyal to Spain throughout the 1790s and into the 1800s, when Spain transferred Louisiana to France, which then sold the colony to the United States. For his particular merit at Fort San Felipe de Placaminas and his constant zeal, activity, and love of royal service, the free moreno captain Manuel Noël Carrière received a commendation from the crown.[66] In 1801 he held the honorable position of Commander of the Battalion of Free Morenos of New Orleans and formed part of the general command staff.[67]

Carrière and other free black militiamen engaged in active combat once more on behalf of the Spanish government during the attack on Fort San Marcos de Apalachee, a Panton and Leslie trading post in West Florida, in June 1800. Responding to the American adventurer William A. Bowles's capture of the fort, the Spaniards sent Vicente Folch, commander at Pensacola, to recapture it. The expedition was successful but expensive; part of the twenty thousand pesos spent went to provision and pay free black troops from New Orleans.[68] Promotions and new commissions abounded in 1801, when Governor Casa Calvo once again reorganized the free black militia into four companies of free pardos and two companies of free morenos.[69] In addition, regulations issued in 1801 (see the appendix) firmly established the rights, responsibilities, and privileges accorded libre militiamen.

In addition to its defensive role, the free black militia in New Orleans functioned as a corporate group in society, and as such, it wielded its organized strength on behalf of all libres. Individual members, especially officers, also utilized their titles, their reputations as loyal, honorable vecinos, and their patronage from leading whites, many of them military members themselves, to attain increased material and social influence. The title that accompanied promotion in rank conferred upon the holder recognition from a white community that honored and valued military service; libre militiamen proudly wore their uniforms during drills and when parading through the city's streets on feast days. Officers of the free black militia also often functioned as leaders among libres, and they prominently placed their titles on public documents.[70] For example, in the 1795 census of New Orleans Francisco Dorville identified his occupation as "capitaine des mulâtres libres," even though he more fully devoted his time to running a tavern and selling goods in New Orleans and Natchitoches.[71]

As was the case throughout Spanish America, many free black officers were artisans and skilled laborers who owned property.[72] Some skilled persons holding rank in the militia have been identified earlier. Others included Carlos Brulé, a free pardo carpenter, who in 1795 possessed three slaves and in 1801 held the rank of grenadier captain, and Vicente Cupidón, a mason and lieutenant in the free moreno militia.[73] Brulé's brother-in-law was Raymundo Gaillard, a free pardo silversmith and grenadier married to María Isabel Destrehan, whose brother Honorato was second lieutenant of the grenadiers. The free pardo butcher Carlos Montreuil owned two slaves and served as a first corporal.[74] The battalion commander Manuel Noël Carrière plied his trade as a cooper and in 1795 owned five slaves.[75] Cupidón Caresse, a moreno sergeant in 1779, hunted to earn his keep; in 1795 he owned five slaves, who also helped support him.[76] The free black officers Carlos Navarro and Vicente Populus both labored as shoemakers, and Pedro Bailly, Gabriel Gerónimo, and Agustín Malet all resided in the Faubourg Ste. Marie, where in 1798 they sold wood and owned a total of twenty slaves.[77]

Other libre officers owned and worked plantations or farms. Commander of the free pardo and moreno militia in the 1770s and 1780s, Simón Calpha lived on his large plantation located twelve leagues upriver from New Orleans but was still considered a vecino of New Orleans.[78] In 1785 Nicolás Bacus and his son Juan Bautista Bacus, both rice and sugar farmers in Tchoupitoulas (about two leagues upriver from New Orleans), sued Doña Mariana Bergeron, the widow Bienvenu, for the cost of damages caused by her slaves. The slaves were hunting rabbits by setting fire to the fields, and when the fire spread out of control it destroyed the Bacuses' houses, fences, and 320 barrels of rice. Nicolás had been promoted from second to first lieutenant of the free morenos in 1781; by 1791 he served as a captain and Juan Bautista as a second lieutenant.[79]

In some respects, however, militia service imposed a substantial burden on many free black soldiers and even officers. Pay rates while on active duty were in many cases lower than what free blacks earned as civilians, and weekly drills consumed a large part of their free time with no monetary compensation. The cabildo usually paid libre militia members at the same daily rate they paid white militiamen: one peso for officers, six reales for non-coms, and four reales for soldiers.[80] In addition, military expeditions pulled libres away from their homes and families and exposed them to danger, hunger, exhaustion, and miserable weather. Upon returning from Fort San Marcos de Apalachee in 1800, free black officers complained to the cabildo about changes in climate and food, "mosquitoes, night-dew, humidity, and many other dangerous inconveniences . . . which they [had] suffered."[81] In a separate case, a free black soldier named Carlos Meunier, whose father's estate was suing him for collection of a debt, replied that he had lost what little he had in the Apalachee expedition and was in a state of poverty.[82]

Despite these drawbacks, militia membership tended to promote group cohesiveness and identity among free blacks. Libre militiamen, most notably officers, married each other's daughters and sisters and loaned money and provided other types of assistance to each other. Officers commonly practiced lucrative trades and thus more likely possessed the means to aid fellow militia members than did the rank and file. For example, in 1803 Pedro Bailly, a former free pardo officer, stood as guarantor of a slave purchase that Luis Dusuau, a free pardo sergeant, made at a public auction. The free pardo corporal Carlos Montreuil did the same for Pablo Cheval, a free pardo *soldado*.[83] In 1791 the pardo captain Francisco Dorville borrowed four hundred pesos from then captain of the free moreno militia, Manuel Noël Carrière. Dorville guaranteed the sum with one of his slaves and used the money to purchase goods that he retailed in Natchitoches.[84] A few years earlier Dorville had loaned money to a slave to purchase his freedom. In 1783 Don Pedro Joseph Favrot freed his pardo slave named Joseph, twenty-four years old and by trade a barber, for eight hundred pesos. Joseph had paid five of the eight hundred, and Dorville agreed to pay Don Pedro Joseph the remaining three hundred within four months. Four years later Favrot wed Modesta Populus, a woman with many relatives in the free pardo militia; in 1794 both she and their eighteen-month-old daughter passed away, leaving Favrot to care for their only other daughter. Before his own death in 1798 Favrot served as a corporal in the free pardo militia, a position Captain Dorville and the Populuses most likely helped him to attain.[85]

Members of the free black militia also served as godparents for the children of other militiamen of color and witnessed each other's weddings. The godfather of Favrot's second daughter was Carlos Brulé, then a first sergeant. In turn, Favrot was godfather to Brulé's oldest son José, born in 1788.[86] Brulé's daughter Margarita—who, like Favrot's daughter, died young—had as her godfather Basilio Gaillard, a fellow militiaman and brother-in-law of Brulé. Captain Hugón stood as godfather to another Brulé daughter (Eulalia).[87] When Brulé had married María Constancia Gaillard much earlier in 1777, Francisco Dorville witnessed the event, along with Raymundo Gaillard, the bride's other brother and, like Basilio, a militia-man.[88] The pardo militiaman Pedro Esteban Aubry—son of Don Pedro Aubry and morena Catalina Emelitte—wed a free cuarterona in 1803 when he was twenty-one and she was thirteen. Standing as witnesses were three pardo officers and noncoms: Dorville, Juan Francisco Durand, and Pedro Baltazar Demasilière. Aubry's sister María Genoveva had married a free pardo corporal two and a half years earlier; Durand and another militia offi-cer witnessed that event.[89] While the pardo soldier Pedro Demouy lay dying and dictating his testament in August 1802, he sent former pardo officer Bailly to fetch his common-law wife of some twenty-five years so he could marry her. Bailly and Commander Carrière then stood as witnesses.[90]

Like brothers and in-laws, the sons of officers frequently followed their relatives' example and joined the militia, often rising through the ranks to officer status. The Hugón-Calpha family discussed in greater detail below offers one example. Others included the Bacus, Tomás, and Carrière families. In the 1790s Nicolás Bacus, a captain of the free morenos, had six sons who were officers or noncoms: Juan Bautista (second lieutenant), Colas (officer of second company), Luis (sergeant), and Zenón, Honoré, and Nicolás (all corporals).[91] The 1801 rosters indicated that sixty-five-year-old Pedro Tomás served as a captain of the free moreno grenadiers, his son Luis Pedro as lieu-tenant, and his other son Felipe Pedro as corporal second class. The Tomás boys' brother-in-law, Manuel Noël Carrière, commanded the battalion of free morenos, while his son of the same name served as second lieutenant of the first company.[92] Loyalty, dedication, and bravery on the part of the father probably influenced royal decisions to promote his offspring. Also, a son who witnessed his father rewarded with titles, prestige, patronage, and community recognition most likely regarded militia service as a positive ex-perience.

Marriages between libres often forged or reinforced the kin and friendship bonds of free black militiamen. In 1778 the above-mentioned Carrière, then a free moreno second lieutenant, married Mariana Teresa Pierre Tomás, the free morena daughter of María Juana and Pedro Tomás. The bride's much younger sister Carlota later wed Vicente Cupidón, a free moreno officer. One of the groom's sisters married militiaman Antonio Conway in 1789, and one of his brothers, Bartolomé Gálvez, also served in the militia. A forceful presence in the free black community, the Carrière-Tomás family frequently stood as godparents and marriage sponsors for many libres and slaves.[93] The pardo libre Benjamín Daigle, a native of London and most recently from Canada, wed María Teresa Malet, a parda libre, in 1802. He was a *miliciano,* and she was the legitimate daughter of the free pardos Jacinta Demasilière and Agustín Malet, a wood vendor and sergeant. The ever popular Dorville stood as a witness to the marriage.[94] Francisco Alexandro Colombé, a cuarterón libre, and María Caterina LaCombe, a parda libre, baptized their son Joseph in 1778. The child's godparents were María's sister Margarita LaCombe and brother-in-law Joseph Casenave, whose militia service dated from French rule. María's male relatives also boasted long service records. After María died in 1789, Colombé married Henriqueta Toutant, the natural parda daughter of morena libre Margarita Leveillé Toutant—sister of Manuel Nöel Carrière—and Don Bartolomé Toutant Beauregard, a white militia officer. Henriqueta's sister María Luisa was married to Esteban Dorville, son of Francisco, and himself a second sergeant in 1801; another sister, María Francisca, had a common-law relationship with Felipe Populus, a free pardo soldier whose many relatives served in the militia.[95]

Some free black militiamen wrote wills that reveal property accumulation over a lifetime and the struggle to improve the next generation's economic and social standing. They also point to strong friendship and kinship ties among free black militiamen. When Joseph Casenave dictated his will in 1779, he left half of his goods to his legitimate wife, Margarita LaCombe, the parda daughter of Joseph LaCombe, another signer of the 1769 oath of allegiance. The other half he left to his two natural sons, Pedro and Carlos, both pardos libres. Casenave's property included two slaves and four arpents of land just upriver from New Orleans.[96] In the years following 1779 he had more natural children and amended his will accordingly. Carlos Casenave, who was a miliciano when he died in 1800 at age thirty-six, noted in his will that his father's estate had totaled 4,291 pesos when Joseph died in 1797. Part of this went to Joseph Casenave's two natural daughters by Carlota Bacus, a morena libre, and part to Carlos, Pedro, and José, whose mother was the morena libre Magdalena Bauré. Carlos's brothers Pedro and José Casenave were also milicianos in the free pardo militia, and all three of them owned land and slaves jointly. Carlos himself possessed three arpents of land with a house, warehouse, and mill, two slaves, three horses, and twelve cows, all of which he left to his natural son, also named Carlos. He owed money to Nicolás Bacus Sr., a retired moreno officer, and to Luis Durand, a pardo corporal first class.[97]

All of these efforts to forge networks between militia members and improve their families' chances for success are exemplified in the Hugón-Calpha family, some of whose members have already been mentioned. When pardo captain Juan Bautista Hugón died in 1792, he had served the Spanish crown in the free pardo militia for twenty-three years, beginning with campaigns against the British at Baton Rouge in 1779. The executor of Hugón's will was Manuel Nöel Carrière; Hugón named as guardian of his minor children Carlos Brulé. Beginning in the 1770s Hugón had purchased the freedom of his morena consort, María, and their five natural children, the final one emancipated with funds from his estate. After paying for the carta, outstanding debts (two of Hugón's creditors were militiamen Brulé and Raymundo Gaillard), and burial and court costs, Carrière turned over 227 pesos 5 reales to the children.[98]

Hugón's children maintained close ties to the libre militia. Juan Bautista's only son Enrique learned the craft of carpentry, like so many other free blacks in New Orleans, and followed his father into militia service; the militia rosters for 1801 listed him as a corporal second class. When Hugón's daughter Celeste married Juan Pedro Claver, a corporal in the free moreno militia, officers in the same unit stood as witnesses: Carrière, Agustín Facende (lieutenant), Rafael Bernabé (corporal), and Marcial Durel (corporal). Claver and Hugón named Carrière godfather of their first child (Manuel) and Carrière's oldest son, Manuel Nöel Jr., was godfather to their second son and third child (Pedro), born in 1801. At the time Carrière Jr. was second lieutenant in the first company of free moreno militiamen. Pedro Claver's godmother was Carrière Sr.'s wife, Mariana Tomás, also from a militia family.[99]

Juan Bautista Hugón's sister, Ana Marta Simón, also married into a militia family, and her husband, one natural son, and two legitimate sons served in the free pardo militia during the Spanish period. Before marrying Simón Calpha in the late 1750s or early 1760s, Ana Marta had a son, Carlos, by an unidentified man, most likely Pedro Simón, the first commander of the

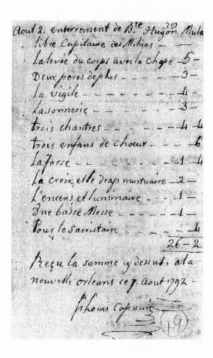

Figure 4.1 Funeral Expenses for Juan Bautista Hugón, 7 August 1792, Courtesy of the Louisiana Historical Society. Hugón, a captain in the free pardo militia, had a more elaborate interment than most libres (or whites for that matter). Itemized expenses totaled 26 pesos, 2 reales, and included raising of the body with its cope, two additional priests, the vigil, ringing of the bells, three cantors, three altar boys, the grave, the cross and pall, the incense and lighting, one low mass, and fees for the sacristan.

free black militia under O'Reilly. By the time he died in 1799 at the age of forty-three, Carlos had risen through the ranks of the free pardo militia to first lieutenant. As a second lieutenant, Carlos had served in the campaigns against the British during the American Revolution and received a medal of honor from the king of Spain. Carlos married his longtime consort, the free parda Francisca Meunier, on his deathbed (he died about three weeks later); witnesses to their wedding included Francisco Dorville and Pablo Mande-ville, a carpenter and corporal first class in the first company of free pardos. This marriage legitimated Carlos and Francisca's five children. The oldest, Carlos Jr., had enlisted in the free pardo militia by the end of the Spanish period. The younger Carlos's godparents were his paternal grandmother, Ana Marta Simón, and her husband, Simón Calpha. Godparents of their second son, Luis, were his half uncle and aunt, the children of Ana Marta and Calpha. Ana Marta was also the godmother of their third son, Simón.[100]

As previously noted, Calpha was captain of the free pardo and moreno militias from the 1770s until his death in 1786 at the age of eighty. He and Ana Marta produced six children, one of whom died at the age of three in

1772 with another perishing at the Battle of Mobile in 1780. Their other four children—Pedro, Luis Jacinto, Constanza, and Genoveva—variably took their mother's or father's or both names in existing documents. Both Pedro and Luis Jacinto served in the free pardo militia, and by 1801 they had advanced to the rank of captain of the first company and lieutenant of the second company respectively. Luis's godfather and namesake was Luis la Nuit, a signer of the 1769 oath of allegiance and by 1779 a free moreno second lieutenant. None of Simón and Ana Marta's children married in the Catholic Church (or at least no record of such exists for the Spanish period), but Luis Jacinto, Constanza, and Genoveva all had natural offspring whose godparents were kin and militia members. Luis Jacinto had one daughter, Catalina, by a parda slave, and her godfather was Luis Jacinto's half brother and fellow militiaman Carlos Simón. Carlos also stood as godfather for Constanza's natural son Carlos. Constanza's oldest daughter Ana Marta was named after her grandmother, who was also her godmother, and had as her godfather the captain of the free pardos Bautista Bogarin. Another member of the free pardo militia, Henrique Populus, stood as Constanza's other daughter's godfather. Constanza's second son Miguel had for godparents his uncle Luis Jacinto and aunt Genoveva. Genoveva in turn named as godparents to her son Luis her brother Luis Jacinto and sister Constanza.[101]

As an organized body, the free militia of color utilized its collective voice to request privileges that might have been denied individuals. Members also called upon their reputation as loyal, honorable servants of the king to assure local authorities that their decision to grant such privileges would not be regretted. Like most New Orleanians, free blacks liked to dance. When large numbers of them flocked to public dances, however, local authorities fretted about problems of social control and illegal admittance of slaves. Libres thus had to petition the cabildo for permission to hold dances. In many cases the cabildo rejected these petitions, but when the free black militia, represented by four officers, submitted its request in 1800, the cabildo approved it.

The militia had just returned from an exhausting but victorious expedition against William Bowles at Fort San Marcos de Apalachee in Florida, and its spokesmen requested a reward in the form of weekly dances conducted at the house of Don Bernardo Coquet. In order not to interfere with the white dances that took place on Sundays, libres offered to hold their dance on Saturdays, from November through the end of the coming carnival season. Well aware that while they were away at Apalachee some unsavory characters had soiled the reputation of free black balls, the petitioners asked that city police forces patrol Coquet's house on Saturday nights to prevent any disturbances. Previous mischievous behavior included provoking arguments, chewing vanilla and spitting it out to produce an intolerable odor, placing chewing tobacco on women's seats to stain their skirts, and "finally, doing and inventing as many evil things as can be imagined." The petitioners promised to reward the sergeant in charge for maintaining discipline. In closing, they noted that throughout the kingdoms of the Americas, as well as of Europe, the carnival season permitted these types of diversions. Not only did the cabildo grant the request, that body renewed it again the following year despite strong protests from the procurador general.[102]

Another example of collective political action on the part of the free black militia is perhaps more significant in that it affected the material well-being of militia members and their descendants and was directed toward Spanish officials in Havana rather than the local cabildo. Through their representative, Francisco Dorville, members of the free pardo militia who had fought with Gálvez to seize Pensacola from the British in 1781 petitioned for a share of the plunder resulting from that action. They did this in 1799, long after the actual event, and directed their request to Spain's royal and military treasury. Dorville specifically asked to recover from the treasury the portion due his unit that had long ago been ordered paid from proceeds resulting from the capture of ships and other effects in the conquest of Pensacola during the American Revolution. Dorville reminded treasury officials that even though some individuals of the pardo militia had died, they had left heirs who were entitled to their share.[103] Although the outcome of Dorville's petition is not known, the Spanish government most likely did compensate the pardo militia with its just portion. The distribution of goods taken in warfare was a tradition that came from medieval Spain during the Reconquest and in more modern times during the exploration and conquest of the New World, where in both cases the primary method for rewarding victorious troops was to promise them a share of the plunder.[104] Petitioning royal officials was also a tradition long employed in the Spanish legal system to achieve political objectives. New World corporate bodies like the free pardo militia, artisans, or native villages could pool their resources and political clout to express grievances and obtain "justice" from higher authorities in situations where individual claims might be ignored or where local officials might deny them. Dorville stood a much better chance of recovering his share of booty by petitioning on behalf of the free pardo militia to officials in Havana than by making a claim on his own to Spanish representatives in New Orleans.

During the waning years of Spanish rule in Louisiana colonial administrators augmented the size and status of the free pardo and moreno battalions, and the free blacks of New Orleans did not surrender their militia rights without a struggle when the United States purchased the colony. Militia officers often functioned as community leaders, and military service, along with property accumulation, skilled trades, and kinship and patronage connections, combined to produce an influential free black group that aspired to attain a high social position in New Orleans. Thus when the United States assumed control of Louisiana in 1803 and attempted to divest the free black militia of its distinctive status and even threatened to disband it, free black leaders protested. Proud of their heritage and determined to preserve it, the militiamen petitioned the United States territorial government, citing their right as free citizens to maintain a military organization. Under United States rule the free black militia remained intact but lost some of its prestige.[105]

Militia service provided free blacks in New Orleans and throughout Spanish America with an important instrument for political expression as a corporate body, an avenue for social advancement, and a means by which to gain honor, prestige, and recognition. Despite the obvious disadvantages created by prejudice and economic sacrifice, "the free colored community ultimately supported their militia units and their right to bear arms as a fundamental right of citizenship."[106] The second half of the eighteenth century constituted a period of extensive, momentous transformations occasioned by crown policy, demographic conditions, and metropolitan and provincial military disturbances. It was during this era that libres advanced their position through the militia; colonial administrators depended on free blacks to defend their provinces, and libres took advantage of the situation. Independent military units commanded by officers of their own phenotype furnished critical support for free blacks and provided them with a significant political organization. Additional political and cultural activities engaged in by libres will be the subject of the next chapter. The militia was probably the most important institution—followed by the family, elite leadership, and cultural expression—in promoting group cohesiveness and identity among libres in colonial New Orleans. Paradoxically, however, the organization of the militia also confirms the idea that libres did not constitute one homogeneous body but rather were divided by distinctions in kin group, wealth, occupation, nearness to slavery, and phenotype. After all, Dorville petitioned to recover spoils only for members of the pardo—not the moreno—militia.

Chapter 5

∎

CULTURAL AND

POLITICAL ACTIVITIES

When in 1791 Pedro Bailly allegedly solicited free pardos at a dance in the home of fellow pardo militiaman Esteban Lalande to join him in overthrowing the hierarchical Spanish social system in favor of revolutionary French equality, he enticed them with the possibility of achieving rights and treatment equal to those enjoyed by white citizens. At the same time he did not advocate abolishing slavery, an institution in which he as a slave owner had a vested interest. Like Dorville when he petitioned for spoils, Bailly sought what he perceived as justice for free pardos, not for slaves or even free morenos. Ironically, in seeking to attain what whites had, libres had to come together as a group with their own agenda, and thus they promoted their distinct identity. Although conservative compared to modern civil rights leaders, New Orleans libres challenged the racist ideology of hegemonic whites, increasingly so during the revolutionary last decade of the 1700s and first decade of the 1800s.

To protest their subordinate status within New Orleans society and at the same time create an identity that emphasized their contributions to that society, libres often used such cultural activities and political actions as carnival balls and parades, protests, and petitions. They wanted to reform, not revolutionize, a system that condemned them outright for being nonwhites and failed to recognize their worth except as measured by skin color. Rejecting race as a basis for placement in the social hierarchy, libre leaders, many of them militia officers and members of the emerging "elite," made an appeal for individual or group efforts and achievements. They emphasized what made them good citizens: military service, church attendance, property accumulation, concern for family, hard work, honest business transactions, orderly conduct. In their pursuit of the rights of citizenship, they, like Bailly, frequently combined cultural and political behavior. They petitioned city authorities to hold dances; marched armed and uniformed in parades on feast days and other religious celebrations; flaunted gold jewelry, headdresses, and clothes that only whites were supposed to wear as they strolled down streets and along the levee and bayou promenades in the evening; and hurled insults and occasional blows at whites who belittled them or questioned their rights in public social spaces. Unlike Bailly, however, most libres sought redress through legal channels, rather than by way of physical or verbal assault.

The cultural behavior and social activities of New Orleans libres at times promoted interdependency between different status groups but increasingly helped create a distinct free black consciousness and culture. Over the last decades of the eighteenth century libres more and more began to define their own cultural enterprises, by necessity and choice. This separation from slave and white forms of cultural play became more pronounced—but never complete—toward the end of the Spanish era, foretelling antebellum and postbellum developments not only in New Orleans but in rural Louisiana as well.[1] With the building of a new theater, dance halls, and cathedral in the 1790s, whites relegated nonwhites, slave and free, to the back rows or upper balconies, or excluded them altogether. To fight this discrimination and prevent wholesale categorization with slaves, libres created separate social spaces, which their growing numbers, affluence, and corporate identity made possible. The process was not finalized, however, at least not during the Spanish era, and might indeed still be ongoing today.[2]

Although they struggled daily to achieve or maintain respectable living standards, free blacks made time to enjoy the company of whites, slaves, and other libres in various ways, most of which strengthened community ties across racial boundaries, though they also reaffirmed the city's patriarchal, Eurocentric social hierarchy. New Orleanians participated in the festivities surrounding carnival season and other religious holidays, and they marked baptisms, confirmations, weddings, and funerals each with some sort of celebration. Libres also joined whites and slaves at the taverns and gambling tables, playing such illegal card games as twenty-one and canasta. Consequently, they all spent time in jail with one another.

With few exceptions, persons of all colors and classes worked and played together. In the still primarily frontier environment of Spanish New Orleans libres, whites, and slaves commonly mingled in the streets, markets, taverns, dance halls, churches, and private homes of the city. Despite the efforts of some religious and secular authorities and individual citizens, New Orleans society refused to function according to any solidified social stratification based on race, class, or legal status. Occasional raids on billiard halls alleged to house illegal card games uncovered "distinguished" and lower-status whites, free blacks, and slaves drinking with and betting against one another. As we have seen, libres and whites formed common-law unions, usually without the church's blessing but at least with its toleration. Free blacks also married or had relations with slaves, but they often had to live apart.

Constant physical interaction between libres, whites, and slaves in the city modified tendencies toward monolithic group identity. Even when a white person or slave did not live in the same household with a free black, he or she most likely resided next door to one. Census and notarial records attest to the lack of residential segregation in colonial New Orleans. Free blacks bought, sold, and rented accommodations adjacent to whites. Though concentrated primarily in the third and then the fourth districts, free blacks occupied houses on almost every city block. Table 5.1 presents population percentages for each group by district in 1795 and 1803.[3] A perusal of census returns indicates that libres resided not only next door to whites and slaves but also in the same households with them. Economic considerations drew free blacks into white households, where they worked as apprentices, domestics, and laborers. In addition, libres rented rooms or floors to and from white persons.[4]

Libres, whites, and slaves also came together within the St. Louis Parish church, after 1794 a cathedral. Most free blacks received baptism in the church, and some were married and buried there too. They also attended mass and celebrated religious holidays, as did other "upstanding" members of society. Whether slave or free, persons of African descent in New Orleans practiced the Catholic faith, at least in name. They most likely preserved some African and Caribbean rituals that were reinforced by mass importations of slaves in the 1780s and early 1800s, but in the urban setting

TABLE 5.1   Population Percentages by Quarter, New Orleans, 1795 and 1803

Group	1795			1803		
	1st	2nd	3rd	1st	3rd	4th
Whites	48	39	33	50	35	50
Free blacks	9	11	35	14	38	25
Slaves	43	49	28	37	28	25
Total	100	99[a]	100	101[a]	101[a]	100
N	1,480	1,335	1,513	1,494	2,088	884

Sources: 1795 Census; Census of the City of New Orleans, 1803, New Orleans Municipal Papers, box 6, folder 14, HTML, Tulane University.
Note: Returns for the fourth quarter of 1795 and for free blacks in the second quarter of 1803 are missing.
a. Rounding error.

whites surrounded and intervened in almost all personal activities of black persons. White apprehension of subversive activity among large groups of African slaves and libres in the context of the Saint-Domingue rebellion forced the performance of African religious practices into the back rooms or outskirts of the city. The "sight of twenty different dancing groups of the wretched Africans, collected together [in the rear of the town] to perform their *worship* after the manner of their country" compelled one early nineteenth-century eyewitness to recount the gathering's music and dancing to a correspondent.[5] On one Sunday in 1799 another visitor remarked on the "vast numbers of negro slaves, men, women, and children, assembled together on the levee, . . . dancing in large rings" at the edge of town.[6] Such observers rarely mentioned the presence of libres in these groups, but of course someone unfamiliar with the participants would not be able to distinguish slave from free.

Although slaves and newly freed Africans practiced their non-Catholic religious beliefs overtly—but cautiously and usually within a controlled setting—most libres followed the prescriptions of the dominant Catholic religion. Astute free blacks were well aware that "Spaniards, and especially hispanised Frenchmen, consider all who are not Catholics as beasts."[7] They aspired to white acceptance and patronage. The historian Thomas Marc

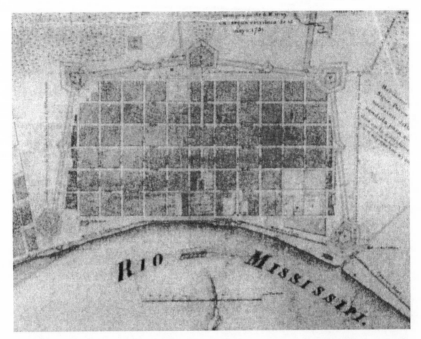

Figure 5.1 Plano de la Ciudad de Neuva Orleans, 1798, by Carlos Trudeau, Detail, Courtesy of the Louisiana State Museum. If one divides the city into four equal parts, the first quarter is on the lower right side, the second quarter on the lower left side, the third quarter on the upper left side, and the fourth quarter on the upper right side.

Fiehrer perceives many divisions between slaves and libres, with religion prominent among them, "the free colored generally adhering to orthodox Catholicism, the slaves frequently retaining their original religious orientation."[8]

In New Orleans, however, it appears that both free blacks *and* slaves constituted the city's most active churchgoers. One contemporary observer noted that "women, Negroes, and officers of the governor's staff are almost the only people who go to church."[9] Records of fees collected for services show that between 1791 and 1795 the St. Louis Cathedral garnered 6,799 pesos from whites and 4,181 pesos from persons of color, a substantial amount considering that the majority of libres and slaves were impoverished, or at least on average poorer than white parishioners. The church charged all persons equal fees regardless of race or status, a practice not

TABLE 5.2 Comparison of Funerals and Total Population by Race, Status, and Age, New Orleans, 1790–1792

Group	Funerals		Total Population	
	N	%	N	%
White adults	293	30.6	1,349	28.0
White children	164	17.1	716	14.9
Libre adults	120	12.5	481	10.0
Slave adults	235	24.6	1,358	28.2
Libre and slave children	145	15.2	912	18.9
Total	957	100.0	4,816	100.0

Sources: "Statement of Income Earned from Funerals," Records of the Diocese of Louisiana and the Floridas, roll 3, 10 December 1792; 1791 Census.
Note: Adults included persons age fourteen and older, children age thirteen and younger.

observed in most of Latin America.[10] From 1790 through 1792 the church held funerals for 293 white adults, 164 white children, 120 free black adults, 235 slave adults, and 145 slave and free black children. Proportions paralleled those for each group in the total urban population, with whites and free black adults slightly overrepresented and slaves and free black children slightly underrepresented (table 5.2).[11] Given the cost of a funeral—usually around nine pesos—it is remarkable that so many free persons of color and slaves (or their masters) could afford one. Indeed, a priest noted that the lavishness of one free woman of color's funeral eclipsed that of most distinguished white persons. He might have been talking about Fanchon (Francisca) Montreuil, although she died a decade later. Her burial included the services of two priests, three cantors, the sexton, and three altar boys; the benefice and vigil; a cross, burial cloth, bells, candles, and incense; and a medium-sized grave, all totaling forty-three pesos.[12] Exiting the world in proper fashion weighed upon Catholic New Orleanians of all colors.

Additional religious celebrations revolved around baptisms, marriages, and such holy seasons as Christmas and Lent. Pomp and solemnity surrounded the baptism of the natural daughter of Don Juan Antonio Lugar and the parda libre María Juana Prudhome on 24 June 1793. As the organ and church bells played, the midday ceremony attracted a large crowd of white and free black persons. The officiating priest declared that he had not witnessed such a large gathering, even for the baptisms of "los más grandes señores" (the most prominent people). Following the ceremony, a retinue of twenty or thirty individuals accompanied the parents to a private party and banquet in their home. Among them were several military and government officials and leading vecinos, who toasted the baptism, the father, and the mother with such noise and song that they were heard throughout the neighborhood. Eight years later—and a few months before her former white consort died—Prudhome married the pardo libre Joseph Cabaret at the cathedral, in what was probably a much less lavish affair.[13]

Parish priests constantly strove to attend to the moral character of what they considered New Orleans' notoriously decadent, disparate population in whatever way possible. Church-sponsored attempts to direct moral behavior included planned festivities that enticed parishioners into the church and away from "depraved" forms of recreation. For the spiritual benefit of the town the bishop in 1796 arranged to hold a *feria* (fair) in the cathedral on the Sundays of Lent. He urged town magistrates to attend these fairs and establish a commendable standard of conduct for the "hordes of all classes and colors" expected to attend. Cabildo members agreed to attend but on an individual basis and not as a body; they, too, pursued many occupations that consumed their Sundays with nonreligious activities.[14] Apparently parishioners preferred to be entertained rather than subjected to pious preaching in their church, and their spiritual keepers recognized this preference. More than one visitor to New Orleans admired "the policy of such an accommodating system of religion, which, while it provides for the *salvation of the soul,* takes care it shall not interfere with the more important *pleasure of the body.*"[15]

In addition to religious events, New Orleans libres joined whites and slaves in several popular forms of amusement. Scholars of early modern European societies have attempted to make sense of such popular recreations, refusing to dismiss them merely as "means of blowing off steam." In particular, Natalie Zemon Davis argues that instead of serving only to deflect "attention from social reality, festive life can on the one hand perpetuate certain values of the community (even guarantee its survival), and on the other hand criticize the political order."[16] In many ways the behavior of Davis's artisans and lower classes in the villages of France paralleled that of libres and slaves in eighteenth-century New Orleans. When free blacks and slaves wore masks and dressed in costumes during carnival season, they disguised their second- or third-class status and mimicked socially superior whites. This "turning the world upside down" actually reinforced the legitimacy of the social order. Persons of African descent recognized their place and temporarily escaped it. At the same time, however, they condemned an order that discriminated against them solely on the basis of their skin color.

Aware of this criticism and its potential dangers, government officials and white colonists in Louisiana sought to diffuse it through regulation. As paranoia about a second Saint-Domingue sweeping Louisiana spread in the 1790s, official proclamations prohibited free blacks and slaves from masking during carnival and established separate balls for whites and libres. Under United States rule these divisions were further cemented. In 1808 Christian Schultz noted that "the fashionable part of the city is divided into two parties [whites and free blacks], who have each their respective ballrooms."[17] Racially segregated dance halls replaced the tricolor balls held during the Spanish period at "the famous house of Coquet, located near the center of the city, where all that scum is to be seen publicly." Pierre-Louis Berquin-Duvallon also lamented that the balls were "not at all secret," noting that he had "several times seen the printed announcements posted at the street corners, with the express permission of Monsieur, the civil governor"[18] Don Nicolás María Vidal who himself had several casta children by different free black women.

In late-eighteenth-century New Orleans forms of cultural play included cockfights, fireworks displays, card games, billiards, parades, fêtes, and dances. Governor Miró's 1786 Bando de buen gobierno (Edict for Good Government) stipulated that in the interest of public tranquility the government would not allow fiestas or large gatherings without official notice.[19] Magistrates periodically issued permits to free blacks to stage cockfights and other amusements, and these permits were transferable. After Governor Carondelet granted a license to José María Jacques, a pardo libre, and Francisco Barba, a moreno libre, to set off fireworks and stage cockfights on "los días de fiesta," Jacques sold his share of the lucrative privilege to the free pardo Francisco Hardy for 110 pesos 4 reales.[20]

Residents of New Orleans also enjoyed the company of their neighbors and guests along thoroughfares in and around the city. Walking and riding along the banks of the levee, the Bayou Road (leading to Bayou San Juan), and the Carondelet Canal, New Orleanians enjoyed cool evening breezes, picturesque scenery, and chats with acquaintances all dressed in their best attire. One sarcastic traveler reported that pretentious colonials on the Louisiana frontier used these roads as promenades

> where it is stylish to go out riding when the weather is fine, either on horseback or in carriages more or less elegant, for one or two hours in the evening—not indeed to enjoy the advantages and pleasures accompanying that exercise, . . . but to make a show . . . of some appearance of luxury.[21]

Lamenting the absence of public gardens in New Orleans, another contemporary noted that "the Levee after sunset is crowded with company, who having been confined all the day to their homes, seldom miss this favourable opportunity of breathing a little fresh air."[22] The promenaders surely included libres, most of whom could not afford the luxury of remaining in their homes during the day but who liked to mingle socially with each other, their white patrons and friends, and slave acquaintances.

New Orleanians of both races also patronized the city's one theater, which opened in 1792. Listed in the census returns for the 1790s were comedians, musicians, and actors who performed until 1803, when city officials razed the dilapidated building that housed the theater. By the next year, however, a white Saint-Domingue refugee had remodeled and reopened the popular entertainment center. Among the actresses performing in New Orleans during the 1790s and 1800s were several cuarteronas from Saint-Domingue. Their talents bothered such colonial leaders as Governor Miró, who wrote to Don Joseph Delfau de Pontalba: "You are right in saying that if the quadroon actresses continue to receive public favor in the theater, they and others of their class might be encouraged to aspire to greater privileges than good custom dictates."[23] Following the pattern of dance halls in the late eighteenth and early nineteenth centuries, the theater was segregated by color; whites sat on the lower floor and nonwhites in the balcony. As was true of most forms of entertainment in New Orleans, "the fullest and most brilliant audience is always collected together on a *Sunday* evening."[24] During the Spanish period proceeds from the lottery and licensing fees for public dance halls financed the upkeep of this playhouse, called El Coliseo, the Coliseum.[25]

Dancing was by far the most favored public diversion and played a large part in carnival celebrations lasting from the first of the year until Lent. Eat-ing, drinking, and dancing all combined at private fêtes, where according to the French visitor Berquin-Duvallon "a stupid uproar reigns . . . in the assemblage of the guests who go thither without any order. I can not accustom myself to those great mobs, or to the old custom of the men . . . of getting more than on edge with wine." Berquin-Duvallon observed that such parties enlivened the slow, dull, inactive winter months in urban and rural areas and that all sorts of persons participated. On plantations outside New Orleans slaves gathered after laboring all day in order to perform African and European dances. These nocturnal assemblages became so widespread as to incite official concern: Miró's Bando prohibited slave gatherings unless the master gave his or her permission and there were no slaves from other plantations who did not have written permission from their masters. Within the city Miró also forbade until after vespers "los tangos, o bailes de Negros" (tangos or slave dances) that ordinarily convoked in the Plaza de Armas (today's Jackson Square) on fiesta days.[26]

Free blacks in New Orleans organized balls that attracted all sorts of persons and increased in size and frequency as the number of libres in the city rose. The dances allowed free blacks to vent emotions and stress, provided them with opportunities to plan events over which they had primary control and responsibility, and encouraged a sense of comradery and group identity. Free blacks valued these public dances and continually petitioned the cabildo for permission to hold them on a weekly basis. Just as regularly, the attorney general, claiming to act in the public interest, requested that the governor and cabildo prohibit the dances. He usually did not succeed,[27] primarily because financial matters overrode worries about undesirable libre and slave activities and tied the fate of El Coliseo to the continuance of free black balls. Although it attracted large audiences, the theater lost money with each season; in 1799 leading arts supporters appealed to the governor and cabildo for subsidies. Seizing the opportunity, Bernardo Coquet and José Boniquet, proprietors of the St. Peter Street ballroom where free blacks held their dances, offered to underwrite El Coliseo for one year if officials would grant them the exclusive right to hold public dances for libres. Over protests from the procurador general, the governor issued Coquet and Boniquet permits to operate public dances each year, an activity they pursued into the American period. In addition to frequenting this official ballroom, free blacks in New Orleans also danced at the city's many taverns, billiard halls, and private residences.[28]

Figure 5.2 Esplanade, or Place of Arms, 1803, by J. S. Boqueta de Woiseri, Detail, Courtesy of The Historic New Orleans Collection. Called the Plaza de Armas during Spanish rule and Jackson Square today, the Plaza was the physical and symbolic center of New Orleans. Libres sought salvation in the Cathedral and justice in the newly completed Cabildo on the left. They also bought, sold, and manufactured goods in the shops along the two sides of the Plaza and in stalls upon the levee that ran in front of the square. On weekends and fiesta days, the free moreno and pardo militia units drilled and paraded there, and free blacks and slaves held dances.

Although local authorities preferred separate dances for whites, libres, and slaves, residents of New Orleans usually cavorted in mixed company. Free blacks provided the music at many white gatherings. Masked slaves and libres occasionally disrupted carnival balls, their identities hidden behind ingenious disguises. In 1781 the procurador general noted that the war between Spain and England had deposited a great multitude of troops and ships' crews in New Orleans. On account of this influx of strangers and the growing number of free blacks and slaves in the city, he recommended that the cabildo prohibit all forms of masking and public dancing by blacks during the carnival season.[29] Officials also complained that slaves attended some free black balls without the permission of their owners. One snobbish white commentator was especially bitter:

A public ball, where those who have a bit of discretion prefer not to appear, organized by the free people of color, is each week the gathering place for the scum of such people and of those slaves who, eluding their owner's surveillance, go there to bring their plunder.[30]

Prosperous whites and libres mingled at a dance held at the home of Esteban Lalande, a pardo libre; a visitor noted that the guests were not wearing masks and thus had to guard their words and actions.[31] On another occasion Lalande entertained only libres at a ball in his home.

Free persons of all colors and statuses also danced—and apparently did much more—at the home of Juan Reyes, whose illegal activities were the subject of a court case and subsequent fines in 1794. The free pardo Juan Bautista Gómez sued several persons at Reyes's party for defrauding him of his possessions after they "liquored him up" and enticed him to gamble at card games he knew not how to play but was too proud to admit ignorance. Gómez, his pardo companion, and several other white and libre residents joined their host and a man whom witnesses identified as a professional billiard player and card shark in a night of dancing, drinking, and gambling. The court fined the latter and ordered him to return his ill-gotten gains to Gómez; Reyes was fined for allowing illegal games in his home.[32]

Gómez and the others who gathered at Reyes's house were not alone in their penchant for gambling. Free blacks, most of them males, frequently joined whites and slaves at the gaming tables commonly located in private homes, dance halls, and taverns. Visitors to New Orleans commonly commented on the love that New Orleanians of all social stations possessed for sites of recreation that combined billiards, card playing, drinking, dancing, and prostitution. Berquin-Duvallon once again critically observed:

At the corners of almost all the cross streets of the city, and its suburbs, are to be seen nothing but taverns, which are open at all hours. There the canaille, white and black, free and slave, mingled indiscriminately, go to bear the fruit of their swindlings, and to gorge themselves with strong drink.[33]

He also noted that generations of males gave "themselves to their passion for play, and to squander more or less their moderate resources," or they chose "to revel and dance indiscriminately and for whole nights, with a lot of men and women of saffron color, or quite black, either free or slave."[34] His jaundiced view of "the canaille" paralleled that of most upper-class New Orleanians, who could afford to partake of liquor, games, and illicit women in the privacy of their own homes. Even "gentlemen," though, amused themselves with "billiards abroad, and cards at home, or at some appointed house: and it is said they are generally too much attached to the bottle after dinner."[35]

A municipal law sanctioned in 1771 and a royal decree of 1778 prohibited the playing of games of chance in establishments dealing with the public, such as taverns, inns, and houses that also served as business establishments. Miró's Bando reiterated the provisions of these laws and also imposed a curfew; police patrols could arrest anyone seen on the streets of New Orleans after nine o'clock in the evening during winter months and after eleven o'clock during summer. According to one observer, however, the "government is aware of and permits all of that; and woe unto the minor official who would want to stop it."[36] Besides, police patrols probably could not make out furtive shapes slipping along the city's streets, where "lanterns . . . placed only at each cross-street and consisting of three small lights on winter nights, illumine for only ten paces and leave all the rest of the space in total darkness."[37]

In the early 1790s the newly appointed governor Carondelet intensified official raids on taverns and billiard halls. Police patrols usually arrived at the suspected institution at night and barged into a back room to find "gente de todas clases y colores" (people of all classes and colors) drinking and playing prohibited card games or participating in raffles. Most offenders escaped through back doors, but the police often caught at least one free black. In March 1791 the sergeant major snared three whites, one slave, and the moreno libre Luis Carrière. He later discovered two white soldiers and the owner of the billiard hall, Pedro Alarcón, who was fined fifty pesos and released. The others spent ten days in jail.[38]

Five months later the intendant, acting on a tip, inspected a billiard hall and tavern operated by Juan Freyre, known as Juanico el Gallego, where he found "negros, mulatos, paisanos, artilleros, y soldados del Regimento." The intendant arrested Freyre, a white corporal, a white hospital employee, and a pardo libre named Francisco Livaudais. Freyre paid a twenty-five-peso fine and the others an undisclosed amount of money, but Livaudais possessed no goods and thus had to serve a jail sentence of ten days.[39] A raid in 1792 turned up no libres, but the sergeant major seized an unusual prize:

the distinguished vecino, Don Diego de Silveyra.[40] One year later officials discovered fourteen or fifteen persons playing cards at the house and shop of a young shoemaker, Agustín Díaz. They apprehended four whites and a free moreno named Pedro Larronde, age fifty. A patron at Díaz's shop, the moreno libre Matheo Cotilla, testified that he had not seen anyone playing twenty-one or canasta that night. Larronde admitted to playing cards but stated that he had not recognized anyone else who was playing. He most likely "played dumb" to prevent the arrest of his accomplices and to ensure a position at gaming tables in the future.[41]

Like cultural behavior, some of the political actions in which libres engaged were also deemed antisocial by white officials and labeled as subversive resistance. One of the more popular forms of resistance, especially among women, was the hurling of *palabras infuriosas,* or slander, sometimes accompanied or provoked by physical attacks. Frustrated with a patriarchal, racist society that discriminated against them both as nonwhites and as women, female libres occasionally lashed back at their oppressors with venomous tongues. Anyone could be accused of slander, but libres in particular were targeted because the law demanded that they show respect for all whites, their actual and symbolic former "masters."[42] One woman who resented this preferential treatment for whites and the humiliating behavior expected of libres was María Cofignie (Coffiny), a free parda. In May 1795 Don Pedro Favrot, a captain of the fixed regiment, brought charges against Cofignie for insulting his daughter Josefina.[43] According to the testimony of white neighbors who witnessed the incident, Cofignie's young pardo son[44] was playing with some children on the sidewalk in front of the Favrot home on Conti Street. They told the *mulático* to leave them alone, he threw dirt in Josefina's face, and the other children chased him to his mother's house on the same street, whereupon Cofignie furiously confronted the señorita and referred to her as an "hija de puta" (daughter of a whore or prostitute)—a definite insult. Berating Josefina for threatening her son, Cofignie decried the actions of Josefina and other persons of French descent like her who, "just because they are white, believe that we [libres] are made to be scorned, spurned, and slighted. I am free and I am as worthy as you are; I have not earned my freedom on my back" (i.e., as a prostitute). These egalitarian sentiments upset the white witnesses and the Favrot family, who considered Cofignie's pronouncements "the most vile atrocities that were as outrageous . . . as those that have caused a revolution" in France and its Caribbean colonies. Like libres in Saint-Domingue, Cofignie "talked of the whites in general with disdain and great contempt."

By accusing Cofignie of criminal behavior in a public arena, Don Pedro sought to quell these inflammatory ideas and restore the reputation of his daughter and wife, the former insulted to her face and the latter by implication labeled a whore. He ably played the part of the influential patriarch defending the honor of his female charges. As a nonwhite single mother of illegitimate children, Cofignie had to rely on her own efforts; according to the Hispanic code of values that prevailed in New Orleans, she had no honor and was left unprotected and vulnerable. Although she probably enjoyed more independence than the Favrot women, she also had greater responsibilities. After more than two months of languishing under house arrest (the women's prison had been destroyed by fire in December 1794) without any sign of a resolution to the case, Cofignie pleaded with the court to release her so that she could work to sustain her family. She claimed to be "a miserable poor person burdened with . . . four children"; four months later she gave birth to another.[45] While repeatedly denying the charges brought against her, Cofignie reluctantly accepted Favrot's proposal to drop the case provided she humble herself and apologize to Señora and Señorita Favrot. She had no choice if her family was to keep from starving. Cofignie's independent spirit, like that of so many libres, was restrained by material necessities.[46]

Although white witnesses considered Cofignie's words and manner of speaking "incendiary" and "revolutionary," the free pardo Pedro Bailly offered a much greater actual threat to Louisiana's hierarchical system and to a plantation society based on racial deference and control, not to mention to the tenuous balance of international politics between imperial rivals Spain, France, and Great Britain. In 1794, at the height of the French and Haitian Revolutions, Governor Carondelet tried Bailly before a military tribunal, found him guilty of "having burst into tirades against the Spanish government and of being a manifest follower of the maxims of the French rebels," and sentenced him to prison in Cuba. A court presided over by Governor Miró had acquitted Bailly of similar charges in 1791, when fears of interracial conspiracies against Spanish authorities and Louisiana's slave-holding system were not so rampant.[47] Bailly definitely was an exception among libres, however, although he voiced concerns held by many — many, that is, of those who had risen above poverty and could afford the luxury of worrying about such abstract concepts as equality and justice. And judging from his behavior before and after the trials, it is not outside the realm of possibility that he was falsely accused of doing anything more than talking. According to standards of the time, his cause was not even very radical, and his aims closely paralleled those of the gens de couleur of Saint-Domingue, that is, to gain citizenship rights for free pardos equal to those of whites but not to abolish slavery.[48]

Bailly, Cofignie, and other libres reflected the conflicting sentiments that prevailed in Louisiana and other parts of the Americas during the Age of Revolution. As loyal Spanish subjects and members of the free pardo and moreno militias, many libres defended Louisiana against a likely invasion by French radicals attacking from both the Gulf and the upper Mississippi, as well as from internal disturbances fomented by pro-French agitators and discontented African and creole slaves.[49] Throughout Spanish America administrators continued to rely on free blacks to contribute to their colonies' defensive and labor needs. In Louisiana organized groups of libres labored on fortifications, kept guard at strategic points, pursued runaway and rebellious slaves, and revealed "seditious" Jacobin activities to authorities.[50] A few, like Bailly, joined the Jacobins in advocating the overthrow of a discriminatory Spanish government and the institution of liberal French laws that guaranteed free blacks equal rights as citizens. As Bailly discovered, most libres were reluctant to go so far as to take up arms against white persons, not only because whites could call on well-trained police forces, but also because many libres were linked to whites by kinship and patronage networks and had a direct stake in Louisiana's slaveholding system. Nevertheless, they could concur with much of what he said.

During the years of the French and Haitian Revolutions the Spanish government increased enforcement of its system of checks and balances among several corporate groups in society in order to avert mayhem, especially in the unstable Caribbean. These entities were components of "a hierarchical order, to be manipulated and counterbalanced against one another."[51] An absence of overt rebellion and the failure of insurrectionary plots in late eighteenth-century Louisiana indicate in part that Spanish officials triumphed in their handling of the various interest groups. French and Spanish wariness of collusion between libres and slaves predated the Saint-Domingue rebellion, and Louisiana governments had enacted mechanisms

for the control and separation of these two groups from the colony's beginning. Throughout the Americas white colonials considered free blacks to
have a detrimental effect on orderly slave societies and suspected them of
plotting with slaves to overthrow the "natural" hierarchical order.[52] Spanish
authorities in Louisiana were similarly apprehensive regarding fraternization between radical whites and free blacks. With insurrection expected from
almost every social group, "Spanish prescriptions for safety touched white
as well as black behavior," and most crown officials agreed with Governor
Carondelet that "in the course of a war with France . . . little or nothing
could be counted on from most of the inhabitants."[53]

In such a setting, the words and actions of libres came under even closer
scrutiny than usual. Free black immigrants and sailors from Saint-Domingue
brought news of the latest developments and inflammatory notions of liberty and equality, or at least officials and leading vecinos feared they did.
During his term Governor Carondelet banished a free black tailor who
had recently arrived from Saint-Domingue, and his explanation conveys the
anxiety, even paranoia, of the time:

> He is a native of that part of Santo Domingo that belongs to the French
> and is mixed up in all the intrigues and harassments of the French
> colony, besides being ungovernable and audacious. Having such a char-
> acter around under the present circumstances in which I am placed
> might produce bad results.[54]

Crown representatives associated any pro-French sentiment with the possibility of radicalism and revolt; to them this libre "seemed a direct link
between the events in St. Domingue and Jacobin attempts to disrupt Spanish rule in Louisiana." Other libres played roles in the 1791 and 1795 Pointe
Coupée slave conspiracies and a 1795 conspiracy among soldiers of the fixed
regiment.[55]

Testimony from the two Bailly trials reveals many of the frustrations free
blacks experienced in a racially stratified society and their desire to obtain
the equality and brotherhood that France appeared to offer.[56] While they resented being treated as second-class citizens, most merely wanted to reform
the system rather than overthrow it and remained loyal to the crown. In
October 1791 some whites and free pardos accused Bailly of trying to gather
support among the free pardos to instigate a rebellion like that just breaking
out in Saint-Domingue. In particular, they claimed that he had asked two

free pardos if they would consider leading such a movement and be willing to take up arms against the whites if violence were necessary. Within a month the free pardo witnesses modified their testimony, and Miró acquitted Bailly. Two and a half years later, when the radical phase of the French Revolution was at its peak, a Carondelet tribunal tried Bailly for espousing notions of equality among whites and free pardos, defaming the Spanish government and its policies, and conspiring to murder the free pardo commander in order to place himself at the head of the company. These charges were much more serious, the testimony much more convincing, and royal anxiety about pro-French subversive activity more exaggerated than in 1791. Consequently, in March 1794 Carondelet found Bailly guilty "por haver profesado especies sugestivas de revolución" (of having professed ideas suggestive of revolution) and sent him to prison in Havana's Morro Castle for more than two years.

Bailly utilized New Orleans' patrimonial, hierarchical social structure and legal system for his and his family's benefit, and his military career appeared as exemplary as his personal and material accomplishments. Between 1779 and 1793 he advanced from corporal second class to first lieutenant in the free pardo militia and served with that unit in the Baton Rouge, Mobile, and Pensacola expeditions against the British during the American Revolution. He and other free pardos also captured runaway slaves, repaired cracks in the levee, and patrolled the streets of New Orleans at night. His most recent service to the crown was at Fort San Felipe de Placaminas. In order to protect Louisiana from an anticipated French invasion from the Gulf by way of the Mississippi River, in late 1793 Governor Carondelet dispatched regular and militia troops to Placaminas, located below New Orleans near the river's mouth, where they were stationed until the threat dissipated two or three months later.

When the free pardo commander and captain of the first company, Francisco Dorville, and the captain of the second company, Carlos Simón, brought charges against Bailly in 1794, they cast a much less favorable light on Bailly's militia service. According to Dorville and Simón, Bailly consistently feigned illness in order to shirk his responsibilities as a militia officer, duties these two officers took very seriously.[57] Corporal Bailly reluctantly joined the 1779 Baton Rouge expedition led by Governor Gálvez, complaining that he was ill and had other, more important things to do. Bailly frequently refused to parade through the city with his company on the annual feast day of Corpus Christi, and he substituted one of his slaves to work in his place when called to repair cracks in the levee, a tactic usually practiced by wealthy white persons and resented by libres. During these years Dorville and Simón claimed to have questioned royal officials about the promotions in rank that Bailly received despite his disrespectful, insubordinate behavior. Authorities turned down their repeated requests to examine the commission records.[58] Most recently, Bailly disobeyed Dorville's orders to assemble the pardo company in order to march to Placaminas. Once again he claimed to have better things to do than march.

Indeed, the report Dorville and Simón made contrasted sharply with Bailly's record of rapid promotión in the pardo militia. During the 1791 trial Bailly emphasized his long and loyal service to the Spanish crown and his excellent reputation as a hardworking vecino of New Orleans. Either the pardo officers exaggerated Bailly's insubordination, or white officials chose to ignore it. Bailly's white superiors also might have rewarded his material success with promotions; it has already been noted that wealth and military titles often accumulated simultaneously in such strategic areas on the colonial frontier as Louisiana. The pardo officers, however, resented what they considered Bailly's flippant disrespect for an institution they highly esteemed. In addition, long-standing personal conflicts probably tainted Dorville's and Simón's opinion of Bailly. Their 1794 report noted that in the early 1780s and at Placaminas Bailly had gathered supporters in order to murder Dorville. In the 1790s Dorville experienced several economic failures and owed money to numerous creditors, one of the most persistent being Bailly.[59] Relations between these men were not harmonious, and each sought to discredit the other. Still, one wonders why they waited until 1794 to malign Bailly; perhaps Dorville and Simón, for personal and professional reasons, concocted this entire rationalization ex post facto in order to distance themselves from an individual some ruling whites considered dangerous, and not without concrete proof to that effect. In the end both triumphed: Dorville rose to command a battalion composed of four companies of free pardos; Bailly spent two years in prison in Havana but returned to New Orleans and resumed his fruitful pursuit of material gain.

In the early 1790s Bailly was also involved in monetary disputes with Don Luis de Lalande Daprémont, a *negociante* (merchant or dealer) who later accused Bailly of seditious activity. In September 1791 Daprémont sued Bailly to collect a series of debts incurred in the years 1787 and 1788 and totaling

1,270 pesos. The court seized two of Bailly's properties but returned them to Bailly when he satisfied the debt ten days later. Daprémont concurrently sued Bailly for a debt of 2,346 pesos 4 reales, but Bailly argued that he had already paid Daprémont the sum. Daprémont admitted his error and paid all court costs.[60] One month later Bailly prosecuted Daprémont for rental payments. For a period of three years Daprémont had stored some iron at Bailly's warehouse, and now Bailly demanded he pay rent of one peso per month, an amount Daprémont considered too high. Daprémont called three master blacksmiths to testify that they never charged their customers rent for storage of iron at their warehouses or shops, even if they had completed the work long before the iron was removed. Nevertheless, in June 1792 officials ruled in Bailly's favor; Daprémont paid Bailly the thirty-six pesos rent and almost one hundred pesos in court costs.[61]

It was while these cases were before the court that Daprémont presented evidence to Governor Miró accusing Bailly of making criminal statements against the Spanish government. Much of the testimony was hearsay: some free pardos overheard Bailly talking with Esteban Lalande at a dance at Lalande's house, the latter subsequently related the conversation to a white man who then told Daprémont, and Daprémont in turn went to the army surgeon. This man and Daprémont proceeded to write letters to the colonel of the royal armies, who presented them to the governor. According to these witnesses, Bailly had told Lalande that he was anxiously awaiting letters from the pardos at Cap Français (el Guarico)[62] "para dar el golpe" (in order to start the coup). He wanted to conduct in Louisiana an uprising similar to theirs. Before talking with Lalande, Bailly had asked a gentleman who had just arrived from el Guarico if he had any information; the gentleman answered that he had good news about the rebels' success. Bailly then informed Lalande that the morenos and pardos of el Guarico had conducted themselves well against the whites and speculated that in the future a similar movement would take place in New Orleans. The movement lacked only a leader. Lalande replied that he would never lead or even participate in such a rebellion, primarily because he refused to sacrifice his life in what he considered a futile effort. He further assured the court that he had informed Bailly that he could never resolve to take up arms against the whites and that, on the contrary, he would sacrifice his life to defend them. At that moment Lalande's cousin and fellow militiaman Carlos Brulé had joined Bailly and Lalande's conversation, and he, too, had allegedly sworn to defend the whites.

Lalande, Brulé, and other pardo witnesses modified their statements about a month after Daprémont made the initial charges. Lalande substantiated Bailly's innocence and denounced the accusations as malicious hearsay. He pointed out the unlikelihood of Bailly initiating a conversation in which he expressed support for a revolution like that of libres in Cap Français, considering that Bailly had a family and owned slaves. In addition, given all the unmasked morenos, pardos, and blancos in the house, Lalande doubted that Bailly would have been foolish enough to express overt hostility toward Lalande's white guests. Besides, the governor and other officials had previously trusted Bailly to command several expeditions for the apprehension of runaway slaves and other "wrongdoers," and he continued to merit their trust. Perhaps the white parties in this suit had taken some of the pressure off these pardo witnesses, or Bailly had exerted even greater influence over them.

On the basis of this altered testimony, Miró acquitted Bailly. He declared that the judicial inquiry had not established that Bailly was guilty of uttering ideas opposed to the public tranquility. Also in Bailly's favor were his honorable conduct, dependability, and good reputation, merits that were not to be discredited by these proceedings. Furthermore, Miró faulted Lalande for instigating court proceedings and distorting the content of his and Bailly's conversation and with presuming its criminal intent. Testimony from Bailly's second trial in 1794 reveals, however, that he most likely had awaited communication from Saint-Domingue and had advocated racial warfare. Several persons who had offered testimony in the 1791 case and others who claimed to have observed Bailly and Lalande conversing without coming forward at that time served as character witnesses in the later trial.

Newly accused of maligning the Spanish government and advocating radical French maxims, Bailly stood trial once again in February and March 1794. As decreed in a royal ordinance of 14 May 1793, anyone who espoused ideas that disturbed public order and tranquility was to be charged with treason and punished accordingly. Late in 1793 Bailly had allegedly denounced Spain's social hierarchy and discrimination based on color and praised the equality he perceived in the new French constitution.[63] In Governor Carondelet's opinion, officials had to restrain Bailly in order to prevent the spread of such pernicious ideas and their inculcation in the souls of the discontented. Unfortunately for Bailly, Carondelet expressed these beliefs even before beginning an investigation.

The setting for Bailly's renewed struggle against inequality was Fort San

Felipe de Placaminas. In November 1793 Carondelet dispatched members of the regular army, the white militia, and the free pardo and moreno militias to reinforce that fort. Several of these white and free pardo officers and enlisted men testified to what transpired at Placaminas. After arriving, officers divided the free pardo company between guard duty and manual work on the fortifications. Although troops supposedly volunteered for manual labor, they often were coerced, and they resented it, especially Bailly. He counseled his fellow soldiers to present themselves en masse to the commanding officer, Colonel Gilberto Antonio de St. Maxent, and claim they were too ill to work on the fort. Bailly naturally set an example, disdaining work and remaining in his tent under the pretext of poor health, thereby confirming what Dorville and Simón had said about his entire military career. Indeed, some pardos refused to work together as an organized body or perform their assigned tasks, a tendency the white officers attributed to Bailly's harmful influence.

Bailly allegedly encouraged insubordination in other ways as well. He preached to whoever would listen that the Spanish government valued the pardos at this time only because they were needed to defend the colony; under usual circumstances officials degraded them. He even had the audacity—or courage, depending on one's perspective—to explain to one white officer that Colonel St. Maxent would use *mon fils* (my son) and other similar terms to refer to the pardos during this time of crisis but afterward would treat them as if they were dogs. Were they among the French against whom they had been called to arms, however, Bailly believed that pardos would be treated as the equals of whites, as they should be. St. Maxent's reluctance to drink coffee at the free pardo officers' table and preference for dining with white officers especially irritated Bailly. Although St. Maxent gave the pardo militiamen all the coffee, salt, butter, sugar, and medicinal wine they requested, Bailly thought that a simple sign of respect, expressed by giving the pardo officers a cup of coffee at his table, would mean more than all these other presents.

Bailly also publicly criticized the actions and demeanor of Dorville, the free pardo commander. Simón testified that Bailly so widely disseminated seditious and insubordinate ideas among the pardo company that he put it in a state of complete disorder. Dorville found it necessary to arise from his sickbed in order to reassert control over his men and remind them of their duty. He also humiliated some of the soldiers and forced them to work on the fortifications. As a result, Bailly's dislike of Dorville intensified, and he poisoned the others against their commander, even encouraging them to murder him. One pardo corporal heard Bailly criticize Dorville several times and refer to him as an ass or fool, using the French expression "sot." Bailly intimated that if he were heading the company, everyone would benefit because he knew many things of which the others were ignorant. With the inept Dorville gone and Bailly in charge, the corps would win respect. Bailly hinted that he and others could easily arrange for Dorville's demise; on one occasion he remarked that if rope were needed to hang Dorville, he would gladly supply it, and at another time he offered to fire the first shot into Dorville's head. Dorville himself testified that persons had informed him of Bailly's designs on his life, and he complained about Bailly's attempts to humiliate him publicly, without any respect for his age or rank or for the royal medal he had earned.

Testimony given by Don Luis Declouet, second lieutenant of the Louisiana regiment and Ayudante de las Milicias de Pardos, y Morenos, provided the clearest insights into Bailly's thoughts, words, and actions, in particular his resentment of being the target of discrimination simply because he had African ancestry.[64] While at Placaminas, Bailly approached Declouet and asked for his opinion concerning information about the French enemy. Certain that the French rebels would attack the colony, Declouet responded that Louisiana troops had to prepare to meet and defeat the French, not only because they were enemies of the state and religion, but also because they constituted a foe to all humanity. An aroused Bailly replied: "Humanity! Humanity! I am going to speak frankly to you, sure that you are a man of honor. Sir, I do not see that any acts of inhumanity have been committed. It is true that they have done wrong by murdering their king, but sir, the French are just; they have conceded men their rights."

Declouet asked Bailly to elaborate, to what rights did he refer? Bailly answered: "A universal equality among men, us, people of color. We have on the Island of Saint-Domingue and other French islands the title *ciudadano activo* (active, participatory citizen); we can speak openly, like any white persons and hold the same rank as they. Under our [Louisiana] rule do we have this? No, sir, and it is unjust. *All of us being men, there should be no difference. Only their method of thinking—not color—should differentiate men* [author's italics]. Under these circumstances of war the governor treats us with certain semblances, but we are not deceived. Señor Maxent politely received us here at Fort Placaminas, telling us that on this occasion there would be no differences between us and the whites, implying that at other times there are distinctions. Every day Señor Maxent invites officials of the white militia to eat at his table. And why are we not paid this same attention? Are we not officers just as they are?" Declouet tried to calm Bailly and dismiss what he considered ridiculous pretensions by noting that among whites themselves distinctions had existed since the beginning of time. This differentiation constituted one of the most indispensable and sacred characteristics of human society, one that all should honor rather than reject or scorn, without which the Spanish corporatist system could not function.

Declouet's words failed to satisfy Bailly, however; he still maintained that "whites derive excess benefits from their rights." Bailly demonstrated his point by providing examples of the inferior status and unjust treatment he had experienced as a person of African descent. One day a Mr. Bernoudy had approached Bailly on the levee and said, "My mulatto, you are a good man, do me a favor." This expression upset Bailly, and he responded: *"Mi mulato! Mi mulato!* When was I ever *your* mulatto?" Bailly resented Bernoudy treating him in this "foolish way," in other words, as a slave. On another day Bailly had been at the notary's office when a Mr. Macarty had had the audacity to remark that the free pardos were ruined by their associations with slaves and that if pardos wished to be regarded more highly, they ought to discontinue any fraternization with the tainted slaves. Macarty had referred to free pardos as "riffraff, thieves whom the governor should expel from the colony." With good reason these words angered Bailly; he told Mr. Macarty that if there were among them such persons, he should name them and not insult everyone. To which Macarty replied that Bailly was the principal thief and threatened him with his walking stick.

Bailly in this instance can be said to have further illuminated the legal and social systems' lack of justice. Although he brought charges against Macarty, officials punished the white offender with a mere fine, not for insulting free pardos as a group and Bailly in particular but rather for showing disrespect for the government by criticizing the governor's policies. Bailly then asked Declouet the rhetorical question of what the government would have done to him if he had talked to a white person the way Macarty had spoken to him. "And you call this justice? No, sir, and I am as much an officer as you are."

Bailly also discussed this topic of racial equality, or lack of it, with another white officer, Don Manuel García. Following his usual complaint about St. Maxent's unwillingness to share his table with pardo officers, Bailly proceeded to state that one's skin color was an accident or chance occurrence. Pigmentation should not constitute a reason to differentiate between pardos and whites. Bailly then praised the French because they rewarded or punished subjects only on the basis of their merit and conduct.

The commanding officers, both white and pardo, considered Bailly's ideas, expressions, and example a dangerous threat to their control over the troops and to the effective defense of the fort. Dorville and Simón repeatedly informed their white superiors about Bailly's insubordination, arrogance, and disrespect, especially toward Dorville. Commanding officer St. Maxent lacked only a pretext to rid the encampment of Bailly, and this opportunity arose when Bailly complained of another illness. St. Maxent issued Bailly a passport, and he immediately returned to New Orleans. After Bailly's departure, St. Maxent noted more tranquility and subordination among the pardo militia than ever before. From this observation he reasonably assumed that previous tension had stemmed from Bailly's influence. Both St. Maxent and the pardo captain Simón refused to lead any other expeditions if Bailly joined them; Simón even threatened to resign if Bailly were not discharged from the pardo militia.

On 26 March 1794 Governor Carondelet rendered his judgment. He found Bailly guilty of having followed and adopted the new constitution of the French rebels, especially concerning the notion of equality, with such determination that he had not hesitated to make known his sentiments even to the white officers. Moreover, Bailly freely shared his beliefs with individuals of his own color, persuading them personally to adopt his pernicious ideas as well as execute them. They consequently resisted voluntary service and weakened the colony's ability to defend itself from external and internal foes. Bailly also displayed insubordination and lack of respect for his immediate superiors, thereby setting a bad example for others in his company.

Carondelet promptly remitted Bailly to prison in Havana, where he remained until 1796.[65] When Bailly returned from Havana, he resumed his business transactions with whites and libres, evidently restoring his former honorable reputation as a diligent, trustworthy worker. Although Bailly never served in the militia again, he continued to value his prior rank. Before a notary in 1798 he registered his record of promotion to second lieutenant on 18 September 1792; it stated that he was an industrious and worthy person, an estimation he obviously wanted others to appreciate publicly and formally. Both Bailly and his son Pedro, a soldier in the free pardo militia, signed an "Address from the Free People of Color" to Governor William C. C. Claiborne on 17 January 1804. In this petition several members of the free pardo and moreno militias clearly outlined their expectations of the new United States government; they emphasized their personal and political freedom as full-fledged citizens and vowed to provide loyal military service, as they had under the previous regime.[66] Thus, even into the American period, Bailly continued his untiring, undaunted struggle to achieve just treatment within a society stratified by race and color, though following his imprisonment he did so through legitimate legal channels.

Testimony and events surrounding the Bailly and Cofignie cases reveal the discrimination, desires, and frustration most libres experienced in New Orleans' hierarchical society. These two defendants expressed in words and deeds what most free blacks probably felt like doing on an almost daily basis but generally refrained from in view of the kind of retribution to which Bailly and Cofignie were subjected. Through various forms of political action and cultural play, in both covert and overt ways, they and other libres resisted oppression based on their race and status. At the same time, however, these and other cases also disclose the loyalty many libres sustained for their white patrons and kin and for the Spanish government, no matter how unequal its system of privileges and rewards. Militiamen Dorville and Simón contrasted their zealous service to the crown with Bailly's insubordination and disrespect for military duty. Lalande's words at the dance expressed what most free blacks recognized, that pardos had received favorable treatment from whites during the period when France ruled the colony and liberty under the Spanish regime.[67] Emphatically asserting that they were the sons of whites and had their blood, Lalande, Brulé, Simón, and other free pardos testified that they were incapable of murdering their white relatives and benefactors. They opted for peaceful paternalism rather than revolutionary equality, as eventually did María Cofignie when she decided to soothe the wounded pride of the Favrot family and save her children from starvation rather than fight for an assessment of her worth based on merit instead of race.

Both Bailly and Cofignie longed for the utopian society that revolutionary France appeared to espouse, one founded on liberty, equality, and fraternity. White witnesses to the altercation between Cofignie and Josefina Favrot decried as an "atrocity" María's assertion that she was "free and . . . as worthy as you are"; in their minds such notions were as "outrageous" as those that had started the revolution in Haiti. The ideals of radicals in France and the example set by rebellious free blacks in Saint-Domingue and the other French islands, coupled with his own personal experiences of racial discrimination, also motivated Bailly to speak out against local injustice, even advocating violent revolution if necessary. Like that of Cofignie, Bailly's determined effort to secure equal rights for free pardos did not succeed: he landed in jail, Louisiana never experienced a revolution like the one in Saint-Domingue during its early phase, and free black rights and privileges deteriorated even further under United States rule. Without the protection of a paternalistic Spanish government, as race-conscious as it was, libres in New Orleans encountered continuing attacks on their status as a distinct group; as the nineteenth century unfolded, local whites stepped up efforts to define and treat all persons of African descent as slaves.[68] Despite their failed attempts, Bailly and Cofignie voiced many of the issues free blacks confronted as they individually and collectively contested the ambiguous, often tenuous status they held in a complex society, demanded rights equal to those of whites, and through it all came to identify as a group.

Epilogue

On 20 December 1803 free blacks in their militia units and as part of the multitude watched officials raise the Stars and Stripes over New Orleans' Plaza de Armas and ceremoniously transfer the former French and Spanish colony to the United States. They could not foresee the dramatic increase in their numbers and cultural influence that thousands of Saint-Domingue refugees would bring within a few short years. Nor, ironically, did many libres anticipate the drastic reductions in their rights, privileges, social and material status, and freedom of assemblage and movement that world events, Anglo laws and attitudes, and economic and demographic trends would prompt over the next few decades. With the Americanization of Louisiana and the commercialization of sugar and cotton production, free blacks encountered increasing discrimination and legal restrictions that would draw them together and more clearly define their position in New Orleans society. They, like the "large *mulato* populations of Saint-Domingue and Cuba, suffered persecution and exclusion during periods of rising expectations, sugar boom, and self-generated economic competition." [1]

The rising group consciousness among the libre population of New Orleans, a sense of identity that was beginning to take shape in the latter years of Spanish rule, came into focus more sharply in the nineteenth century. During the antebellum era in particular, free blacks participated in what one scholar has convincingly argued was the "formation of a three-caste society," with definite distinctions created between whites, libres, and slaves. [2] While these divisions were present in colonial New Orleans, they were not so well demarcated as they would become in the antebellum period. For example, increasingly restrictive manumission laws passed in the first decades of the nineteenth century meant that few slaves entered the libre population and thus alienated the two groups even further. In fact, affluent Creoles of Color resented the loss of their identity as a "third caste" between whites and slaves when they were lumped together with all other freedmen following the Civil War. Forced by political necessity or the machinations of reemerging white leaders into the same social category as ex-slaves, many Creoles of Color in New Orleans, Natchitoches, Opelousas, Attakapas, and other Louisiana locales withdrew even further into their own group, practicing racial endogamy, or migrated to Mexico and California, returning several generations later as "white" persons.[3]

During the early decades of the nineteenth century sugar and cotton production and trade exploded, profit-oriented planters and merchants introduced thousands of African American slaves to Louisiana, and Caribbean refugees, European reactionaries, and American laborers poured into the lower Mississippi Valley. A rising tide of racism accompanied an influx of white women, a more intense competition between free black and white labor in the antebellum period, and the closing and more precise defining of white society. Unaccustomed to a large, influential group of libres, Anglos and even Latins in New Orleans regarded their numbers, skills, and military power, all primarily gained during the era of Spanish rule, with trepidation.[4]

White New Orleanians quickly moved to disband the city's prestigious armed free black militia units, to limit manumission procedures, and to keep libres out of the territory and state. Although Governor Claiborne tried with federal approval to retain but not enlarge New Orleans' free militia of color, territorial legislators omitted the battalion from militia acts passed in 1804, 1805, 1806, and 1807, thereby inactivating it. Like most local whites, Claiborne suspected the loyalty of trained, well-equipped free blacks who might very readily join with rebellious slaves and Spanish conspirators to challenge Louisiana's planter-merchant-bureaucrat elite. He did not want to alienate influential libres, however, and thus walked a thin line of compromise. To that end Claiborne accepted and forwarded militia members' expressions of fealty, recognized their right to organize, appointed two white officers to command the free black battalion, and awarded it a standard.[5] A petition presented to Claiborne and other United States officials within a month of the transfer best conveys free black militia members' sense of their heritage and hope for future equality under the American republic:

> We are Natives of this Province and our dearest Interests are connected with its welfare. We therefore feel a lively Joy that the Sovereignty of the Country is at length united with that of the American Republic. We are duly sensible that our personal and political freedom is thereby assured to us for ever, and we are also impressed with the full-

est confidence in the Justice and Liberality of the Government towards every Class of Citizens which they have here taken under their Protection.

We were employed in the military service of the late Government, and we hope we may be permitted to say, that our Conduct in that Service has ever been distinguished by a ready attention to the duties required of us. Should we be in like manner honored by the American Government, to which every principle of Interest as well as affection attaches us, permit us to assure your Excellency [Governor Claiborne] that we shall serve with fidelity and Zeal. We therefore respectively offer our Services to the Government as a Corps of Volunteers agreeable to any arrangement which may be thought expedient.

Referring to themselves as "free Citizens of Louisiana," free black militia members voiced their "Sentiments of respect & Esteem and sincere attachment to the Government of the United States."[6]

Faith in the American government's goodwill eroded, however, as local whites enacted harsh Black Codes. Unrestrained by a paternalistic Spanish government, fearful of slave unrest, and increasingly disposed toward Anglo racial attitudes and legal traditions emphasizing individual property rights, Louisianians moved to control every action of their bondpersons, including interaction with libres. The Black Code of 1806 and various other rulings decreed that slaveholders could not free slaves under the age of thirty, that they had to post bond upon manumission, and that the newly freed had to leave the territory. Laws also required free black residents to carry proof of free status with them at all times and forbade marriage between whites and blacks and even between libres and slaves. In addition, free blacks from the West Indies or anywhere else could not enter Orleans Territory under threat of a twenty-dollar fine for every week they stayed.[7] In 1809 the United States Congress overrode local legislation to allow 9,059 Saint-Domingue refugees evicted from Cuba to land at New Orleans free of penalties. Among these exiles were 3,226 slaves and 3,102 free persons of African descent.[8]

Several dissatisfied libres chose either to flee or to fight. Some accepted the asylum Spain proffered in the bordering territories of Florida and northern New Spain. Their wealth, education, and manners the target of envy and harassment, other propertied free blacks migrated to Mexico and the West Indies, "where they hoped to resume planting and commerce unfettered by

American legal and social discrimination."⁹ More drastic measures included plotting with Spanish officials to overthrow the American regime. In January 1806 a libre named Stephen informed Governor Claiborne that almost every free black man living in the city's environs had joined with others like him at various homes, taverns, and businesses to discuss actions libres could take against the territorial government. All possessed guns, ammunition, and training. These free black friends of the Spanish awaited orders from the marqués de Casa Calvo, a former governor of Louisiana, to unite with Spanish troops, Indian allies, and black slaves in toppling Anglo dominion in the Mississippi Valley. While Claiborne did not entirely believe Stephen's accusations and thus did not investigate further, he did place a white militia company on nightly guard duty.¹⁰

In light of these activities, authorities questioned the allegiance of a free black population embittered by official neglect. Despite elite apprehension, however, most libres continued to demonstrate their fidelity to both the still-fledgling union and local white rule. In January 1811 slaves on the Andry plantation forty miles upriver from New Orleans rose in rebellion, killing whites and gathering adherents as they marched from St. John the Baptist Parish toward New Orleans. As they had for Spain, free black volunteers offered their services and joined union regulars and local militia in quelling this insurrection, the largest slave revolt in United States history. Through their actions libres attempted to show white community leaders that they valued their individual free status and stake in Louisiana's slave society over general emancipation for black bondpersons; they continued to support a three-tiered society.¹¹

Libres further demonstrated their loyalty to Louisiana and the United States during the War of 1812, specifically in the Battle of New Orleans. Following the 1811 slave uprising, Claiborne noted that free black militiamen had performed "with great exactitude and propriety," and he urged legislators to organize a militia strong enough to protect the territory from internal and external attacks. Finally, compelled by the impending threat of war against Britain, Louisiana lawmakers approved on 7 September 1812 a militia act that included "a certain portion of chosen men from among the free men of color."¹² Four companies of sixty-four men each, officers included, made up the newly formed Battalion of Chosen Men of Color, a unit limited to men who had paid a state tax and for the two preceding years had owned real property worth at least three hundred dollars. A white man commanded the battalion, but libres held lower-ranking positions.

Louisiana was the first state in the union to commission a military officer of African descent—Second Lieutenant Isidore Honoré—even though Spain, France, and Portugal had been doing so for centuries. The state's 1812 militia act also constituted "the first time in the United States that a Negro volunteer militia with its own Negro line officers was authorized by state legislative enactment."[13] This measure basically reactivated, with some modifications, the militia organization Louisiana had inherited from Spain. Furthermore, in New Orleans on 19 December 1814 General Andrew Jackson appointed Joseph Savary to the rank of second major in the United States Army, the first free African American accorded this high position. A distinguished officer of France's army in the former colony of Saint-Domingue, Savary recruited enough refugees to form the Second Battalion of Free Men of Color.

Desperately short of manpower, Jackson welcomed both battalions to his Louisiana campaign forces and sought to expand their size and involvement. In a September 1814 address, "To the Free Coloured Inhabitants of Louisiana," Jackson appealed to that group's patriotism, summoned them to serve the United States valiantly and selflessly as they had Spain during the colonial era, and invited them to join in the "glorious struggle for National rights" in pursuit of "the path to glory." In promising them separate but equal quarters and provisions, Jackson guaranteed free black militia forces the same treatment and rewards accorded white soldiers, and in general he fulfilled that obligation.[14]

Military service in the Battle of New Orleans, though it did not elevate the status of Louisiana's libre population, helped to preserve its legal, social, and economic position up to the 1830s, when white opposition to abolitionists and free blacks emerged as a strong force in the state. The free black militia continued to muster and train after the Battle of New Orleans until the state legislature disbanded it in 1834. The demise of the militia resulted from libre indifference as well as growing white hostility: veterans grew old and died, and potential recruits struggling merely to survive no longer had the time or desire to participate in military service. Sometime during the 1830s one libre who had served in the Battle of New Orleans composed a poem under the pseudonym of Hippolyte Castra. Consisting of five stanzas of eight verses in French, the poem relates the fraternization of white and black heroes drawn together by their common experience, a camaraderie that gradually gave way to the "disillusionment and bitterness of the colored men who subsequently felt the sting of race prejudice, persecution, and rejection."[15]

In fact, the city's free blacks did not develop a strong sense of group identity until the antebellum period, especially after 1830, when they coalesced to combat attacks on their intermediary position in New Orleans' three-caste society. Similar instances of group solidification occurred in eighteenth-century Saint-Domingue and nineteenth-century Cuba.[16] During much of New Orleans' colonial period free blacks "generally accepted and identified with the colonial status structure."[17] Interpersonal relations in this small community on Spain's northern frontier ameliorated prejudice, fostered interaction and understanding among the races, and enabled individuals to advance, always within acceptable limits, on their own merit or with the aid of kin and patronage connections. As in Spanish St. Augustine, "a fairly fluid social system" and "relaxed personal relations" characterized colonial New Orleans.[18] Free blacks in New Orleans and throughout the Americas imitated white vecinos in manner and attitude in order to distance themselves from slave status, gain acceptance, and cultivate patronage.[19]

When the dominant white society moved to define free blacks as inferior or equal to slaves, however, libres commonly united in order to resist or withdraw. In late-eighteenth-century Saint-Domingue the gens de couleur met their dashed expectations of equality with violence. In antebellum New Orleans free blacks combated discrimination by distancing themselves from it. Spurned by a white society that relegated them to the vastly inferior social and legal level of bondpersons, Creoles of Color formed their own congregations, neighborhood associations, mutual-aid organizations, religious orders, schools, and literary and musical societies. Free blacks joined these organizations in increasing numbers before and after the Civil War in part to elude the humiliation of discrimination, boost afflicted feelings of self-worth, and pass beliefs and value systems on to future generations.[20]

Even in the face of the escalating repression that spread throughout the southern United States in the antebellum era, the free black population of New Orleans was renowned for its size and prosperity, much like that of Charleston. Louisiana had "the highest proportion of freedmen to slaves in the ante-bellum South in the first three decades of the [nineteenth] century," in large part owing to Spain's guarantee of manumission rights for slaves and its promotion of growth among the free black population. Throughout the antebellum period libres made up about 45 percent of New Orleans' nonwhite population.[21] Travelers frequently commented on

> the large proportion of blacks seen in the streets, all labor being per-formed by them; the grace and beauty of the elegant Quadroons. . . . [New Orleans society] contained two distinct sets of people, both celebrated, in their way for their social meetings and elegant entertain-ments. The first of these is composed of Creole families, who are chiefly planters and merchants. . . . The other set consists of the excluded but amiable Quadroons. . . . Of all the prejudices I have ever witnessed, this appears to me the most violent, and the most inveterate. Quadroon girls, the acknowledged daughters of wealthy American or Creole fathers, educated with all the style and accomplishment which money can procure at New Orleans . . . are not admitted, nay, are not on any terms admissible, into the society of the Creole families of Louisiana.[22]

At about the same time, in the 1820s, the German visitor Paul Wilhelm, Duke of Württemberg, noted that "the Negroes, Mulattoes, and such, clas-sified as either free or slave, constitute the major population of the city and the flat country." Two decades later Sir Charles Lyell of England wrote that "when passing through the stalls [of the New Orleans marketplace], we were surrounded by a population of negroes, mulattos, and quadroons, some talking French, others a patois of Spanish and French."[23]

As they had in the colonial period, New Orleans libres owned planta-tions, urban properties, slaves, livestock, jewelry and other personal goods, boats, carriages, and small businesses. Saint-Domingue was not the only re-gion that could claim to have a "significant group of landowners emerge among the free colored class prior to abolition."[24] Louisiana legal codes and courts rarely assailed free black rights to accumulate property and transfer it to their heirs. In addition, refugees from Cuba and Saint-Domingue in the early 1800s augmented the numbers, holdings, and talents of the city's libre population. With secession and war impending, propertied free blacks, especially those who owned slaves, rallied to the Southern cause. They de-clared in an edition of the New Orleans *Daily Delta:*

The free colored population of Louisiana . . . own slaves, and they are ready to shed their blood for her defense. They have no sympathy for abolitionism; no love for the North, but they have plenty for Louisiana. . . . they will fight for her in 1861 as they fought in 1814-'15. All they ask is a chance and they will be worthy sons of Louisiana.[25]

Antebellum New Orleans' unusually large, influential, propertied Creole of Color population derived from circumstances prevailing in the Spanish period. Demographic, economic, political, and military conditions fused with cultural and legal traditions to favor the growth and persistence of a substantial group of free pardos and morenos. Although Spain promoted the rights of free black and slave laborers and potential allies for its own strategic purposes, white and libre colonists and their black slaves utilized Spanish provisions to their own advantage. For example, the implementation of coartación gave slaveholders not only years of slave labor but also compensation for their slave property, usually at inflated values and in one lump sum of hard cash. It also gave slaves incentives to work even harder and save their earnings rather than "squander" them on liquor and entertainment. Like libres throughout the Americas, the majority earned their liberty and whatever property they acquired themselves rather than benefited from the generosity of individual masters.[26] Not all slaves sought freedom, a state that free blacks rarely enjoyed to the extent that white persons did, but those who did yearn for liberty in New Orleans had a better chance of succeeding under Spain's dominion than under that of either France or the United States. Once free, they and other freeborn and immigrant blacks tested and sometimes expanded or breached the boundaries of their lives and their places in colonial New Orleans. These boundaries, in turn, helped define libre identity within a complex, ambiguous social milieu; that same complexity characterizes New Orleans to the present day.

Appendix

REGULATIONS GOVERNING THE FREE BLACK MILITIA

The organization of the white and free black militias of Louisiana was based on Cuba's Reglamento para las Milicias de Infantería y Dragones de la Isla de Cuba . . . , regulations compiled by General Alexandro O'Reilly in 1769. This codification obligated all physically capable men between the ages of fifteen and forty-five to serve. The reorganization plan converted several existing and almost all new militia companies from urban to provincial or disciplined units.[1] Although Louisiana's white and free black militias were officially classified as urban until 29 March 1796,[2] they functioned in practice as disciplined units because of the colony's frontier character and purpose as a defensive bulwark for New Spain.

In Louisiana, as in other Spanish American colonies, colonial administrators were torn between their distrust of the free black man's capacity to command and the need to enhance morale and loyalty among libre troops. They partially resolved this dilemma by adopting the solution used by other officials: a dual system of command. Led by free black noncommissioned officers, first and second lieutenants, captains, and commanders, the free colored militia companies were supervised by white advisers who formed part of the plana mayor (headquarter command and staff group).[3] During the 1780s Louisiana created the post of Garzón de Pardos y Morenos Libres and promoted the white first sergeant Juan Bautista Mentzinger to fill this post at the grade of second lieutenant.[4] Mentzinger was the only person to hold this position; in the 1790s reorganization of the free black militia reinstated the free black commander–white adviser pattern. By 1801, however, the free pardo and moreno militia battalions had both one white commander who formed part of the Plana Mayor de Blancos and two black commanders who formed part of the Plana Mayor de Pardos and the Plana Mayor de Morenos.[5]

The Reglamento para las Milicias de Infantería de Pardos y Morenos, de Nueva Orleans, regulations promulgated by Louisiana's governor, the marqués de Casa Calvo, on 13 April 1801, synthesized and recorded scattered ordinances that had been in practice for several years.[6] As was true for many of the provisions that governed Louisiana, the New Orleans reglamento was modeled on Cuban legislation, in this case the 1780 Reglamento de las Milicias de Havana. It consisted of nine chapters covering such subjects as the foundation, strength, and makeup of the corps; governing and police regulation; discipline; privileges; penalties and punishments; promotion and the filling of positions; marriage regulations; uniforms, badges, and emblems; and requisites for distinguished merit awards.

In order to obtain as many troops as possible, the reglamento ordered colonial officials to prepare a list of all libre men between the ages of fifteen and forty-five capable of carrying arms, compiled according to neighborhood residence or temporary location in other parts of the colony. The list was to detail the age, height, and general health (*robustez*) of each man within one hundred leagues (three hundred land miles) of the city, and the captain of each company was to keep this roster current. Each pardo and moreno company was to consist of one captain, lieutenant, second lieutenant, and sergeant first class, one or two sergeants second class, six corporals first class, six corporals second class, and seventy-four soldiers, although the actual numbers rarely conformed to these guidelines.[7] Each company also had drummers and fifers, who were to be free and of the same phenotype as their unit and who could begin service at age five. The physician Don Domingo Fleytas administered to both the disciplined white militia and the free pardo and moreno militias. For the battalion of free pardos of New Orleans the uniform was a white jacket with inlaid collar and gold buttons, trousers, a round hat with a crimson cockade, and black half boots. Members of the free moreno battalion dressed similarly but in a green jacket with white buttons and lapels.[8]

Included in the qualifications for officers, sergeants, and corporals were literacy, honesty, ability to command, and a decent, proper lifestyle representative of the officer's social position. Even though the reglamento stipulated that administrators prepare service records (*hojas de servicio*) for each officer and noncom, no such records appear to exist for free black units in Louisiana. Accorded the same authority as commanders of other veteran and militia regiments, the commanders of pardo and moreno battalions had the power to arrest and punish any soldier or officer who disobeyed orders, displayed disrespect, or was absent without leave. All militia members could petition for redress of any presumed injustice; royal administrators encouraged them to do so even though the process might be long and expensive. The reglamento instructed all officers to inculcate in their companions a love of royal service and military glory through word and deed.

The reglamento also specified requirements for the recruitment of rank and file. During times of war the age qualification of fifteen to forty-five years could be extended in order to recruit more milicianos. Although soldiers were to stand at least five feet tall, they could be slightly shorter as long as they were in good health. No capable man was exempt from the obligation to defend his *patria* (fatherland) and king, but the rules stipulated that officers enlist lawyers, notaries, scribes, pharmacists, doctors, surgeons, ecclesiastics, schoolmasters, and various local public officeholders only as a last resort. The exemption did not apply, however, to the individual's children, clerks, servants, or other dependents.

Other regulations described privileges, limitations, and responsibilities. Although required to pay many taxes along with other crown subjects, militiamen did not have to pay licensing fees to operate stores, market goods, or practice a trade. Whereas free black militia units had to drill one day each week—whichever day would be least burdensome to the poor—and were subject to a rigorous annual inspection, they could be mustered into active service only during crisis situations or when every vecino concurred. They had to be kept on the move and could remain in any one area for a period no longer than two hours. In all other cases the commander was to render the governor a precise account of the proceedings and pay each soldier two reales per day, each corporal three reales, and each sergeant four reales. When a detachment marched through a region, the commander was held personally responsible for any damage caused. During bimonthly firing practices officials provided free pardo and moreno soldiers with ten cartridges, distributed at the time of the formation so that the bullets were not lost or misused. The same procedure held true for rifles; only in actual campaigns were munitions distributed for long durations of time. The over-all philosophy of the Spanish crown was that although all vassals were born with a definite obligation to serve the king and defend the empire, the utility of any military force depended more on its quality, discipline, subordination, and honor than on its mere numbers.

The 1801 reglamento granted all free black militiamen the fuero militar on an equal basis with regular troops. This privilege was intended to augment their prestige as valuable members of the "distinguido servicio de las armas." In particular, free pardo and moreno militia officials were to be treated with respect; no one, including a white person, was permitted to abuse them through word or action. After twenty years of militia service, free black officers could retire and continue to enjoy the fuero for the rest of their lives. Time served in actual battle counted double toward retirement. If a militiaman was crippled or mutilated in the line of duty, he merited not only the fuero but also the *sueldo de inválidos* (salary of an invalid) for his remaining years; and if he died, the crown provided his wife and children with an invalid's salary for four years, renewable with royal permission. Although officers received a fixed salary, sergeants, corporals, and soldiers earned wages only during active combat. To attain officer rank, soldiers had to advance through the hierarchy, except when combat offered opportunities for advancement through distinguished and notorious acts of valor.

For those militiamen who acted disgracefully rather than valiantly, retribution was swift and harsh. Punishments occasionally varied by rank, phenotype, and social status. The reglamento carefully outlined the penalties incurred by noncommissioned officers for unsavory conduct but rarely mentioned punishments for officers. Spanish administrators trusted officers, even free black ones, more than enlisted men and commonly dealt with each case of officer misconduct on an individual basis. Noncoms and soldiers, regardless of color, were condemned to death if they deserted to the enemy and to two years of public work if they took a leave without permission. Punishment for buying any personal effect, piece of clothing, or ornament associated with the militia varied according to social standing: a noble person paid two hundred ducats, whereas a plebeian or commoner suffered four years of forced labor for the crown. A militiaman who upon retirement lost the fuero militar could not continue to use his uniform, staff, or any other military distinction. If he violated this regulation, he suffered a one-month jail sentence; for the second offense he served two months in jail and relinquished the staff and uniform. Colonial administrators applied proceeds from sales of confiscated uniforms to the support of impoverished prisoners. Each militia member could marry whom he chose without royal permission or license, the only stipulation being that he notify one of his superiors. If the woman he married became unworthy on account of her scandalous behavior, however, the militiaman faced dismissal. The ultimate disgrace that could befall an officer consisted of the failure to control and discipline his troops, or cowardice in actions of war. Such weaknesses constituted incontestable proof of the officer's lack of esprit de corps and inability to command military forces.

The reglamento concluded with a description of the ways in which free pardo and moreno militiamen could qualify for awards of distinguished merit. Rewards, like punishments, varied by rank. Colonial administrators could recommend to the crown commendation of an officer for defeat of an enemy with only two-thirds the number of troops; retreat with permission in the presence of a vastly superior, well-disciplined enemy; detainment of a superior force owing to choice of a favorable position; capture of a battery that defended the post entrusted to it until, through deaths and injuries, two-thirds of the enemy forces were lost; seizure of the enemy's flank by means of talent, skill, and quick wit; success at being the first man to jump a trench, climb a breach, or scale a rampart of the enemy; attainment of a very advantageous position owing to the discipline of one or many regiments and the molding of worthy officers. A sergeant or soldier merited distinction by performing his duty for a long period with one or more wounds; being the first to climb a breach, jump inside a trench or fort, take a flag, break the enemy battalion or squadron, or take possession of the enemy battery; saving the life of one or many of his companions, in particular that of an officer; combating two of the enemy and taking them prisoner; not surrendering to three enemies until wounds made further defense impossible; taking prisoner some officer of note.

The reglamento represented the culmination of a long developmental process occurring in the free black militias of New Orleans, which grew in both size and prestige during the era of Spanish rule.

Notes

Introduction

1. The term Creole of Color was not used in Louisiana during the Spanish period and acquired its distinct meaning in the nineteenth and twentieth centuries. Colonial documents sometimes refer to a person, usually someone of African ancestry, as a "creole of Jamaica," "creole of Martinique," "creole of Louisiana," etc., meaning a native of that particular place. Throughout the New World, creole was applied to anyone of European or African ancestry born in the Americas. For further discussion of the evolving and distinct meaning of the capitalized term Creole in Louisiana, see Gwendolyn Midlo Hall, *Africans in Colonial Louisiana: The Development of Afro-Creole Culture in the Eighteenth Century* (Baton Rouge: Louisiana State University Press, 1992), pp. 157–59; Joseph G. Tregle Jr., "Creoles and Americans," in *Creole New Orleans: Race and Americanization,* ed. Arnold R. Hirsch and Joseph Logsdon (Baton Rouge: Louisiana State University Press, 1992), pp. 136–41.

2. For a definition of upstreaming see Richard White, *The Middle Ground: Indians, Empires, and Republics in the Great Lakes Region, 1650–1815* (New York: Cambridge University Press, 1991), p. xiv, and Inga Clendinnen, *Ambivalent Conquests: Maya and Spaniard in Yucatan, 1517–1570* (New York: Cambridge University Press, 1987), pp. 132–33. Even as recently as 1994 works on the Creoles have appeared that contribute much to our understanding of nineteenth-century populations but slight the eighteenth century. Carl A. Brasseaux, Keith P. Fontenot, and Claude F. Oubre in their book *Creoles of Color in the Bayou Country* (Jackson: University Press of Mississippi, 1994) fill a major void for the southern and southwestern regions of Louisiana but, after a few pages discussing the origins of this population in the colonial era, devote most of the work to the nineteenth and twentieth centuries. The main limitations affecting eighteenth-century studies concern the availability of source materials, their dispersal into many archives, and the need to be familiar with both French and Spanish paleography. To be fair, however, this lack of knowledge about pre-nineteenth-century slave societies is common for most regions of the Americas, including Virginia, South Carolina, Brazil, and the Caribbean, for many of the same reasons.

3. Arnold A. Sio identifies this process in the British Caribbean: "By the late eighteenth century, the larger society was aware that the free coloured had begun to develop a separate identity and were becoming a solitary people" ("Marginality and Free Coloured Identity in Caribbean Slave Society," in *Caribbean Slave Society and Economy,* ed. Hilary Beckles and Verene Shepherd [Kingston, Jamaica: Ian Randle Publishers, 1991], p. 153).

4. Sio, "Marginality and Free Coloured Identity," p. 153.

5. Hall, *Africans in Colonial Louisiana,* p. xiii.

6. Daniel H. Usner Jr. depicts a frontier exchange economy in which Indians, settlers, and slaves participated equally, although certain groups took advantage of others, with their positions of strength shifting through time and place. Natives, whites, and Africans in Louisiana were not homogeneous entities; rather, each group varied internally by ethnicity, economic interest, religion, language, etc. (*Indians, Settlers, and Slaves in a Frontier Exchange Economy: The Lower Mississippi Valley before 1783* [Chapel Hill: University of North Carolina Press for the Institute of Early American History and Culture, 1992]). See also the 1993 work by Derek Noel Kerr, *Petty Felony, Slave Defiance, and Frontier Villainy: Crime and Criminal Justice in Spanish Louisiana, 1770–1803* (New York: Garland, 1993), which is basically Kerr's dissertation from Tulane University of ten years earlier.

7. Obviously, my interpretation does not agree with that of Thomas N. Ingersoll, who argues that in 1805 the number of libres "was so small and so dispersed that they had no core around which to mold a true community" ("Free Blacks in a Slave Society: New Orleans, 1718–1812," *William and Mary Quarterly* 48:2 [April 1991]: 198). I contend in this work that libres had at least begun this process by the end of the Spanish period.

8. Gilberto Freyre, *Casa grande e senzala, formaçao da familia brasileira sob o regimen de economia patriarchal* (Rio de Janeiro: Livario José Olympio Editora, 1933) and *Sobrados e mucambos: Decadencia do patriarchado rural no Brasil* (São Paulo: Livario José Olympio Editora, 1936); Frank Tannenbaum, *Slave and Citizen: The Negro in the Americas* (New York: Alfred A. Knopf, 1947).

9. Stanley Elkins, *Slavery: A Problem in American Institutional and Intellectual Life* (Chicago: University of Chicago Press, 1959). Herbert S. Klein (*Slavery in the Americas: A Comparative Study of Cuba and Virginia* [Chicago: University of Chicago Press, 1967]) also distinguished between mild Latin and harsh Anglo slave systems.

10. An informative analysis of arguments presented by both sides in the debate's early years can be found in Eugene D. Genovese's "Materialism and Idealism in the History of Negro Slavery in the Americas," *Journal of Social History* 1:4 (summer 1968): 371–94. Other works that emphasize material factors include David Brion Davis, *The Problem of Slavery in Western Culture* (Ithaca: Cornell University Press, 1966); Carl N. Degler, *Neither Black nor White: Slavery and Race Relations in Brazil and the United States* (New York: Macmillan, 1971); Thomas Marc Fiehrer, "The African Presence in Colonial Louisiana: An Essay on the Continuity of Caribbean Culture," in *Louisiana's Black Heritage,* ed. Robert R. Macdonald, John R. Kemp, and Edward F. Haas (New Orleans: Louisiana State Museum, 1979), pp. 3–31; Marvin Harris, *Patterns of Race in the Americas* (New York: Walker and Co., 1964); Harry Hoetink, *The Two Variants of Caribbean Race Relations: A Contribution to the Sociology of Segmented Societies* (London: Alfred A. Knopf, 1947); Mary C. Karasch, *Slave Life in Rio de Janeiro, 1808-1850* (Princeton: Princeton University Press, 1987);

Franklin W. Knight, *Slave Society in Cuba during the Nineteenth Century* (Madison: University of Wisconsin Press, 1970); Magnus Mörner, *Race Mixture in the History of Latin America* (Boston: Little, Brown and Co., 1967). David W. Cohen and Jack P. Greene contend in the introduction to their edited work *Neither Slave nor Free: The Freedmen of African Descent in the Slave Societies of the New World* (Baltimore: Johns Hopkins University Press, 1972) that "diversity is . . . much more closely related to specific economic conditions [than to ethos and law] — at times and in particular places opening up extensive opportunities for a free, non-white middle group, while at other times effecting the closure of opportunities for non-whites and the displacement of the free colored" (p. 17).

11. Davis quoted in George Fredrickson, "Comparative History," in *The Past before Us,* ed. Michael Kammen (Ithaca: Cornell University Press, 1980), p. 466.

12. Information presented in chapter 1 seems to indicate that this situation prevailed in lower Louisiana during the Spanish regime. Spanish authorities often protected the rights of slaves and free persons of color against abusive French planters. With a slightly different twist, essays in Cohen and Greene's edited work *Neither Slave nor Free* generally suggest that "a relatively rigorous slave regime, such as that observed in Surinam and the French islands, may have resulted in a relative amelioration of conditions for the free colored as a direct result of the whites' need for allies within the slave society" (p. 11). David P. Geggus also notes that "in Jamaica and Antigua, moreover, which had two of the highest black/white ratios in the British Caribbean, limited political concessions were used to ally free coloured to the regime" (*Slavery, War, and Revolution: The British Occupation of St. Domingue, 1793–1798* [New York: Oxford University Press, 1982], p. 22).

13. Genovese in particular supported this view. See his "The Treatment of Slaves in Different Countries: Problems in the Application of the Comparative Method," in *Slavery in the Americas: A Comparative Reader,* ed. Genovese and Laura Foner (Englewood Cliffs, N.J.: Prentiss-Hall, 1969), p. 203.

14. Herbert S. Klein, *African Slavery in Latin America and the Caribbean* (New York: Oxford University Press, 1986), p. 218. Fiehrer also states that "while racism is a constant in multiracial societies, the level to which it affects class stratification and class relations in a given system varies with economic circumstances. The large *mulato* populations of Saint-Domingue and Cuba suffered persecution and exclusion during periods of rising expectations, sugar boom, and self-generated economic competition" ("African Presence," pp. 23–24).

15. The names are too many to list here, but scholars who have produced works on free blacks include Frederick Bowser, Colin Palmer, Herman Bennett, William Sharp, Patrick Carroll, A. J. R. Russell-Wood, Stuart Schwartz, George Reid Andrews, Carl Degler, Jane Landers, Peter Stern, Joseph Sánchez, Arnold Sio, Thomas Holt, Jerome Handler, David Barry Gaspar, David Geggus, Douglas Hall, Gwendolyn Midlo Hall, John Garrigus, Mavis Campbell, Gad Heuman, Ed Cox, Monica Schuler, Franklin Knight, Herbert Klein, Rebecca Scott, and Manuel Moreno Fraginals for Latin America and the Caribbean; and Ira Berlin, John Hope Franklin, Larry

Koger, Leonard Curry, Michael Johnson, James Roark, Gary Nash, James Horton, Adele Alexander, Judith K. Schafer, L. Virginia Gould, and Loren Schweninger for the United States.

16. Jack D. L. Holmes, *A Guide to Spanish Louisiana, 1762–1806* (New Orleans: A. F. Laborde, 1970), p. xii.

17. Hall, *Africans in Colonial Louisiana*, p. xiii.

18. Brasseaux, Fontenot, and Oubre, *Creoles of Color in the Bayou Country;* Light Townsend Cummins, *Spanish Observers and the American Revolution, 1775–1783* (Baton Rouge: Louisiana State University Press, 1991); Gilbert C. Din, *The Canary Islanders of Louisiana* (Baton Rouge: Louisiana State University Press, 1988) and *Francisco Bouligny: A Bourbon Soldier in Spanish Louisiana* (Baton Rouge: Louisiana State University Press, 1993); Donald E. Everett, "Free Persons of Color in Colonial Louisiana," *Louisiana History* 7:1 (winter 1966): 21–50; Fiehrer, "African Presence"; Laura Foner, "The Free People of Color in Louisiana and St. Domingue: A Comparative Portrait of Two Three-Caste Slave Societies," *Journal of Social History* 3:4 (summer 1970): 406–30; L. Virginia Meacham Gould, "In Full Enjoyment of Their Liberty: The Free Women of Color of the Gulf Ports of New Orleans, Mobile, and Pensacola, 1769–1860 (Ph.D. dissertation, Emory University, 1991); Hall, *Africans in Colonial Louisiana;* Paul F. Lachance, "The 1809 Immigration of Saint-Domingue Refugees to New Orleans: Reception, Integration, and Impact," *Louisiana History* 29:2 (spring 1988): 109–41, "Intermarriage and French Cultural Persistence in Late Spanish and Early American New Orleans," *Histoire Sociale/Social History* 15:2 (May 1982): 47–81, and "The Politics of Fear: French Louisianians and the Slave Trade, 1786–1809," *Plantation Society in the Americas* 1:2 (June 1979): 162–97; Ulysses S. Ricard Jr., "Pierre Belly and Rose: More Forgotten People," *Chicory Review* 1:1 (fall 1988): 2–17; Usner, *Indians, Settlers, and Slaves.*

19. For a discussion of the Tannenbaum thesis as it applied to antebellum Louisiana, see David C. Rankin, "The Tannenbaum Thesis Reconsidered: Slavery and Race Relations in Antebellum Louisiana," *Southern Studies* 18:1 (spring 1979): 5–31.

20. Jane Landers, "Black Society in Spanish St. Augustine, 1784–1821" (Ph.D. dissertation, University of Florida, 1988), p. 6.

21. Klein has observed that "following the Haitian Revolution, British, French, Dutch, and North American legislation became even more hostile to the freedmen" (*African Slavery*, p. 221). He might have added Spanish, particularly Cuban, legislation as well.

22. Fiehrer, "African Presence," p. 4; Genovese, "Materialism and Idealism," p. 248.

23. The following works inform my discussion of Louisiana's political and economic history: Mathé Allain, *"Not Worth a Straw": French Colonial Policy and the Early Years of Louisiana* (Lafayette: Center for Louisiana Studies, 1988); Carl A. Brasseaux, *Denis-Nicolas Foucault and the New Orleans Rebellion of 1768* (Ruston, La.: McGinty Publications, 1987); Caroline Maude Burson, *The Stewardship of Don Esteban Miró, 1782–1792* (New Orleans: American Printing, 1940); John G. Clark, "New

Orleans: Its First Century of Economic Development," *Louisiana History* 10:1 (winter 1969): 35–47, and *New Orleans, 1718–1812: An Economic History* (Baton Rouge: Louisiana State University Press, 1970); Light Townsend Cummins and Glen Jeansonne, eds., *A Guide to the History of Louisiana* (Westport, Conn.: Greenwood Press, 1982); Joseph G. Dawson III, ed., *The Louisiana Governors: From Iberville to Edwards* (Baton Rouge: Louisiana State University Press, 1990); Jack D. L. Holmes, *Gayoso: The Life of a Spanish Governor in the Mississippi Valley, 1789–1799* (Baton Rouge: Louisiana State University Press, 1965), *A Guide,* and "Indigo in Colonial Louisiana and the Floridas," *Louisiana History* 8:4 (fall 1967): 329–49; John Hebron Moore, "The Cypress Lumber Industry of the Lower Mississippi Valley during the Colonial Period," *Louisiana History* 24:1 (winter 1983): 25–47; Joe Gray Taylor, *Louisiana: A Bicentennial History* (New York: W. W. Norton, 1976); Usner, *Indians, Settlers, and Slaves;* Arthur Preston Whitaker, *The Spanish-American Frontier: 1783–1795, the Westward Movement and the Spanish Retreat in the Mississippi Valley* (Gloucester, Mass.: Peter Smith, 1962).

24. Daniel H. Usner Jr., "From African Captivity to American Slavery: The Introduction of Black Laborers to Colonial Louisiana," *Louisiana History* 20:1 (winter 1979): 25–48, and *Indians, Settler, and Slaves,* pp. 13–76.

25. Clark, *New Orleans,* p. 209; Din, *Francisco Bouligny.*

26. Alexander DeConde, "Napoleon and the Louisiana Purchase," in *Napoleon and America,* ed. Robert B. Holtman (Pensacola: Perdido Bay Press for the Louisiana State Museum, 1988), pp. 100–136.

27. For the best analysis of colonial Louisiana's economic activities, see Usner, *Indians, Settlers, and Slaves.* He convincingly argues that most inhabitants, whether there by force, choice, or invasion, resisted crown and elite efforts to draw the colony into an Atlantic commercial system. Over the years they had constructed an elaborate frontier exchange economy that met their needs without too much expenditure of effort.

28. William Bartram, *The Travels of William Bartram,* ed. Mark Van Doren (New York: Dover Publications, 1928), p. 339; Usner, *Indians, Settlers, and Slaves.*

29. Fiehrer, "African Presence," p. 10.

30. Clark, "New Orleans," p. 46.

31. This is just a cursory look at slavery under French and Spanish rule. For more complete information on slaves during the colonial period and free blacks during the French regime see Mathé Allain, "Slave Policies in French Louisiana," *Louisiana History* 21:2 (spring 1980): 127–37; Carl A. Brasseaux, "The Administration of Slave Regulations in French Louisiana, 1724–1766," *Louisiana History* 21:2 (spring 1980): 139–58; Fiehrer, "African Presence"; Foner, "Free People of Color"; Hall, *Africans in Colonial Louisiana;* Thomas H. Ingersoll, "Old New Orleans: Race, Class, Sex, and Order in the Early Deep South, 1718–1819" (Ph.D. dissertation, University of California, Los Angeles, 1990); John S. Kendall, "New Orleans' 'Peculiar Institution,'" *Louisiana Historical Quarterly (LHQ)* 23:3 (July 1940): 864–86; Roland C. McConnell, *Negro Troops in Antebellum Louisiana: A History of the Battalion of Free*

Men of Color (Baton Rouge: Louisiana State University Press, 1968); James Thomas McGowan, "Creation of a· Slave Society: Louisiana Plantations in the Eighteenth Century" (Ph.D. dissertation, University of Rochester, 1976); Gary B. Mills, *The Forgotten People: Cane River's Creoles of Color* (Baton Rouge: Louisiana State University Press, 1977); Charles B. Roussève, *The Negro in New Orleans* (New York: Archives of Negro History, 1969); H. E. Sterkx, *The Free Negro in Ante-bellum Louisiana* (Rutherford, N.J.: Fairleigh Dickinson University Press, 1972); Joe Gray Taylor, *Negro Slavery in Louisiana* (Baton Rouge: Louisiana Historical Association, 1963); Usner, "From African Captivity to American Slavery."

32. Hall, *Africans in Colonial Louisiana,* pp. 12–18, 56–95, 119–55; Usner, "From African Captivity to American Slavery," p. 26. The governor who proposed the exchange was Jean Baptiste Lemoyne, sieur de Bienville, the founder of New Orleans. Although the Spanish governor Alejandro O'Reilly outlawed Indian slavery in 1769, priests were still baptizing mestizo slave infants as late as 1800 (Nonwhite Baptisms, book 6a, no. 712, 19 February 1800).

33. Fiehrer, "African Presence," pp. 7–8; Hall, *Africans in Colonial Louisiana,* pp. 275–315. In arguing for the re-Africanization of Louisiana, Hall emphasizes that "Africans were, by far, the largest group of people introduced into Spanish Louisiana," although "total population figures . . . are difficult to calculate" (p. 277).

34. Lachance, "Politics of Fear."

35. Virginia R. Domínguez, *White by Definition: Social Classification in Creole Louisiana* (New Brunswick, N.J.: Rutgers University Press, 1986), pp. 115–16; Taylor, *Negro Slavery,* pp. 5–6.

36. The Spaniards' figures were no more accurate than those of the French era, however, and usually undercounted free blacks. See examples provided in chapter 1.

37. Domínguez, *White by Definition,* pp. 115–16; Lachance, "The 1809 Immigration." Domínguez's figures for 1791 (1,147 libres, 1,604 slaves) differ from those given in the 1791 Census (862 libres, 1,789 slaves). I prefer to use the numbers enumerated in the original source, the 1791 Census.

38. Klein, *African Slavery,* p. 224; Landers, "Black Society."

39. See Henry Putney Beers, *French and Spanish Records of Louisiana: A Bibliographical Guide to Archive and Manuscript Sources* (Baton Rouge: Louisiana State University Press, 1989) for an overview of documents and archives pertinent to Louisiana history.

40. Beers, *French and Spanish Records of Louisiana,* pp. 30–31.

41. There also exists at the New Orleans Public Library an inventory of the notarial offices of Carlos Ximénez (1768–70) and Pedro Pedesclaux (1770–1804). This is merely an index and does not include the actual notarial acts.

42. As the work of Hall and Usner reveals.

43. This is what Patricia Seed best defines as classification by "social race" in her article "Social Dimensions of Race: Mexico City, 1753," *Hispanic American Historical Review (HAHR)* 62:4 (November 1982): 569–606.

44. On militia rosters the free black officer making the count frequently crossed

out the term "negro libre" or "mulato libre" written on the form and placed "moreno" or "pardo" above it. When free blacks signed documents, in most cases they placed pardo or moreno libre after their names rather than mulato or negro libre.

Chapter 1: Avenues to Freedom

1. Sio, "Marginality and Free Coloured Identity," p. 153.
2. Klein, *African Slavery,* pp. 217–41; Tannenbaum, *Slave and Citizen.*
3. Genovese, "Materialism and Idealism."
4. Harris, *Patterns of Race in the Americas.*
5. These include Fiehrer, "African Presence," pp. 23–24; Foner, "Free People of Color; Karasch, *Slave Life in Rio;* Stuart B. Schwartz, "The Manumission of Slaves in Colonial Brazil: Bahia, 1684–1745," *HAHR* 54:4 (November 1974): 603–35. Karasch argues that "most slaves owed their manumission to their own efforts or those of individual owners" rather than to institutions such as the church or legal system (p. 336). Foner contends that striking differences in the initial growth and position of libres in various regions resulted from both demographic and cultural/idealogical factors.
6. My data for manumissions are derived from the Notarial Acts specified by notary and date in the introduction to this work. The total of 1,921 between 1771 and 1803 includes only those manumissions actually registered before a notary. Contested manumissions in the Spanish Judicial Records and the Court Proceedings of various notaries, as well as emancipations listed in wills, *are not* included in this figure. If a contested case was successful, it was then recorded before a notary, just as a slave's emancipation pursuant to the testament of a deceased master was. By using only the actual Acts, one avoids double-counting or counting a manumission that never took place; for example, many masters wrote wills freeing favored slaves but then did not die or died many years later. If the master died and the slave was freed, it was recorded in the Acts. I believe this is the most accurate way of counting and analyzing manumissions in the Spanish period. My figures differ slightly from those of Ingersoll because that author covers a longer time period: through 1804 or 1809; it is also not clear whether he double-counts the contested and testamentary cases ("Free Blacks in a Slave Society").

This work does not examine Indian slavery in Louisiana and New Orleans. Even though Governor O'Reilly acted on instructions from the Spanish crown and outlawed Indian slavery in Louisiana in 1769, colonists continued to enslave indigenes. In the 1790s Governor Carondelet once again tried to enforce the law against such enslavement, and a number of persons of Native American descent, including individuals with some African ancestry, appealed for their freedom in front of government tribunals. See Stephen Webre, "The Problem of Indian Slavery in Spanish Louisiana, 1769–1803," *Louisiana History* 25:2 (spring 1984): 117–35.
7. Juan José Andreu Ocariz, *Movimientos rebeldes de los esclavos negros durante el dominio español en Luisiana* (Zaragosa, Spain: Cagisa, 1977); Gilbert C. Din, "Cima-

rrones and the San Malo Band in Spanish Louisiana," *Louisiana History* 21:3 (summer 1980): 237–62; Hall, *Africans in Colonial Louisiana;* Jack D. L. Holmes, "The Abortive Slave Revolt at Pointe Coupée, Louisiana, 1795," *Louisiana History* 11:4 (fall 1970): 341–62; Kerr, *Petty Felony.*

8. Antonio Acosta Rodríguez, *La Población de Luisiana española (1763-1803)* (Madrid: Ministerio de Asuntos Exteriores, 1979), pp. 17–226.

9. Quote from Fiehrer, "African Presence," p. 18. Brasseaux, *Denis-Nicolas Foucault;* Foner, "Free People of Color," pp. 415–16, 418–19. A "tenuous allegiance of the dominantly French planters to the Spanish regime" posed perennial challenges to Spanish administrators in Louisiana. An analysis of the correspondence of Governor Carondelet, who served during the era of the French Revolution, particularly highlights this dilemma (see Fiehrer, "African Presence," pp. 16, 25).

10. Gilbert C. Din, "Proposals and Plans for Colonization in Spanish Louisiana," *Louisiana History* 11:3 (summer 1970): 197–213.

11. For example, a count of 97 libres in 1771 was ridiculously low, given that militia rosters for 1770 list 61 free pardos and 283 free morenos between the ages of fifteen and forty-five living within four leagues (twelve land miles) of New Orleans ("Liste de la quantité des naigres libres de la Nouvelle Orléans, 1770," AGI PC 188-A, 22 February 1770).

12. Frederick P. Bowser, "Colonial Spanish America," in Cohen and Greene, *Neither Slave nor Free,* p. 35; Leonard P. Curry, *The Free Black in Urban America, 1800-1850: The Shadows of a Dream* (Chicago: University of Chicago Press, 1981).

13. For example, in 1777 the province of Louisiana counted 536 free blacks (3.0 percent of the total population, 6.0 percent of the free population, and 5.6 percent of the nonwhite population); a province enlarged by inclusion of Mobile and Pensacola numbered 1,701 libres in 1788 (4.0 percent of the total population, 8.0 percent of the free population, and 7.3 percent of the nonwhite population). All these percentages are much lower than for New Orleans (table 1.1). AGI PC 2351, 12 May 1777, and AGI PC 1425, 1788.

14. Bowser, "Colonial Spanish America," p. 33.

15. Domínguez, *White by Definition,* pp. 116–17; Lachance, "The 1809 Immigration."

16. Klein, *African Slavery,* pp. 217–41.

17. Hans W. Baade, "The Law of Slavery in Spanish Luisiana, 1769–1803," in *Louisiana's Legal Heritage,* ed. Edward F. Haas (Pensacola: Perdido Bay Press for the Louisiana State Museum, 1983), pp. 50–55; Bowser, "Colonial Spanish America," pp. 21–22; Lyle N. McAlister, *Spain and Portugal in the New World, 1492-1700* (Minneapolis: University of Minnesota Press, 1984), pp. 25, 435–36.

18. Code noir, applied to Louisiana 23 March 1724, French Judicial Records, Louisiana State Museum Historical Center; Klein, *African Slavery,* p. 195. Although Klein and other scholars of comparative slave societies note the harshness of the Code noir, most Louisiana historiography claims that it was mild (see Baade's discussion of Louisiana scholarship in "Law of Slavery," pp. 43–53). The Code noir

most certainly was more humane than British or Dutch slave law but much more restrictive and favorable to the slave owner than were Iberian codes.

19. Baade, "Law of Slavery," pp. 48–53; Gwendolyn Midlo Hall, "Saint Domingue," in Cohen and Greene, *Neither Slave nor Free*, pp. 172–92.

20. Baade, "Law of Slavery," pp. 64–67. With much research in the primary documents to support him, Baade convincingly argues that "the judicial authorities of Spanish Louisiana routinely applied Spanish rather than French law between 1770 and 1803" (p. 43), and with specific relevance for our study: "when professionally advised, the courts of Spanish Louisiana did *not* apply the *Code Noir* even where there was no contrary Spanish legislation directly in point, and that they *did* apply the Spanish law of freedom-purchase [coartación] which had not been expressly extended to Louisiana" (p. 62).

21. Kerr, *Petty Felony*, p. 152.

22. For example, see Court Proceedings of F. Broutin, no. 11, fols. 74–100, 17 March 1792. Older and even some recent works claim that Spanish administrators continued to apply the French Code noir after assuming control of Louisiana. Din ("*Cimarrones* and the San Malo Band") asserts that O'Reilly's code incorporated the Code noir with only a few alterations, an interpretation initiated by Judge François-Xavier Martin's two-volume *History of Louisiana* in the early nineteenth century (New Orleans: Lyman and Beardslee, 1827). A more thorough examination of primary sources definitively shows, however, that "such a radical 'Francophile' view of the legal history of the Spanish Luisiana cannot still be maintained today" and that "the judicial authorities of Spanish Luisiana routinely applied Spanish rather than French law between 1770 and 1803" (Baade, "Law of Slavery," p. 43). My own research in notarial and judicial documents confirms Baade's findings. The slaves and their representatives repeatedly stated their recognition of a change in slave law and those laws that governed freedmen.

23. Baade, "Law of Slavery"; quotations from McGowan, "Creation of a Slave Society," p. 194.

24. Both white and free black masters and their slaves recognized differences between French and Spanish law and attitudes. When Don Francisco Raquet purchased the parda Francisca from Mr. Leches in September 1769, he promised her freedom after six years of service. The sale and promise were made by an informal note (*papel simple*) according to the ancient customs of the colony. In 1772 Raquet recorded the promise of freedom before a notary. He stated that under the previous rule slaves had been considered movable property or chattel (*bienes muebles*), and there was thus no need to have a notary record transactions dealing with slaves. Raquet wanted to register a formal document with the authorities of the new dominion (Acts of Almonester y Roxas, fol. 35, 11 February 1772). The free morena Angélica Perret also noted a change in the status of slaves. The ancient custom of treating slaves as chattel no longer prevailed, and now even libres could manumit their slaves without seeking special permission from the government. She thus sought a formal recording of the freedom she bestowed upon her daughter and two grandchildren (Acts of

Almonester y Roxas, fol. 165, 4 May 1772). Another slave, the moreno Juan Bely, referred to his right to petition the tribunal for liberty against the wishes of a reluctant
slaveholder. Bely asserted that he had continually asked the widow and testamentary
executor of his late master (Don David Ross) to issue him a carta at the price of
his estimated worth. For this reason he exercised rights conceded him by the Spanish crown according to royal decree in order to name an estimator ("En cuya virtud
usando del derecho que S.M. por Real Cédula me concede, nombro por mi tasador
Don Fernando Alzar"). The court appointed Don Josef de Toca as Bely's *defensor*,
and Ross's estate named its estimator. Unfortunately, the record ended at this point
(Court Proceedings of N. Broutin, no. 60, fols. 1495–1501, 14 September 1803).

25. McGowan, "Creation of a Slave Society," pp. 201–5; Mörner, *Race Mixture*,
pp. 116–18.

26. I agree with Ingersoll that the "creation of the free black population of New
Orleans was dominated by the initiative of blacks, not whites," although it seems he
is referring only to white fathers freeing (or not freeing) their casta offspring when
making this statement. As we will see, whites freed or helped free slaves for reasons
other than paternity, especially those white masters who were female. My findings
do, however, conflict with Ingersoll's with regard to contested manumissions; he
notes them declining over the Spanish period, while I see a rise in the late 1780s,
only tapering off in the early 1800s. See his "Free Blacks in a Slave Society," quotation p. 188.

27. Cohen and Greene, introduction to *Neither Slave nor Free*, p. 7; Ingersoll,
"Free Blacks in a Slave Society," p. 186.

28. Cohen and Greene, introduction to *Neither Slave nor Free*, pp. 7–8; Klein,
African Slavery, p. 228. New Orleans during the colonial period was in what Cohen
and Greene describe as "the early phase of the emergence of the free colored (the first
several generations)," in that free black females overwhelmingly outnumbered libre
males. During this phase "the free colored groups throughout the hemisphere included disproportionately large numbers of females, not only as a result of the manumission of female partners in mixed marriages or sexual unions, but also as a result
of the general tendency to manumit female infants in greater numbers than males."
They note two factors that tended to even the sex ratio: self-purchase, which favored
males, and government offers of freedom for meritorious nonwhite male soldiers.

In New Orleans, however, self-purchase favored females, and the government
freed few deserving males. However, male slaveholders or an interested third party
did often manumit or purchase the freedom of adult and adolescent female slaves, in
particular manumitting gratis pardo and cuarterón slave children, presumably their
own offspring (see table 1.4). After analyzing notarial records for New Orleans from
1770 to 1803, McGowan notes that "three times as many women (123) as men (41) between the ages of 20 and 49 purchased their freedom" ("Creation of a Slave Society,"
p. 202). My numbers are higher than his, but the proportions are about the same.

29. Cohen and Greene, introduction to *Neither Slave nor Free*, pp. 7–8.

30. See the discussion in note 28. Klein generalizes for Latin America that "among

those who purchased their freedom there was an even distribution of women and men" (*African Slavery,* p. 228), but in Spanish New Orleans female self-purchasers greatly exceeded males. In addition to various explanations for the preponderance of females in the free black population offered on the pages above, another factor might be that the lucrative tasks of street and shop vendor, seamstress, and cook were usually performed by female slaves. While these occupations offered opportunities to accumulate funds even after paying the master a stipulated sum, the talents associated with them usually did not raise the slave's value, unlike artisan skills. Also, the more populous free black females often left their possessions to other females, slave and free, when they died, thus giving them the assets with which to purchase freedom.

31. Cohen and Greene, introduction to *Neither Slave nor Free,* p. 8.

32. Hall, *Africans in Colonial Louisiana,* pp. 275–315; Usner, *Indians, Settlers, and Slaves,* pp. 8–9, 142–44.

33. This observed trend conflicts with what Ingersoll notes: "suits became rare once masters understood that the policy could seldom be modified by their resistance" and that "the number of contested cases declined" ("Free Blacks in a Slave Society," pp. 184, 186). I, of course, think my statistics are more reliable.

34. For example, in her will dated 3 September 1781 Doña Pelagia Loireins, the widow Brazilier and current wife of Don Andrés Jung, granted cartas to eight of her twenty-four slaves. She died three days later. Doña Magdalena Brazilier, by contrast, wrote her will in 1793 but did not die until 1801. Three of her slaves waited eight years for their promised freedom (Acts of Mazange, no. 4, fol. 691, 3 September 1781; Acts of N. Broutin, no. 3, fols. 294, 298, 2 October 1801). Thus, the numbers mentioned in the text only include those manumissions that actually took place, which had to be notarized as an act separate from the testament and usually were carried out by the will's executor.

35. Acts of Ximénez, no. 5, fol. 649, 7 November 1793.

36. See for example Acts of Mazange, no. 5, fol. 109, 30 January 1782; Acts of Almonester y Roxas, fol. 97, 15 February 1782; Acts of Rodríguez, no. 7(2), fol. 836, 20 September 1783, and fol. 1037, 12 December 1783; Acts of Pedesclaux, no. 16, fol. 23, 14 January 1793. Of particular interest is a case in which two free pardo siblings and their natural white father, José, manumitted their morena mother and consort named María, whom they had inherited from Jorge Beaulieu, grandfather of the pardos and father of José. A few months later the two pardos, plus three other pardo siblings, manumitted their two grifo half siblings, whose mother was also María and whom they had also inherited from Jorge Beaulieu (Acts of Pedesclaux, no. 42, fol. 915, 13 December 1802, and no. 43, fol. 61, 27 January 1803).

37. Acts of Pedesclaux, no. 43, fol. 221, 21 March 1803. Examples of libres freeing slaves after the money borrowed to purchase them had been repaid included a libre woman who manumitted her mother after seven months and a free parda who liberated her sister after one year (Acts of Mazange, no. 3, fol. 115, 17 February 1781; Acts of Ximénez, no. 1, fol. 438, 30 September 1791).

38. Acts of Almonester y Roxas, fol. 462, 27 August 1779.

39. Acts of Mazange, no. 6, fol. 833, 3 October 1782.

40. Acts of Almonester y Roxas, fols. 58, 62, 13 March 1773; Acts of Garic, no. 4, fol. 243, 3 September 1774, and fol. 245, 4 September 1774.

41. Acts of Pedesclaux, no. 12, fol. 269, 29 March 1791.

42. Acts of Pedesclaux, no. 3, fols. 505–16, 520, 15 and 16 April 1788.

43. Acts of Almonester y Roxas, fol. 188, 31 July 1773; Acts of Garic, no. 6, fol. 240, 7 October 1775; 1778 Census; Acts of Pedesclaux, no. 41, fol. 445, 16 June 1802, and no. 42, fol. 923, 20 December 1802. According to Marion's 1802 testament, the three children by Bauptista were Isabela (about forty-eight years), Roseta (about forty-six), and Elena (about forty-four). Five surviving children by Gaillard were Constanza (married to Carlos Brulé, pardo libre), Adelaida (about thirty-six), Helena (about thirty-four), Raymundo (about thirty-two, militiaman), and Basilio (about twenty-eight).

44. Acts of Almonester y Roxas, fol. 291, 10 November 1772; Acts of Garic, no. 3, fol. 366, 5 December 1772; 1778 Census.

45. Everett, "Free Persons of Color," p. 46.

46. Acts of Rodríguez, no. 7(1), fol. 362, 22 April 1783; Acts of F. Broutin, no. 30, fol. 143, 14 June 1794.

47. Nonwhite Baptisms, books 4a, 5a, 6a, 7a, 8a, and 9a, 1788 to 1806; White Burials, 6 June 1811. For additional information on the Lemelle family, many of whom moved to Opelousas, Louisiana, see Brasseaux, Fontenot, and Oubre, *Creoles of Color in the Bayou Country*, pp. 19–20, 28–29; Gould, "In Full Enjoyment of Their Liberty," pp. 161, 301–3, 332–33.

48. Acts of Pedesclaux, no. 18, fol. 666, 16 August 1793, and fol. 747, 18 September 1793.

49. Acts of Almonester y Roxas, fol. 131, 6 March 1782; Acts of Pedesclaux, no. 16, fol. 25, 14 January 1793, and fol. 77, 31 January 1793; Nonwhite Baptisms, books 4a, 5a, 6a, and 7a, 1792–1802.

50. Acts of Almonester y Roxas, fol. 49, 26 January 1776.

51. Acts of Garic, no. 3, fol. 339, 20 November 1772.

52. "Bernardo Izurra, curador y tutor del menor Carlos, mulato, hijo natural del difunto Carlos Begin su padre y de la Negra María Esclaba que fue de este, declarando sus derechos," SJR, 19 May 1794.

53. Acts of Pedesclaux, no. 19, fol. 904, 30 October 1793; Acts of N. Broutin, no. 5, fol. 238, 13 May 1803.

54. Acts of N. Broutin, no. 4, fol. 463, 6 November 1802.

55. Acts of Ximénez, no. 1, fols. 497, 501, 25 November 1791.

56. Acts of Pedesclaux, no. 38, fol. 118, 19 February 1801.

57. Acts of Mazange, no. 3, fol. 89, 9 November 1781. Broutin freed Carlota for services, especially "dando el pecho a mis dos últimos hijos pupilos." Both Francisco in the 1790s and his son Narciso in the 1800s served as notaries for the Spanish government.

58. Acts of Pedesclaux, no. 13, fol. 681, 2 November 1791, and no. 43, fol. 283, 30 March 1803.

59. Acts of Ximénez, no. 14, fol. 211, 2 March 1799.

60. Acts of Garic, no. 6, fol. 274, 22 November 1775.

61. Ira Berlin, *Slaves without Masters: The Free Negro in the Antebellum South* (New York: Pantheon Books, 1974); Degler, *Neither Black nor White;* Peter Kolchin, *American Slavery, 1619–1877* (New York: Hill and Wang, 1993). Evidence from New Orleans shows that slaves over fifty years of age were manumitted at about four and a half times their proportion of the slave population.

62. Recent scholarship questions the conventional view that slaveholders discarded many of their elderly, incapacitated slaves. Klein points out that "although it was initially thought that the more economically minded Iberians were simply freeing their old and infirm slaves, this was not the case. . . . All recent studies have found that approximately two-thirds of the manumitted were women (from 60 to 67%), and few were found to be 45 years of age or older" (*African Slavery*, p. 227). For example, Schwartz ("Manumission of Slaves in Colonial Brazil") analyzed a sample of almost seven thousand manumission cases and concluded that the average age of those manumitted was a mere fifteen years of age.

63. Acts of Garic, no. 8, fol. 106, 11 March 1777.

64. Acts of Almonester y Roxas, fol. 434, 11 June 1776. Another interesting case combined manumission by will and self-purchase. In 1782 Juan Bautista Roux donated one hundred pesos to his morena slave Catarina in his will. Roux also stipulated that at his death his executor was to allow Catarina to purchase her freedom for five hundred pesos (Acts of Almonester y Roxas, fol. 177, 1 April 1782).

65. Acts of Almonester y Roxas, fol. 312, 16 July 1778, and fol. 313, 17 July 1778. This case also indicates that persons of Native American ancestry (in this instance a mestiza) were still being held as slaves in Louisiana.

66. Acts of Almonester y Roxas, fol. 96, 9 March 1772; fol. 199, 10 May 1772; and fol. 267, 25 October 1773.

67. Karasch, for example, found that in Rio ex-slaves who "had antagonized former owners and had been thrust into their new lives without patron or profession" faced a bleak struggle just to survive. Indeed, "since so many freedpersons were women, many continued to work as servants for their previous owners and so maintained old patterns of dependency. . . . By continuing dependent relationships with her former owner, a freedwoman seldom experienced a change in her living conditions and personal security, since her former owner would serve as her protector," not always an adverse situation. On the other hand, "for slaves who had been given their freedom gratuitously and turned out of their owner's house, life was quite difficult," especially without kin or friends to lend support (Karasch, *Slave Life in Rio*, pp. 362–64).

68. Acts of Garic, no. 5, fol. 245, 23 December 1774.

69. Acts of Mazange, no. 6, fol. 872, 18 October 1782; Acts of Rodríguez, no. 7(2),

fol. 791, 5 September 1783. Other examples of conditional manumission include Eugenio, an eight-year-old pardito, freed with the condition that he serve his mistress's friend for the rest of her lifetime. Don Luis de Berducat, captain of the Fixed Infantry Regiment of Louisiana, manumitted his morena slave Martón on condition that she serve him for six more years (Acts of Mazange, no. 6, fol. 830, 2 October 1782; Acts of Ximénez, no. 4, fol. 26, 23 January 1793). In addition, Fray Bernabé of the Capuchin mission freed his twenty-five-year-old moreno slave and creole of New Orleans named Pedro in exchange for the slave's promise of service for the rest of Bernabé's life. Pedro was the son of the free morena Marta, who had died in 1774 and willed her belongings to Father Bernabé for the care of her son ("Successión intestado de una Negra libre llamada Martón o Marta," SJR, 17 January 1774; Acts of Garic, no. 6, fol. 257, 20 October 1775).

70. Acts of Garic, no. 9, fol. 176, 11 April 1778.

71. Acts of Garic, no. 8, fol. 485, 15 December 1777, and no. 9, fol. 583, 22 December 1778. For additional information on the Ursulines and their slave transactions see Karen Greene, "The Ursuline Mission in Colonial Louisiana" (M.A. thesis, Louisiana State University, 1982).

72. Acts of Garic, no. 4, fol. 172, 14 May 1773.

73. Acts of Garic, no. 6, fol. 109, 26 April 1775.

74. Acts of Garic, no. 6, fol. 86, 3 April 1775.

75. Acts of N. Broutin, no. 3, fol. 239, 7 August 1801.

76. Acts of Pedesclaux, no. 40, fol. 127, 23 February 1802.

77. Acts of F. Broutin, no. 7, fol. 357, 3 November 1791.

78. Acts of F. Broutin, no. 7, fol. 253, 24 May 1791.

79. Acts of Pedesclaux, no. 45, fol. 739, 6 September 1803.

80. Acts of Almonester y Roxas, fol. 251, 10 September 1772.

81. Acts of Ximénez, no. 2, fols. 229, 231, 5 May 1792, and fols. 234, 235, 237, 7 May 1792. The slaveholder, Doña María Julia de la Brosse, the legitimate wife of Don Francisco Carrière and childless, let several other slaves purchase their cartas at the same time. Two months later she wrote her will and donated to Magdalena, now a free morena, a fully outfitted bed and to Magdalena, her three daughters, and another former slave all the clothes of her use, divided equally five ways (Ximénez, no. 2, fol. 331, 6 July 1792).

82. Acts of Almonester y Roxas, fol. 140, 10 March 1775.

83. Acts of Garic, no. 8, fol. 382, 20 October 1777; Acts of Almonester y Roxas, fol. 282, 18 May 1779.

84. Acts of Almonester y Roxas, fol. 23, 12 January 1781, and fols. 41, 42, 27 January 1781.

85. Acts of Perdomo, fols. 432, 433, 434, 29 November 1782.

86. Acts of Garic, no. 4, fol. 88, 17 March 1773.

87. Karasch, *Slave Life in Rio,* pp. 211, 243.

88. For additional cases see Ingersoll, "Free Blacks in a Slave Society," p. 184.

89. See, for example, the case of Honoré, the pardo slave of Mr. Beralleft, who

had purchased him coartado twenty years earlier but had appropriated as his own all of Honoré's wages and treated him as a normal rather than a coartado slave. Honoré requested that the court verify his status by pulling the bill of sale from the archives, which is where the documentary record ends. Without a written agreement, he probably did not prevail ("Honoré mulato solicitando Ser Libre," SJR, 6 August 1792).

90. Acts of Almonester y Roxas, fol. 361, 23 June 1779.

91. "Información producida por el Negro Antonio Esclavo de Don Juan Pedro Decuir para hacer constar haver entrepada a esta Cantidad de pesos acuenta de su Libertad," SJR, 25 February 1795.

92. Although my figures differ from Ingersoll's, because he looks at a slightly longer time period (through 1809 rather than 1803), the percentages are similar. He found 200 of 612 third-party purchasers to be white men (32.7 percent) ("Free Blacks in a Slave Society," p. 188).

93. Acts of Pedesclaux, no. 38, fol. 288, 7 May 1801. Another white who did not explicitly state his paternity but obviously was the slave's father was Don Juan Josef Calmona. He paid Don Juan Bautista Mercier two hundred pesos to manumit Carolina, the eighteen-month-old cuarterona daughter of Mercier's parda slave Pognon (Acts of N. Broutin, no. 3, fol. 338, 27 October 1801).

94. Acts of Pedesclaux, no. 45, fol. 881, 14 November 1803, and fol. 796, 1 October 1803.

95. Acts of Pedesclaux, no. 39, fol. 569, 20 October 1801. For other examples of third parties purchasing cartas for unborn slaves see Acts of Pedesclaux, no. 16, fol. 23, 14 January 1793, and Acts of N. Broutin, no. 3, fol. 23, 26 January 1801.

96. Acts of Pedesclaux, no. 16, fol. 79, 31 January 1793.

97. Acts of Garic, no. 9, fols. 595, 597, 29 December 1778.

98. Acts of Perdomo, fol. 279, 4 June 1782, and fol. 362, 16 September 1782.

99. Acts of Pedesclaux, no. 15, fol. 487, 29 August 1792.

100. Acts of N. Broutin, no. 15, fol. 353, 15 November 1792.

101. Acts of Garic, no. 10, fol. 78, 1 February 1779; Acts of Ximénez, no. 9, fol. 13, 14 January 1795.

102. Acts of Pedesclaux, no. 17, fol. 312, 24 April 1793.

103. Acts of Ximénez, no. 17, fol. 348, 2 June 1802.

104. Acts of N. Broutin, no. 3, fol. 146, 4 May 1801.

105. "Ultimo testamento de Margarita, Parda libre," SJR, 1 March 1770.

106. Acts of Pedesclaux, no. 12, fol. 47, 21 January 1791; no. 17, fol. 474, 14 June 1793; and no. 18, fol. 562, 9 July 1793.

107. Acts of Rodríguez, no. 4, fol. 119, 29 January 1785.

108. Din, *Francisco Bouligny,* pp. 132–40; Hall, *Africans in Colonial Louisiana,* pp. 212–36; chapter 4 in this work.

109. Acts of Rodríguez, no. 8, fol. 671, 25 May 1786; Usner, *Indians, Settlers, and Slaves,* pp. 19, 96–100.

110. For use of this phrase in a disputed case see Court Proceedings of F. Broutin, no. 16, fols. 446–70, 16 February 1793.

111. Acts of Mazange, in Acts of Garic, no. 12, fol. 553, 9 December 1779, and fols. 583, 591, 18 December 1779.

112. Acts of N. Broutin, no. 3, fol. 126, 15 April 1801.

113. Acts of Ximénez, no. 2, fol. 213, 25 April 1792. In all fairness, one must also acknowledge the few cases in which *women* bypassed slave mothers in favor of freeing their children. In 1779 the morena libre Angélica petitioned a tribunal for the freedom of her four-year-old granddaughter María Antonia, the cuarterona slave of Don Santiago Porta. Angélica had petitioned for and won her own carta eight years earlier. Her daughter Francisca, mother of María Antonia, remained a slave of Porta ("Autos hechos por fin y muerte de doña María Bienvenue," SJR, 23 September 1771; "Autos hechos por Angélica, Negra libre, por la libertad de María Antonia, Cuarterona esclaba de don Santiago Porta, por precio de su estimación," SJR, 29 July 1779; Acts of Almonester y Roxas, fol. 431, 5 August 1779).

114. Acts of Almonester y Roxas, fol. 33, 16 January 1779.

115. Acts of Almonester y Roxas, fol. 362, 18 September 1781.

116. Acts of Almonester y Roxas, fol. 151, 11 April 1781.

117. Acts of Almonester y Roxas, fol. 287, 6 November 1773.

118. Acts of Pedesclaux, no. 18, fol. 629, 2 August 1793. Some valuations were so high that the slave never did purchase his or her freedom. One such slave was María. In 1803 the moreno libre Juan Pedro appeared before the court to demand the carta of his daughter, a twelve-year-old morena slave of Doña Isabel Proffit. When both appraisers valued María at 700 pesos, Juan Pedro protested that she was not worth more than 350 pesos; the former was an enormous sum, and he could not pay it. Thus the court denied María her carta and made Juan Pedro pay 17 pesos in court costs (Court Proceedings of N. Broutin, no. 58, fols. 781–90, 27 May 1803).

119. Acts of Pedesclaux, no. 15, fol. 375, 26 June 1792.

120. Court Proceedings of F. Broutin, no. 6, fols. 105–15, 29 January 1791.

121. Acts of Almonester y Roxas, fol. 586, 21 August 1776.

122. Acts of Almonester y Roxas, fol. 264, 14 July 1781.

123. A probably small but important part of this growth was no doubt due to the running away and passing as free that some slaves successfully accomplished. Their numbers are even more difficult to estimate than those associated with natural growth or immigration, but we can gain some notion of their size from the numerous court cases that mention runaways, notations in plantation records, and the reiteration of laws to prevent and punish the efforts of runaways and their accomplices. For more on runaways and the "chaos" that characterized colonial Louisiana, see Hall, *Africans in Colonial Louisiana,* pp. 201–36.

124. See, for example, the Reverend Monsignor Earl C. Woods's discussion of the many places of birth listed in baptismal, marriage, and funeral records for the early nineteenth century, especially among males, in Woods and Charles Nolan, eds., *Sacramental Records of the Roman Catholic Church of the Archdiocese of New Orleans,* 10 vols. (New Orleans: Archdiocese of New Orleans, 1987–95), 7:xix–xxi.

125. This is a very rough measure, to be sure. Absolute numbers of births and

deaths per year cannot be ascertained from this data, or from any other source, in this era before civil records; not everyone was Catholic, even though they were supposed to be, nor did they all take the sacraments of baptism and burial. Also, even though some people lived in New Orleans, they were baptized or buried in another parish. Finally, although New Orleanians usually were buried the same year they died (usually even on the same day in that semitropical climate), they were often baptized several months or years after being born. When a child was baptized soon after birth, that commonly meant he or she was in danger of imminent death. However, I have found that in general the number of persons born in one year and baptized in another is fairly constant over time and thus offsets the discrepancy in any given series of years. When spread over a number of years, calculation of the number of births based on number of baptisms is quite reliable. The experienced demographer Paul Lachance has also observed the same tendency (personal conversation, 9 November 1995). Thus, when the data are expressed as a ratio of baptisms to burials—rather than an absolute number—I feel fairly comfortable using them to get a rough sense of natural increase or decrease.

126. Nonwhite Baptisms, books 4a and 5a, 1787–97; data for computing the median age at death for whites were drawn from funeral records dated 1785 through 1803 (except for a few entries between 1772 and 1776, all funeral records for whites dated earlier than October 1784 perished in the Great Conflagration of 1788) concerning 1,526 males and 741 females; an additional 179 and 69 entries respectively gave no ages and thus were not used in computations. For free nonwhites the funeral records date from 1774 through 1803 and cover 441 males (plus 61 with no given age) and 574 females (plus 116 with no given age).

127. Nonwhite Baptisms, books 4a, 5a, 6a, 7a, 8a, 9a, and 10a, 1790–1808; Nonwhite Funerals, books 2 and 3, 1791–1802.

128. Thomas Ashe, *Travels in America Performed in 1806*, 3 vols. (London: Richard Phillips, 1808), 3:242–43.

129. Paul Alliot, "Historical and Political Reflections," in *Louisiana under the Rule of Spain, France, and the United States, 1785–1807: Social, Economic, and Political Conditions of the Territory Represented in the Louisiana Purchase,* trans. and ed. James Alexander Robertson, 2 vols. (Cleveland: Arthur H. Clark, 1911), 1:71.

130. Don Pedro Dulcido Barrán to the Cabildo, PDLC, book 4088, doc. 337, 24 January 1800.

Chapter 2: Work and Property Accumulation

1. Quote from Pierre-Louis Berquin-Duvallon, *Vue de la colonie espagnole du Mississipi, ou des provinces de Louisiane et Floride occidentale, en l'année 1802* (Paris: Imprimerie Expédite, 1803), p. 252. See also Claude C. Robin, *Voyages dans l'intérieur de la Louisiane, de la Floride occidentale, et dans les isles de la Martinique et de Saint-Dominque, pendant les années 1802, 1803, 1804, 1805 et 1806,* 3 vols. (Paris: F. Buisson, 1807), 2:75. The French physician Paul Alliot wrote in 1804 that libre women in New Orleans "inspire such lust through their bearing, their gestures, and their dress, that

many quite well-to-do persons are ruined in pleasing them" ("Historical and Political Reflections," 1:85).

2. Foner, "Free People of Color," pp. 416–17.

3. Quote from Fiehrer, "African Presence," p. 21; Baade, "Law of Slavery," p. 49.

4. Burson, *Stewardship of Don Esteban Miró*, p. 253.

5. Cohen and Greene, introduction to *Neither Slave nor Free*, p. 16. Lyman Johnson ("The Impact of Racial Discrimination on Black Artisans in Colonial Buenos Aires," *Social History* 6:3 [1981]: 301–16) notes the development of guilds in colonial Argentina, whereas Karasch (*Slave Life in Rio*, p. 200) finds few guild restrictions operating in early-nineteenth-century Rio. The only restrictions I have found for Spanish New Orleans were requirements for the licensing of doctors by a panel of their peers. In 1801, when licenses were reviewed, the free moreno médico, Santiago Derom, was limited to the curing of throat ailments and nothing else (RDC, vol. 1, 8 May 1772, and vol. 4, no. 4, 14 August 1801).

6. Geggus, *Slavery, War, and Revolution*, p. 19. Cohen and Greene further note a link between self- and third-party purchase and opportunities for artisans and traders: "Certainly the evidence suggests that where the 'pulling up' of wives and relatives by newly freed men was a relatively common practice it was a reflection of the opening of the economy to colored traders and artisans" (introduction to *Neither Slave nor Free*, p. 8). In New Orleans many of these traders were females, who also purchased cartas for themselves and loved ones.

7. Burson, *Stewardship of Don Esteban Miró*, p. 253.

8. Examples of such behavior are presented in this chapter and chapter 5. Researchers have noted such a division among free blacks and alliances with either whites or slaves throughout the Americas. For a summary see Cohen and Greene, introduction to *Neither Slave nor Free*, pp. 11–16.

9. As noted before, censuses for the period were often incomplete and undercounted the free black population as well as its contributions; nevertheless, returns offer valuable information on a broad spectrum of occupational pursuits. In 1791 and 1795 officials in New Orleans compiled information on each household head, including his or her name, occupation, age category, and race. In addition, they indicated the number (but not the names or occupations) of persons residing in each household by age group, sex, race, and status. Census takers in 1791 went street by street, whereas in 1795 they went district by district, thereby generating slightly different perspectives. Unfortunately, for female and free black heads of household the 1791 returns provided little or no information on occupation. While the 1795 census did not so severely slight women and nonwhites, returns for the fourth quarter of the city, which had the second highest percentage of free black residents (see table 3.1), are nonexistent. Officials primarily concentrated on gathering data for white males, a shortcoming common to many colonial censuses (Celia Wu, "The Population of the City of Querétaro in 1791," *Journal of Latin American Studies* 16:2 [November 1984]: 279).

10. I have used Jacob Price's model for the grouping of occupation by sector in

American port cities ("Economic Function and the Growth of American Port Towns in the Eighteenth Century," *Perspectives in American History* 8 [1974]: 123–86). Compare total figures and percentages with those of Price for late-eighteenth-century Boston, Philadelphia, and New York City (p. 137). He uses slightly different terms for the same sectors: his governmental = my public, industrial = manufacturing, maritime = commerce. Compared to Price's cities, Spanish colonial New Orleans had a much larger public sector and a much smaller manufacturing sector, to be expected in a colonial capital of a mercantilist, monarchical empire.

11. Karasch (*Slave Life in Rio*) also finds in early-nineteenth-century Rio that skilled slaves and freedmen were most likely to be carpenters or to take up another construction-related craft, including that of joiner, caulker, and mason (p. 200). Most females served as domestics and/or vendors (pp. 206–8).

12. Census of Faubourg Ste. Marie, 1798, AGI PC 215-A. Organized and subdivided beginning in 1788, the Faubourg Ste. Marie (Arrabal Santa María, Suburb St. Mary) was located just outside the city walls upriver. By 1798 240 whites, 96 libres, and 256 slaves resided in the suburb.

13. Cohen and Greene, introduction to *Neither Slave nor Free,* p. 16; Robin, *Voyages,* 2:59–61.

14. Karasch, *Slave Life in Rio,* pp. 185–213, 335–69.

15. RDC, vol. 3, no. 2, 1787; Court Proceedings of Ximénez, fols. 243–45, 30 November 1804.

16. Robin, *Voyages,* 2:75.

17. Berquin-Duvallon, *Vue,* p. 253; Robin, *Voyages,* 2:75. Ironically, in another section of his account Berquin-Duvallon perpetuated the myth (see note 1).

18. Acts of Mazange, no. 7(1), fol. 303, 2 April 1783; "Executivos seguidos por Santiago Derom, Negro libre contra doña Isavel de Trean, sobre el cobro de pesos," SJR, 30 April 1791; RDC, vol. 4, no. 4, 14 August 1801; Charles B. Rousseve, *The Negro in Louisiana: Aspects of His History and His Literature* (New Orleans: Xavier University Press, 1937), pp. 9–10. In the eighteenth century doctors were not esteemed as highly as they are today and usually ranked well below government officials, planters, merchants, and even lawyers on the colonial social scale. In the New World colonies of many nations barbers often doubled as surgeons and dentists, many of whom were free people of color. For examples, see Karasch, *Slave Life in Rio,* p. 202.

19. Hall, *Africans in Colonial Louisiana,* p. 162.

20. Acts of Ximénez, no. 16, fol. 146, 24 July 1799.

21. Berquin-Duvallon, *Vue,* p. 253.

22. Acts of Garic, no. 8, fol. 399, 5 November 1777.

23. Acts of F. Broutin, no. 15, fol. 251, 3 August 1792.

24. Acts of F. Broutin, no. 25, fol. 275, 24 October 1793.

25. Acts of Almonester y Roxas, fol. 287, 2 November 1772; Court Proceedings of Quiñones, no. 1, fols. 87–103, 8 February 1779; AGI SD 2548, 18 January 1782. Calpha's militia service is detailed in chapter 4.

26. "Tableau des habitations . . . Metairie," AGI PC 211, 12 March 1796.

27. Karasch finds the same for Rio (*Slave Life in Rio,* p. 200).

28. "Relación de la pérdida que cada Yndividuo ha padecido en el Yncendio de esta Ciudad acaecido el 21 de Marzo del presente año . . . ," AGI SD 2576, 30 September 1788; Acts of F. Broutin, no. 7, fol. 222, 7 May 1791; Militia Roster, AGI PC 160-A, 1 May 1801 (hereafter 1801 Militia Rosters).

29. Acts of F. Broutin, no. 7, fol. 20, 17 September 1790; 1801 Militia Rosters.

30. Acts of Garic, no. 6, fol. 171, 26 June 1775; Acts of F. Broutin, no. 46, fol. 125, 19 June 1797; 1801 Militia Rosters. Bernabé's marriage to the free morena Francisca Malbroux in 1800 legitimated a relationship that had lasted at least ten years and produced three living children. Two others had died prior to their parents' wedding and another child born in 1801 died four days after birth (Nonwhite Baptisms, books 4a, 5a, and 6a, 1790–1801; Nonwhite Marriages, book 1, no. 57b, 9 June 1800).

31. Robin, *Voyages,* 2:61. The governor and cabildo also contracted with the free black carpenter Juan Bouquin in 1796 to work on the cemetery and Carondelet Canal. The canal linked New Orleans with Bayou St. John (Bayou San Juan) and gave the city an outlet to the Gulf of Mexico via Lake Pontchartrain. Slave and prison labor primarily constructed the canal. Bouquin charged the cabildo twelve reales per day for his labor, four reales per day for labor performed by his slave, and the cost of materials (Cabildo Records, box 2a, folders 7a and 7b, 14 September 1796 and 3 November 1796, LLMVC; John Pintard, "New Orleans, 1801: An Account by John Pintard," ed. David Lee Sterling, *LHQ* 34:3 (July 1951): 223.

32. Usner, *Indians, Settlers, and Slaves,* p. 202.

33. City Treasury Accounts for 1787, Cabildo Records, box 1, folder 4, LLMVC. In New Orleans, as well as in Rio, "one of the most important peddling operations was the vending of all types of foodstuffs, fresh and prepared" (Karasch, *Slave Life in Rio,* p. 207).

34. Ashe, *Travels in America,* 3:260. In addition to poor libres and whites, other marginal economic groups—"primarily city slaves engaged in selling the surplus of their gardens and loot from nocturnal activities, or Indians peddling vegetables, fish, blankets, and trinkets"—participated in the city's retail industry (Clark, *New Orleans,* p. 256).

35. Acts of Almonester y Roxas, fol. 97, 15 February 1782; 1795 Census.

36. RDC, vol. 3, no. 1, 10 September 1784; PDLC, book 4079, doc. 234, 2 September 1794. Both French and Spanish local officials actively involved themselves in ordering daily living, their most vital task being the regulation of colonial food supplies. Authorities attempted to provide adequate, edible foodstuffs to the population at fair prices for both producer and consumer. During the Spanish period, government supervision of the New Orleans market intensified as the cabildo began exercising "a direct and increasing influence upon the daily economic life of the town." In this capacity town council members "set prices, inspect[ed] for quality, assure[d] the use of standard weights and measures, and prevent[ed] recurrent food

shortages from benefiting monopolists and forestallers at the expense of the public welfare" (Clark, *New Orleans,* p. 257).

37. Report from Juan de Castañedo, City Treasurer, 1795, Cabildo Records, box 2, folder 6, LLMVC.

38. Acts of Pedesclaux, no. 29, fol. 262, 25 April 1797.

39. Pintard, "New Orleans, 1801," p. 232. United States officials increased restrictions on license holding with similar results: "In the month of January, 1823, thirty-two vending licenses were issued by authorities. Only free males could procure the licenses, but the license-holders seldom did the actual selling. That task was generally reserved for black slaves: many plantation owners regularly sent their slaves into town to hawk surplus produce in the street. Most of these hawkers were women" (Lilian Crété, *Daily Life in Louisiana, 1815–1830,* trans. Patrick Gregory [Baton Rouge: Louisiana State University Press, 1981], p. 64). Travelers to Rio imparted the general impression that city market stalls were the domain of African women. These women actually owned the stalls, however. Karasch surmises that "since so many stall owners were freedpersons, perhaps they had acquired a stall and freedom" (*Slave Life in Rio,* p. 207).

40. PDLC, book 4079, doc. 287, 6 October 1797. The merchants referred to the "crecido número de Mulatas y Negras tanto libres." The New York merchant Pintard wrote that "one finds however but very little interchange of courtesy among the merchants   too great jealousy of each other prevails" ("New Orleans, 1801," p. 232).

41. Comparative data on Boston and Philadelphia obtained from Price, "Economic Function and the Growth of American Port Towns"; 1791 Census.

42. "Proclamación por Governador Unzaga y Amezaga para regular las casas de Trujos, Posadas, y Tabernas," AGI PC 110, 26 August 1770; Jack D. L. Holmes, "Spanish Regulation of the Tavern and the Liquor Trade in the Mississippi Valley," in *The Spanish in the Mississippi Valley,* ed. John Francis McDermott (Urbana: University of Illinois Press, 1974), pp. 149–82. In 1791 New Orleans boasted more tavern-keepers than members of any other occupation—a full seventy heads of household (1791 Census).

43. Acts of Almonester y Roxas, fol. 268, 27 October 1773, and fol. 85, 16 February 1775; City Treasury Accounts for 1787, Cabildo Records, box 1, folder 4, LLMVC; "Relación de la pérdida . . . ," AGI SD 2576, 30 September 1788; 1795 Census; City Treasury Accounts for 1799, Cabildo Records, box 2a, folder 8, LLMVC; "List of Duties of Tavernkeepers," SJR, 31 Dec. 1800; Acts of Pedesclaux, no. 39, fol. 513, 9 September 1801.

44. Karasch, *Slave Life in Rio,* p. 201.

45. Acts of F. Broutin, no. 7, fol. 89, 23 December 1790; Court Proceedings of F. Broutin, no. 23, fols. 277–88, 20 August 1793; Acts of Ximénez, no. 6, fol. 162, 25 April 1794. Don Francisco also donated a house and land to the free pardo carpenter Pablo Cheval and Pablo's sister Luison Cheval, the mother of seven cuarterones by Don Carlos Vivant (Acts of F. Broutin, no. 25, fol. 169, 9 June 1793, and no. 40, fol. 177, 31 May 1796).

46. Court Proceedings of F. Broutin, no. 16, fols. 48–115, 12 January 1793.

47. Court Proceedings of F. Broutin, no. 22, fols. 518–27, 23 September 1793.

48. "Copia de las condiciones . . . ," AGI PC 548, 1766 and 1767; "Lista y asientos de la Maestranza . . . ," AGI PC 548, 1767. Some wages were accorded on a daily basis, but for comparative purposes I have converted them to a monthly rate, on the basis of a twenty-four-day work month (six days per week).

49. Acts of Almonester y Roxas, fol. 19, 18 January 1782.

50. Court Proceedings of N. Broutin, no. 48, fols. 319–37, 6 August 1801.

51. Acts of Almonester y Roxas, fol. 207, 22 April 1782.

52. See, for example, the report presented by Carlos de la Chaise to the cabildo listing salaries to be paid to slave owners and free blacks for labor performed on constructing a fence along the levee and hauling soil to the city in order to repair the streets and build houses (Cabildo Records, box 2, folder 6a, 26 June 1795, LLMVC).

53. Court Records of Fermín Hernández, no. 1, fols. 99–100, 21 August 1791.

54. AGI Estado 14, no. 60 and 5, no. 107, 1794. More detail on Bailly's life and activities can be found in chapters 3 and 5.

55. Court Proceedings of F. Broutin, no. 3, fols. 139–45, 29 January 1791.

56. Acts of Almonester y Roxas, fol. 23, 12 January 1781. Cecilia is also listed in documents as an india libre and provides but one of many examples of masters reclassifying their Indian slaves as African when the Spaniards outlawed enslavement of native peoples. For additional information on Cecilia and her efforts to free members of her family on the basis of Indian descent, see Hall, *Africans in Colonial Louisiana*, pp. 337–41.

57. Court Proceedings of N. Broutin, no. 47, fols. 76–96, 22 January 1801.

58. At the turn of the nineteenth century Berquin-Duvallon wrote that a father, mother, several children, and three to four servants required an annual income of two thousand pesos merely "for the maintenance of necessary decency and without any superfluity" (*Vue*, p. 43).

59. Henry Plauche Dart, "Public Education in New Orleans in 1800," *LHQ* 11:2 (April 1928): 24–52; Roger Philip McCutcheon, "Libraries in New Orleans, 1771–1833," *LHQ* 20:1 (January 1937): 152–58; Minter Wood, "Life in New Orleans in the Spanish Period," *LHQ* 22:3 (July 1939): 642–709.

60. "Diligencias promovidas por don Joseph Dusuau de la Croix . . . ," SJR, 21 July 1801.

61. Alliot, "Historical and Political Reflections," p. 85.

62. Acts of F. Broutin, no. 15, fol. 245, 27 July 1792.

63. Acts of Pedesclaux, no. 7, fol. 480, 7 May 1789.

64. Acts of F. Broutin, no. 15, fol. 70, 17 March 1792.

65. Acts of Pedesclaux, no. 44, fols. 421 and 423, 20 May 1803, and fol. 428, 21 May 1803. The sisters' mother, Jung's former slave, had either died or been sold to another person.

66. Though the list presented here is not all-inclusive, some studies that discuss slaveholding by free blacks are Berlin, *Slaves without Masters;* Frederick P. Bowser,

The African Slave in Colonial Peru, 1524–1650 (Stanford: Stanford University Press, 1974); James R. Brewer, "Negro Property Owners in Seventeenth-Century Virginia," in *The Making of Black America: Essays in Negro Life and History,* ed. August Meier and Elliott Rudwick (New York: Atheneum, 1969), pp. 201–5; Léo Elisabeth, "The French Antilles," in Cohen and Greene, *Neither Slave nor Free,* pp. 134–71; E. Horace Fitchett, "The Traditions of the Free Negro in Charleston, South Carolina," *Journal of Negro History* 25:2 (April 1940): 139–52; John Hope Franklin, *The Free Negro in North Carolina, 1790–1860* (Chapel Hill: University of North Carolina Press, 1943); Eugene D. Genovese, "The Slave States in North America," in Cohen and Greene, *Neither Slave nor Free,* pp. 258–77; Jerome S. Handler and Arnold A. Sio, "Barbados," in Cohen and Greene, *Neither Slave nor Free,* pp. 214–57; Michael P. Johnson and James L. Roark, *Black Masters: A Free Family of Color in the Old South* (New York: W. W. Norton, 1974); Karasch, *Slave Life in Rio;* Klein, *African Slavery;* Knight, *Slave Society in Cuba;* Larry Koger, *Black Slaveowners: Free Black Slave Masters in South Carolina, 1790–1860* (Columbia: University of South Carolina Press, 1985); John H. Russell, "Colored Freemen as Slave Owners in Virginia," *Journal of Negro History* 1:3 (July 1916): 233–42; William F. Sharp, *Slavery on the Spanish Frontier: The Colombian Chocó, 1680–1810* (Norman: University of Oklahoma Press, 1976); Carter G. Woodson, ed., *Free Negro Owners of Slaves in the United States in 1830* (New York: Negro Universities Press, 1924).

A few scholars have addressed the topic of free black slaveholders in Louisiana, but they concentrate on the antebellum period: Alice Dunbar-Nelson, "People of Color in Louisiana," *Journal of Negro History* 1:4 (October 1916): 361–76; Foner, "Free People of Color"; Joseph Karl Menn, *The Large Slaveholders of Louisiana—1860* (New Orleans: Pelican Publishing, 1964); Loren Schweninger, *Black Property Owners in the South, 1790–1915* (Urbana: University of Illinois Press, 1991) and "Prosperous Blacks in the South, 1790–1880," *American Historical Review* 95:1 (February 1990): 31–56; Sterkx, *Free Negro;* and Taylor, *Negro Slavery.*

For the British Caribbean, Sio notes that "most recent research indicates that the free coloured owned relatively few slaves, were no more than 20 per cent of the owners in 1832, and owned a much smaller proportion of the slave population than did the whites" ("Marginality and Free Coloured Identity," p. 156).

67. Hall, "Saint Domingue," p. 177.

68. Elisabeth, "The French Antilles," p. 166.

69. Russell, "Colored Freemen."

70. Genovese, "The Slave States in North America," p. 267; Menn, *Large Slaveholders of Louisiana,* pp. 92–94.

71. For the British Caribbean Sio finds that "more free coloured females than males owned slaves. They were most likely to have owned slaves in units of rarely more than 10, many of whom would have been domestics" ("Marginality and Free Coloured Identity," p. 156). The sample years referred to here were the first three years in each decade of Spanish rule: 1771–73, 1781–83, 1791–93, and 1801–3.

72. Acts of Pedesclaux, no. 17, fol. 295, 18 April 1793, and fol. 297, 19 April 1793;

Kimberly S. Hanger, *"Personas de varias clases y colores:* Free People of Color in Spanish New Orleans, 1769–1803" (Ph.D. dissertation, University of Florida, 1991), pp. 203–7.

73. Acts of Pedesclaux, no. 4, fols. 981 and 982, 21 August 1788, and fol. 986, 23 August 1788.

74. Acts of Almonester y Roxas, fol. 683, 22 December 1779, and fol. 684, 23 December 1779.

75. Acts of F. Broutin, no. 15, fol. 344, 14 November 1792.

76. Acts of Garic, no. 9, fol. 91, 27 February 1778; Acts of Pedesclaux, no. 13, fol. 764, 18 December 1791. Olivares was buried on 20 December 1791 (White Funerals, book 2).

77. Acts of Garic, no. 8, fol. 67, 21 February 1777; Acts of N. Broutin, no. 25, fol. 108, 4 May 1793.

78. Acts of Ximénez, no. 19, fol. 76, 2 April 1803, and fol. 152, 11 August 1803.

79. Acts of Mazange, no. 5, fol. 283, 18 March 1782.

80. "Lists of Slave Ownership," AGI PC 205 [1790s]. From the first years of the Spanish regime administrators established a tax on all slaves (commonly four reales per slave), with the proceeds from which the government repaid slave owners for any losses incurred when officials killed runaways or slave rebels or when slaves were lawfully executed for crimes committed. Periodic censuses recorded the number of slaves each subject possessed. In the 1790s local authorities also taxed land frontage, chimneys, market stalls, and taverns, inns, and dance halls to fund upkeep of the city's police force, hospital, theater, and street lighting system. For examples see PDLC, book 4083, doc. 33, 6 August 1773; RDC, book 1, 27 October 1775, 17 November 1775, and 9 April 1779; RDC, book 3, vol. 3, 27 June 1794; RDC, book 4, vol. 1, 22 May 1795, and vol. 3, 21 February 1800.

81. Acts of Ximénez, no. 17, fol. 55, 22 April 1801.

82. Acts of N. Broutin, no. 5, fol. 11, 18 January 1803.

83. Acts of Pedesclaux, no. 14, fol. 188, 22 March 1792.

84. Testaments taken from the Notarial Records.

85. Acts of Pedesclaux, no. 41, fol. 578, 20 August 1802; Nonwhite Marriages, book 1, no. 75b, 20 August 1802.

86. Acts of N. Broutin, no. 5, fol. 622, 7 November 1803.

87. Acts of N. Broutin, no. 3, fol. 78, 5 March 1801. Rita was the child baptized with much pomp and circumstance in the St. Louis Cathedral, an event discussed in chapter 5; Nonwhite Baptisms, books 4a, 5a, 6a, 1789–99; Nonwhite Funerals, book 2, 1790–96.

88. Karasch, *Slave Life in Rio,* p. 211.

89. Acts of Almonester y Roxas, fol. 169, 26 February 1777.

90. For further information concerning economic patterns, particularly in commerce and agriculture, during the Spanish era of Louisiana's history see Clark, *New Orleans;* Robin F. A. Fabel, *The Economy of British West Florida, 1763–1783* (Tuscaloosa: University of Alabama Press, 1988); Holmes, "Indigo in Colonial Louisiana

and the Floridas"; Lachance, "Politics of Fear"; McDermott, *The Spanish in the Mississippi Valley;* McGowan, "Creation of a Slave Society"; J. Carlyle Sitterson, *Sugar Country: The Cane Sugar Industry in the South, 1753–1950* (Lexington: University of Kentucky Press, 1953); Usner, *Indians, Settlers, and Slaves.* One early-nineteenth-century traveler noted that "the price of negroes at New Orleans is dearer than it has been in any colony. This is because the fear born of the insurrection of San Domingo has rendered the importation of that *merchandise* extremely difficult, and there is so much land to cultivate that no one has enough negroes. Also they are hired out for a dearer figure here than at Martinique even. . . . A new negro, that is to say one coming from Africa, is sold for four or five hundred piastres [the piastre was equivalent to the peso]; and a creole negro with talents is sold for as much as a thousand or fourteen hundred piastres" (Robin, *Voyages,* 2:112–13). The impact of the French Revolution on Louisiana is examined in greater detail in chapter 5.

91. Schweninger has observed similar endeavors among free blacks for a later time period in Louisiana and the rest of the antebellum southern United States (*Black Property Owners in the South* and "Prosperous Blacks in the South").

92. One must exercise caution when calling any oppressed group "elite," but seen from the perspective of libres, who were starting to form a group identity, this was an elite, or at least privileged, sector.

93. For examples, see Karasch, *Slave Life in Rio,* pp. 362, 364.

94. "Elena Negra libre sobre darle la Libertad a su hijo Esclabo de Dn. Henrique Despres por el precio de su estimación," SJR, 12 August 1780.

95. Free and slave persons of African descent could inherit property from whites. According to the Code noir, which governed slaves and libres in Louisiana under French rule, free blacks could not inherit property. Louisiana judges rarely enforced this provision of the code, and when Spain established its rule in Louisiana, Spanish codes replaced French ones (Baade, "Law of Slavery"). In 1774 the free morena Angélica Perret tested the extent of Spanish law regarding free black inheritance rights. She petitioned to obtain the goods and property that Juan Perret had left her in his will. One of Perret's white grandchildren requested that the court deny Angélica's petition on the basis of Article 52 of a royal French edict pertaining to persons of African descent, which stated that free or not, they could not receive property from whites. The judge ruled in favor of Angélica ("Angélica v. Heirs of Juan Perret," SJR, 25 May 1774).

96. "Criminales seguidos de oficio contra el Pardo libre Pedro Bailly," SJR, 7 October 1791. Bailly was tried and convicted on similar charges in 1794 (see chapter 5).

97. Acts of Almonester y Roxas, fol. 389, 1 September 1775.

98. Court Proceedings of N. Broutin, no. 53, fol. 225–98, 11 June 1802. As an aside, it is interesting to note that the will listed each of the oxen by name.

99. Acts of F. Broutin, no. 30, fol. 328, 23 December 1794.

100. Acts of Rodríguez, no. 3, fol. 573, 6 August 1784, and Acts of F. Broutin, no. 15, fol. 39, 27 February 1792. Toutant Beauregard died in March 1792, a month after writing his will.

101. Cohen and Greene, introduction to *Neither Slave nor Free,* pp. 12–13; Karasch, *Slave Life in Rio,* p. 363.

102. Acts of F. Broutin, no. 15, fols. 370–71, 14 December 1792.

103. Henry Plauche Dart, "Courts and Law in Colonial Louisiana," *LHQ* 4:3 (July 1921): 255–89, and "The Place of the Civil Law in Louisiana," *Tulane Law Review* 4:1 (February 1930): 163–77; Judith K. Schafer, "'Open and Notorious Concubinage': The Emancipation of Slave Mistresses by Will and the Supreme Court in Antebellum Louisiana," *Louisiana History* 28:2 (spring 1987): 165–82.

104. Acts of Almonester y Roxas, fols. 4, 5, 8 January 1775, and fols. 17, 19, 10 January 1777. Francisca apparently only thought she had manumitted Carlos. According to a notarial instrument recorded in 1799, she stated that she had purchased Carlos with the intent to free him but had never officially done so even though he was regarded as a libre. This document formalized the manumission (Acts of Ximénez, no. 16, fol. 29, 27 February 1799).

105. Court Proceedings of N. Broutin, no. 59, fols. 1028–76, 28 June 1803; Court Proceedings of Ximénez, fols. 246–63, 28 May 1804.

106. Acts of N. Broutin, no. 2, fol. 13, 29 January 1800; Acts of Almonester y Roxas, fol. 25, 25 April 1778; Nonwhite Baptisms, book 2, 17 July 1782, book 3, 31 May 1784, and book 4, 15 April 1791; AGI PC 211-A, fol. 160, 1796.

107. Acts of Pedesclaux, no. 12, fol. 47, 21 January 1791. Riche's household goods included (besides the silver harness): a walnut armoire, a bedstead with two feather mattresses and two Spanish moss mattresses, two feather pillows, four pairs of sheets, one linen mosquito net, two woolen blankets, one cotton blanket, four chairs, eight pots, one frying pan, and her personal clothing.

108. Acts of Garic, no. 2, fol. 181, 1 June 1771; Acts of N. Broutin, no. 3, fol. 367, 24 November 1801.

109. Acts of Pedesclaux, no. 21, fol. 728, 1 August 1794; "Autos hechos por fallecimiento de Martona Belair," SJR, 15 August 1795.

110. Marriage contracts, like wills, indicate that on average free blacks were not as prosperous as whites and that females possessed fewer assets than males. For the Spanish period there was a total of ten marriage contracts between free blacks recorded in the notarial registers. Of these, one listed property for both parties but no assessed value for this property. Three other contracts did not include property the male party brought to the marriage. The average value of goods for libre women was 787 pesos ($N = 9$), while the average for libre males was almost twice that amount ($1,487$ pesos; $N = 6$).

A sample of twenty marriage contracts negotiated between white partners (six of which did not include property assessments for the groom) shows an average of 3,270 pesos brought by women—more than four times the average contribution of free black brides—and 4,113 pesos brought by men—almost three times the marriage portion of free black grooms.

111. Nonwhite Marriages, book 1, no. 11, 10 January 1779; Acts of Almonester y Roxas, fol. 57, 23 January 1779. For a discussion of dowry rights under Spanish law

see Edith Couturier, "Women and the Family in Eighteenth-Century Mexico: Law and Practice," *Journal of Family History* 10:3 (fall 1985): 294–304, and Ann Twinam, "Honor, Sexuality, and Illegitimacy in Colonial Spanish America," in *Sexuality and Marriage in Colonial Latin America,* ed. Asunción Lavrin (Lincoln: University of Nebraska Press, 1989), pp. 118–55.

112. Acts of F. Broutin, no. 25, fol. 144, 22 May 1793. The couple had wed four days earlier (Nonwhite Marriages, book 1, no. 65, 18 May 1793).

113. Acts of Almonester y Roxas, no. 1, fol. 224, 15 June 1781. Marriages absent from the sacramental records were not all that rare. For example, the union of Pedro Bailly with Naneta Cadis does not appear in the records, even though their marriage contract was registered in a notarial act and the baptismal records of their children state that they were legitimate offspring. Other documents also indicate that Bailly and Cadis were officially married.

114. "Liberation of Luison, *Mulatresse*," SJR, 9 May 1770; Nonwhite Marriages, book 1, no. 25, 1 April 1785; Acts of Rodríguez, no. 4, fol. 297, 2 April 1785; Acts of N. Broutin, no. 2, fol. 165, 23 June 1800; Nonwhite Baptisms, book 7, fol. 65, 6 March 1802.

115. Nonwhite Marriages, book 1, no. 27, 27 September 1785; Acts of Ximénez, no. 6, fol. 27, 27 January 1794. In 1799 Brouner's youngest daughter Clarisa (Clara) López de la Peña instituted proceedings before an ecclesiastical tribunal to prove that she was of Indian descent and to have her daughter Luisa's baptismal record transferred from El Libro de los negros y mulatos to El Libro de los blancos. Luisa's natural father was Don Luis Declouet, a lieutenant in the Fixed Infantry Regiment of Louisiana. The court granted Clarisa's request (Proceedings by Clara López de la Peña, Records of the Diocese of Louisiana and the Floridas, roll 8, 14 September 1799).

116. Acts of Pedesclaux, no. 41, fol. 1500, 14 July 1802.

117. "Relación de la pérdida que cada Individuo ha padecido en el Incendio de esta Ciudad . . . ," AGI SD 2576, fol. 532, 30 September 1788. The document gives phenotype and status for libres but not for whites, yet other documents indicate that some individuals who were not identified as free blacks were such. For example, in a separate petition for damage remuneration, María Methode is identified as a parda libre, whereas in the "Relación" she is not. Thus the "Relación" may include more free blacks and fewer whites than those who appear.

Chapter 3: "Family Values" and Kinship Strategies

1. For example, see Ramón A. Gutiérrez, *When Jesus Came, the Corn Mothers Went Away: Marriage, Sexuality, and Power in New Mexico, 1500–1846* (Stanford: Stanford University Press, 1991); Patricia Seed, *To Love, Honor, and Obey in Colonial Mexico: Conflicts over Marriage Choice, 1574–1821* (Stanford: Stanford University Press, 1988); and several of the essays in Lavrin, *Sexuality and Marriage.* One of these essays indicates that only one-third of the adult population in Caracas, Venezuela, was married

in 1792 (Kathy Waldron, "The Sinners and the Bishop in Colonial Venezuela: The *Visita* of Bishop Mariano Martí, 1771–1784," p. 163).

2. Marriage of José Fich and Moneta Arlu, Records of the Diocese of Louisiana and the Floridas, roll 5, 1 June 1796.

3. RDC, vol. 4, no. 3, 11 July 1800.

4. Gutiérrez, *When Jesus Came, the Corn Mothers Went Away,* pp. 315–18; Verena Martínez-Alier, *Marriage, Class, and Colour in Nineteenth-Century Cuba: A Study of Racial Attitudes and Sexual Values in a Slave Society,* 2nd ed. (Ann Arbor: University of Michigan Press, 1989), pp. xiv–xv; Mörner, *Race Mixture,* pp. 38–39; Seed, *To Love, Honor, and Obey,* pp. 205–56.

5. Again turning to Caracas, Venezuela, Waldron notes that "the eighteenth-century traveler François Depons stated that union between free pardos and whites was frowned upon, even though it had not been 'prohibited' until recently. He probably understood the Pragmática [of 1778] as a prohibition of such marriages, although it was not" (Waldron, "The Sinners and the Bishop," p. 164).

6. Hall, "Saint Domingue," p. 187.

7. Seed, *To Love, Honor, and Obey,* pp. 148–52.

8. Court Proceedings of Quiñones, no. 1, fols. 30–44, 12 April 1779.

9. Nonwhite Baptisms, book 5a, 1 October 1792–29 April 1798; Nonwhite Marriages, book 1, no. 66a, 10 March 1801; Acts of Pedesclaux, no. 39, fol. 444, 20 July 1801.

10. Nonwhite Marriages, book 1, no. 13, 1 May 1779.

11. Clara's parents were Luison Marigny de Mandeville, also known as Brouner, and Don José López de la Peña, a native of Galicia in Spain and an officer in the Spanish military. Luison is alternately listed as a mulata libre, a cuarterona libre, and a mestiza libre in documents, and her mother, María Juana, as a negra and an india slave. After bearing four daughters and one son by Don José, Luison married Francisco Durand, a free pardo widower with four children. Their marriage lasted nine years, with both partners dying in 1794, and produced no children (Nonwhite Marriages, book 1, no. 27, 27 September 1785; Acts of Ximénez, no. 6, fol. 27, 27 January 1794). Like Prudhome, Mandeville first had a relationship with a white man and then married a free black.

12. Proceedings initiated by Clara López de la Peña, Records of the Diocese of Louisiana and the Floridas, roll 8, 14 September 1799; White Baptisms, book 3 (3 April 1796–7 March 1802), St. Louis Parish; White Marriages, book 2 (2 May 1784–9 June 1806), St. Louis Parish, 1 October 1797.

13. Nonwhite Marriages, book 1, 20 January 1777–29 July 1830.

14. Sister Antonia de Sta. Monica Ramos to Hassett, Records of the Diocese of Louisiana and the Floridas, roll 11, 21 and 24 March 1803.

15. Court Proceedings of Quiñones, no. 5, fols. 357–61, 22 September 1789, and fols. 362–88, 29 September 1789; Nonwhite Marriages, book 1, no. 47, 31 October 1789.

16. "Bartlomé Bta. Grifo libre; contra Juan [*sic*] Lafrance sobre impedir este el

matrimonio de su hija con el dicho Bartolomé," SJR, 6 September 1788; Nonwhite Marriages, book 1, no. 41, 12 September 1788.

17. Acts of Mazange, no. 4, fol. 891, 5 November 1781.

18. Nonwhite Marriages, book 1, no. 11, 10 January 1779; Acts of Almonester y Roxas, fol. 57, 23 January 1779.

19. Nonwhite Marriages, book 1, 1777–1803; Nonwhite Baptisms, books 3a, 4a, 5a, 6a, 7a, 8a, 9a, 10a, and 11a, 1786–1809.

20. Brasseaux, Fontenot, and Oubre, *Creoles of Color in the Bayou Country,* pp. 8–13; Lachance, "The Formation of a Three-Caste Society: Evidence from Wills in Antebellum New Orleans," *Social Science History* 18:2 (summer 1994): 211–42.

21. Nonwhite Marriages, book 1, 1777–1803; Nonwhite Baptisms, books 3a, 4a, 5a, 6a, and 7a, 1784–1803; "List of Duties on Tavernkeepers," SJR, 31 Dec. 1800; Acts of N. Broutin, no. 5, fol. 245, 18 May 1803.

22. For a discussion of the images whites held of black women, see Barbara Bush, *Slave Women in Caribbean Society, 1650–1838* (Bloomington: Indiana University Press, 1990), pp. 11–22.

23. Robin, *Voyages,* 2:112.

24. Alliot, "Historical and Political Reflections," 1:146–47.

25. "Magdalena Canella, Mulata libre contra don Luis Beaurepos para la posseción de su esclava Adelaida," SJR, 20 January 1777.

26. "Criminales Seguidos por Carlos Budé, contra la Negra Libre Nombrada Rosa, sobre palabras Infuriosas," SJR, 16 February 1786.

27. Acts of N. Broutin, no. 5, fol. 291, 18 June 1803.

28. Acts of F. Broutin, no. 46, fol. 118, 17 June 1797; Nonwhite Baptisms, book 6a, 1800.

29. "Testamentaria de don Francisco Hisnard que falleció en el Puesto de Opellousas," SJR, 27 August 1798.

30. Acts of Pedesclaux, no. 31, fol. 289, 25 April 1798; William S. Coker and Thomas D. Watson, *Indian Traders of the Southeastern Spanish Borderlands: Panton, Leslie and Company and John Forbes and Company, 1783–1847* (Pensacola: University of West Florida Press, 1986), pp. 330–49; Holmes, "Do It! Don't Do It! Spanish Laws on Sex and Marriage," in Haas, *Louisiana's Legal Heritage,* p. 23. The third daughter, Irene Thomasa de Villanueva, was born on 18 September 1798, after her father's will was written; she is rarely mentioned in documents and secondary works on the family and possibly died young as had her brother.

31. Nonwhite Marriages, book 1, no. 60a, 21 January 1801.

32. Acts of N. Broutin, no. 4, fol. 447, 26 October 1802, and fol. 512, 14 December 1802.

33. Acts of N. Broutin, no. 2, fol. 94, 3 April 1800.

34. Acts of Rodríguez, no. 7(2), fol. 1016, 5 December 1783.

35. Acts of F. Broutin, no. 7, fol. 203, 19 April 1791; Acts of N. Broutin, no. 1, fol. 163, 28 June 1799; Acts of N. Broutin, no. 3, fol. 212, 7 July 1801, and no. 5, fol. 260, 28 May 1803.

36. Acts of N. Broutin, no. 4, fol. 112, 18 February 1802.

37. "Rosa, Parda libre contra don Josef Bonneville," SJR, 27 July 1791.

38. Court Proceedings of N. Broutin, no. 58, fols. 791–99, 11 June 1803.

39. Court Proceedings of N. Broutin, no. 59, fols. 955–84, 20 June 1803.

40. "Criminales seguidos contra María Luisa, Negra Libre," SJR, 18 October 1793.

41. In April 1795 Ysabel Robín, a parda libre, gave power of attorney to Don Pedro Bertonère to represent her against her son-in-law, Bernardo Mayeaux, a pardo libre, who had petitioned the tribunal to have Robín declared mentally deranged (*enajenación mental*) (Acts of Ximénez, no. 9, fol. 229, 27 April 1795).

42. Acts of N. Broutin, no. 2, fol. 78, 24 March 1800; Court Proceedings of N. Broutin, no. 48, fols. 319–37, 6 August 1801. Carlos Meunier had gained his freedom thanks to the generous act of his mother, the free morena María Juana Meunier, who purchased and freed her son graciosa in 1788, when he was thirty-one (Acts of Pedesclaux, no. 3, fol. 785, 16 June 1788). One indication that Carlos had a better relationship with his mother than with his father was that he took her surname.

43. Acts of Rodríguez, no. 13, fol. 1143, 6 December 1787.

44. Acts of Pedesclaux, no. 13, fol. 436, 30 June 1791. Don Francisco had also donated property and money to Jacinta Demasilière in his will.

45. Acts of Mazange, no. 5, fol. 12, 7 January 1782; Acts of Mazange, no. 7, fol. 282, 29 March 1783, and fol. 290, 1 April 1783; Acts of Ximénez, no. 7, fol. 325, 18 August 1794; Acts of N. Broutin, no. 3, fol. 131, 22 April 1801.

46. Acts of Mazange, no. 5, fol. 12, 7 January 1782; Acts of Mazange, no. 7, fol. 282, 29 March 1783, and fol. 290, 1 April 1783; Acts of Ximénez, no. 7, fol. 325, 18 August 1794; Acts of N. Broutin, no. 3, fol. 131, 22 April 1801; "Diligencias promovidas por don Joseph Dusuau de la Croix . . . ," SJR, 21 July 1801. Gould elaborates further on the life of Jaquelina Lemelle in "Urban Slavery—Urban Freedom: The Manumission of Jaqueline Lemelle," in *More Than Chattel: Black Women and Slavery in the Americas,* ed. David Barry Gaspar and Darlene Clark Hine (Bloomington: Indiana University Press, 1996), pp. 298–314.

47. Stephen Gudeman and Stuart B. Schwartz, "Cleansing Original Sin: Godparenthood and the Baptism of Slaves in Eighteenth-Century Bahia," in *Kinship Ideology and Practice in Latin America,* ed. Raymond Smith (Chapel Hill: University of North Carolina Press, 1984), p. 55. Other studies that discuss the role of fictive kinship in the Americas include Jane Landers, "Gracia Real de Santa Teresa de Mose: A Free Black Town in Spanish Colonial Florida," *American Historical Review* 95:1 (February 1990): 11, 23–25; Sidney W. Mintz and Eric Wolf, "An Analysis of Ritual Co-Parenthood (Compadrazgo)," *Southwestern Journal of Anthropology* 6 (winter 1950): 341–67; Hugo G. Nutini and Betty Bell, *Ritual Kinship: The Structure and Historical Development of the Compadrazgo System in Rural Tlaxcala* (Princeton: Princeton University Press, 1980).

48. Acts of Perdomo, no. 16, fol. 575, 7 December 1790; Acts of Ximénez, no. 15, fol. 526, 21 July 1798; Acts of Pedesclaux, no. 37, fol. 491, 7 August 1800.

49. Acts of Garic, no. 4, fol. 264, 16 September 1773, and fol. 358, 23 December 1773; Acts of Perdomo, no. 7, fol. 189, 21 April 1786.

50. Acts of N. Broutin, no. 2, fol. 197, 6 August 1800.

51. For further information on Bailly see chapter 5 and Hanger, *"Personas de varias clases y colores,"* pp. 288–329.

52. Nonwhite Baptisms, books 2a, 3a, 4a, 5a, 1777–98.

53. Clarence Edwin Carter, ed., *The Territorial Papers of the United States,* 28 vols., vol. 9, *The Territory of Orleans, 1803–1812* (Washington, D.C.: United States Government Printing Office, 1940), pp. 174–75.

Chapter 4: A Privilege and Honor to Serve

1. McConnell, *Negro Troops,* pp. 24–25. The author states that Governor Carondelet expressed a preference for militia forces "because of their dexterity in traversing the swamps and their skill in the use of muskets." In a 1792 report Carondelet stated that "the colored people served during the last year with much valor" and that during peacetime "they are the ones used in pursuing runaway Negroes (slaves) and destroying their hideouts," which were built "in places too impenetrable for regular troops."

2. Studies of the free black militia in Spanish America include Christon I. Archer, *The Army of Bourbon Mexico, 1760–1810* (Albuquerque: University of New Mexico Press, 1977); Leon Campbell, "The Changing Racial and Administrative Structure of the Peruvian Military under the Late Bourbons," *The Americas* 32 (July 1975): 117–33; Herbert S. Klein, "The Colored Militia of Cuba: 1568–1868," *Caribbean Studies* 6 (July 1966): 17–27; Allan J. Kuethe, *Military Reform and Society in New Granada, 1773–1808* (Gainesville: University Presses of Florida, 1978) and "The Status of the Free Pardo in the Disciplined Militia of New Granada," *Journal of Negro History* 56:2 (April 1971): 105–17; Lyle N. McAlister, *The "Fuero Militar" in New Spain, 1764–1800* (Gainesville: University Presses of Florida, 1957) and "The Reorganization of the Army of New Spain, 1763–1767," *HAHR* 33:1 (February 1953): 1–32; and Joseph P. Sánchez, "African Freedmen and the *Fuero Militar:* A Historical Overview of *Pardo* and *Moreno* Militiamen in the Late Spanish Empire," *Colonial Latin American Historical Review* 3:2 (spring 1994): 165–84.

3. Campbell, "Changing Racial and Administrative Structure," pp. 118–19.

4. McConnell, *Negro Troops,* pp. 24–25. For Saint-Domingue Geggus remarks that "the white colonists were to regret this military education [acquired in the United States War of Independence] given to such naturally gifted soldiers" (*Slavery, War, and Revolution,* p. 22).

5. Sánchez, "African Freedmen," p. 165.

6. Kuethe, "Status of the Free Pardo," p. 117.

7. Sánchez, "African Freedmen," pp. 166–67.

8. For further discussion of the fuero militar see Campbell, "Changing Racial and Administrative Structure," pp. 118–19; Jack D. L. Holmes, *Honor and Fidelity: The*

Louisiana Infantry Regiment and the Louisiana Militia Companies, 1766–1821 (Birmingham: Author, 1965), p. 76; Klein, *African Slavery,* p. 232; Kuethe, *Military Reform and Society,* p. 30; McAlister, "Reorganization of the Army," pp. 25–27; Sánchez, "African Freedmen," pp. 165–82.

9. Sánchez, "African Freedmen," p. 165.

10. Quotation from Sánchez, "African Freedmen," p. 169; Kuethe, "Status of the Free Pardo," p. 109.

11. Klein, "The Colored Militia of Cuba," pp. 17–18, and "Status of the Free Pardo," pp. 105–17. For a practical application see regulations in the appendix.

12. Campbell, "Changing Racial and Administrative Structure," pp. 127–31; Kuethe, *Military Reform and Society,* p. 28; McAlister, "Reorganization of the Army," pp. 6, 14, 20–27.

13. Holmes, *Honor and Fidelity,* p. 55.

14. AGI PC 182-A, 16 January 1783; AGI SD 2568, 21 August 1797; 1801 Militia Rosters; AGI PC 203, 7 July 1788; Sánchez, "African Freedmen," pp. 170–82.

15. Campbell finds, though, that in Peru pardos were considered more loyal than mestizos. For information on social prejudice see Klein, "The Colored Militia of Cuba," p. 25; Kuethe, "Status of the Free Pardo," pp. 112–15; and Sánchez, "African Freedmen," p. 165.

16. Klein, *African Slavery,* p. 232, and "The Colored Militia of Cuba," pp. 22, 24–27; Kuethe, "Status of the Free Pardo," pp. 110–13; McAlister, "Reorganization of the Army," p. 27; Roland C. McConnell, "Louisiana's Black Military History, 1729–1865," in Macdonald, Kemp, and Haas, *Louisiana's Black Heritage,* pp. 39–41.

17. AGI PC 193-A, September 1779; AGS GM 6912, 16 October 1779; 1801 Militia Rosters.

18. 1778 Census; Matthew Flannery, comp., *New Orleans in 1805: A Directory and a Census Together with Resolutions Authorizing Same Now Printed for the First Time* (New Orleans: Pelican Gallery, 1936).

19. Sterkx, *Free Negro,* p. 33.

20. AGI PC 188-A, 22 February 1770.

21. 1778 Census; AGI PC 1425, 1788; AGI PC 2362, 1791; Acosta Rodríguez, *La Población de Luisiana española,* pp. 51, 121, 354, 387.

22. AGI PC 193-A, September 1779.

23. AGS GM 6912, 16 October 1779.

24. AGI PC 2351, 11 January 1780; AGS GM 6912, 14 March 1780; Holmes, *Honor and Fidelity,* p. 33.

25. AGI PC 159-A, 3 July 1791.

26. AGS GM 6912, 12 January 1780; AGI PC 182-A, 16 January 1783; AGI PC 159-A, 3 July 1791; 1801 Militia Rosters.

27. We cannot know for sure if pardos were increasing more rapidly than morenos, because although the 1791 census broke libres down by phenotype, the 1805 one did not. Emancipation data show, however, that more pardo males were manumitted

between 1791 and 1801 than moreno males (150 and 114 respectively); there were also about four and a half times more pardo than moreno males baptized between 1790 and 1797 (288 as compared to 63 respectively). Sources for these observations are the Notarial Records and Nonwhite Baptisms, books 4a and 5a, 1790–1797.

28. Din, *Canary Islanders*, p. 16.

29. McConnell, "Louisiana's Black Military History," p. 32.

30. For more information about the militia during the French period see McConnell, "Louisiana's Black Military History," pp. 32–35, and *Negro Troops*, pp. 3–14.

31. Holmes, *Honor and Fidelity*, p. 10.

32. AGI SD 2656, April 1769.

33. Oath of Allegiance Given by Company of Free Pardos and Morenos, SJR, 20 September 1769.

34. Brasseaux, *Denis-Nicolas Foucault*, pp. 75–90; McConnell, *Negro Troops*, pp. 8–11, 16.

35. Holmes, *A Guide*, p. 6.

36. Holmes, *Honor and Fidelity*, pp. 47, 67; McConnell, *Negro Troops*, p. 24.

37. AGI PC 188-A, 22 February 1770.

38. Acts of Almonester y Roxas, fol. 287, 2 November 1772.

39. RDC, vol. 1, 15 October 1773.

40. Several scholars have researched and written on free black armed participation in these campaigns. See, for example, Holmes, *Honor and Fidelity*, pp. 29–36, 54–55; McConnell, *Negro Troops*, pp. 17–22.

41. Sánchez, "African Freedmen," pp. 182–84.

42. Kolchin, *American Slavery*, pp. 63–76, quotation p. 72. For additional information on slaves and free blacks during the Revolutionary era, see Ira Berlin and Ronald Hoffman, eds., *Slavery and Freedom in the Age of the American Revolution* (Charlottesville: University of Virginia Press, 1983); Silvia R. Frey, *Water from the Rock: Black Resistance in a Revolutionary Age* (Princeton: Princeton University Press, 1991); Gerald W. Mullin, *Flight and Rebellion: Slave Resistance in Eighteenth-Century Virginia* (New York: Oxford University Press, 1972); and Benjamin Quarles, *The Negro in the American Revolution* (New York: W. W. Norton, 1973).

43. Slighting of Spain's role in the American Revolution has been allayed most recently by the work of Cummins, *Spanish Observers and the American Revolution* (1991).

44. AGI PC 603-A, 28 August and 28 September 1779; AGS GM 6912, 16 October 1779; Holmes, *Honor and Fidelity*, pp. 30–31; McConnell, *Negro Troops*, pp. 17–19; W. James Miller, "The Militia System of Spanish Louisiana, 1769–1783," in *The Military Presence on the Gulf Coast*, ed. William S. Coker (Pensacola: Perdido Bay Press, 1975), pp. 46–50. Miller only fleetingly mentions that eighty free pardos and morenos accompanied Gálvez with no other references to free black troops.

45. In *Negro Troops* McConnell states that Calpha was a white man (p. 18). Primary documents convincingly indicate, however, that Calpha was a free black man. For example, when he emancipated his black slave Gabriela and her son, Calpha was

listed as a pardo libre and "comandante de las milicias pardas de esta provincia" (Acts of Almonester y Roxas, fol. 287, 2 November 1772). In addition, Calpha's predecessor, Pedro Simón, was also a free pardo.

46. AGI PC 193-A, September 1779; AGS GM 6912, 21 October 1779, 12 January 1780, and 13 February 1780; AGI PC 182-B, 12 January, 20 July, and 22 July 1780.

47. AGI PC 2351, 2 January, 11 January, and 20 March 1780; AGS GM 6912, 14 March 1780; Holmes, *Honor and Fidelity,* pp. 31–33; McConnell, *Negro Troops,* pp. 19–20.

48. Sánchez, "African Freedmen," pp. 182–84. Sánchez states that "two companies [of Cuban free blacks] served in the successful Spanish attacks against British forces at Pensacola and Mobile, and later were assigned to the Fixed Regiment of Louisiana at New Orleans, where they patrolled the streets of the present-day French Quarter and Jackson Square" (p. 184). I have not found any evidence of this presence of Havana libre troops in New Orleans, however, and Sánchez does not cite his source(s) for this information.

49. AGS GM 6913, 26 May and 18 August 1781; AGI PC 182-A, 9 August 1781; AGI SD 2548, 18 January 1782; Holmes, *Honor and Fidelity,* pp. 33–36; McConnell, *Negro Troops,* pp. 20–22.

50. AGI SD 2657, March 1787; Holmes, *Honor and Fidelity,* pp. 23–36.

51. AGI PC 159-A, August 1784; AGI SD 2553, 12 June 1789. Mentzinger lived with a free morena named María and had three natural sons with her, to whom he donated property in 1800. By that time he was a lieutenant in the Spanish regiment (Acts of Pedesclaux, no. 37, fol. 381, 14 June 1800).

52. Kuntz Collection, Spanish Colonial Period, 15 February 1782, HTML; RDC, vol. 2, 15 February and 20 September 1782.

53. Din, *Francisco Bouligny,* pp. 132–39, and "*Cimarrones* and the San Malo Band"; Hall, *Africans in Colonial Louisiana,* pp. 212–34. The two authors offer differing interpretations of San Maló's and Bouligny's actions.

54. RDC, vol. 2, 28 May and 4 June 1784; Charles C. Thompson Collection, box 2, folder 9, 1784, LLMVC; Din, *Francisco Bouligny,* pp. 138–39, and "*Cimarrones* and the San Malo Band"; McConnell, *Negro Troops,* pp. 22–23.

55. AGI PC 201, 24 March 1788; AGI SD 2576, 30 September 1788.

56. RDC, vol. 3, no. 2, May 1790.

57. McConnell, *Negro Troops,* p. 23.

58. AGI PC 188-A, 22 February 1770; AGI SD 2553, 28 May 1789; AGI PC 184-A, 24 November 1789; AGI PC 196, 10 September 1789; AGI PC 202, 19 March 1791.

59. AGI PC 159-B, 7 November 1793.

60. The subject of the French and Saint-Domingue Revolutions and their impact on free blacks in Louisiana is discussed in greater detail in chapter 5 and in Kimberly S. Hanger, "Conflicting Loyalties: The French Revolution and Free People of Color in Spanish New Orleans," *Louisiana History* 34:1 (winter 1993): 5–33.

61. Ernest R. Liljegren, "Jacobinism in Spanish Louisiana, 1792–1797," *LHQ* 22:1 (January 1939): 47–97. Liljegren's account is very pro-French; he uses evidence from

Carondelet's correspondence to support his contentions, while at the same time he admits that Carondelet was prone to exaggeration.

62. Kolchin, *American Slavery,* pp. 89–90, 156.

63. Klein, *African Slavery,* pp. 217–42; Liljegren, "Jacobinism in Spanish Louisiana," p. 58.

64. Liljegren, "Jacobinism in Spanish Louisiana," pp. 59, 60.

65. AGI PC 159-B, 7 November 1793; AGI PC 191, 6 November 1793; Holmes, *Honor and Fidelity,* pp. 45–51, 53–58, 60; McConnell, *Negro Troops,* pp. 24–47.

66. AGI PC 23, 13 February 1796.

67. 1801 Militia Rosters.

68. AGI SD 2617, 22 June 1800; Letter from the Free Black Militia to the Cabildo, PDLC, book 4088, doc. 367, 24 October 1800; Holmes, *Honor and Fidelity,* p. 72; McConnell, "Louisiana's Black Military History," p. 37.

69. 1801 Militia Rosters.

70. See Acts of Almonester y Roxas, fol. 287, 2 November 1772; Acts of F. Broutin, no. 30, fol. 143, 14 June 1794; Court Proceedings of N. Broutin, no. 53, fols. 225–98; Acts of Mazange, no. 6, fol. 644, 6 July 1782; Acts of Ximénez, no. 2, fol. 137, 26 March 1792, and no. 9, fol. 1, 1 January 1795.

71. City Treasury Accounts for 1787, RDC, vol. 3, no. 2; 1795 Census.

72. Bowser, "Colonial Spanish America," pp. 46, 52, 58.

73. 1795 Census; 1801 Militia Rosters.

74. 1795 Census; 1801 Militia Rosters; Court Proceedings of N. Broutin, no. 61, fols. 380–85, 20 December 1804.

75. 1795 Census; 1801 Militia Rosters.

76. AGI PC 188-A, 1779; 1795 Census.

77. The 1795 Census and the Census of Faubourg Ste. Marie, 1798, AGI PC 215-A, indicated the occupation and number of slaves owned by these men. Their ranks in the militia were as follows: Populus was captain of the third company of pardos (1801 Militia Rosters); Navarro was second lieutenant of the *milicias de color,* promoted from sergeant (AGI PC 182-B, 1 September 1783); Bailly was a pardo lieutenant (AGI PC 159-B, 6 November 1792); Gerónimo was second lieutenant of the second company of pardos; and Malet was lieutenant of the first company of pardos (1801 Militia Rosters).

78. Court Proceedings of Quiñones, no. 1, fols. 87–103, 8 February 1779.

79. AGI PC 182-B, 31 July 1781; "Nicolás Bacus y Juan Bautista, negros libres v. Mme Guillome," SJR, 20 January 1785; AGI PC 159-B, 7 November 1793.

80. Kuntz Collection, Spanish Colonial Period, 15 February 1782, HTML; Charles C. Thompson Collection, box 2, folder 9, 1784, LLMVC.

81. Letter from the Free Black Militia to the Cabildo, PDLC, book 4088, doc. 367, 24 October 1800.

82. Court Proceedings of N. Broutin, no. 48, fols. 319–37, 6 August 1801.

83. 1801 Militia Rosters; Acts of N. Broutin, no. 5, fol. 219, 5 May 1803, and fol. 425, 31 August 1803.

84. Acts of F. Broutin, no. 7, fol. 202, 18 April 1791.

85. Acts of Rodríguez, no. 7(2), fol. 756, 16 August 1783, and fol. 767, 27 August 1783; AGI PC 204 [early 1790s]; Nonwhite Marriages, book 1, no. 38, 13 October 1787; Acts of Pedesclaux, no. 32, fol. 611, 17 August 1798.

86. Nonwhite Baptisms, book 4a, 19 October 1788 and book 5a, 11 January 1793; AGI PC 159-B, 1792.

87. Nonwhite Baptisms, book 4a, 17 March 1791, and book 5a, 16 March 1793.

88. Nonwhite Marriages, book 1, no. 2, 10 May 1777; 1778 Census.

89. Nonwhite Marriages, book 1, no. 83a, 3 September 1803, and no. 65a, 7 February 1801.

90. Acts of Pedesclaux, no. 41, fol. 578, 20 August 1802; Nonwhite Marriages, book 1, no. 75a, 20 August 1802.

91. AGI PC 159-B, 7 November 1793; AGI PC 206, 17 January 1797.

92. 1801 Militia Rosters.

93. Oath of Allegiance Given by Company of Free Pardos and Morenos, SJR, 20 September 1769; Nonwhite Marriages, book 1, no. 9, 17 November 1778, and no. 47, 31 October 1789.

94. 1795 Census; 1801 Militia Rosters; Court Proceedings of N. Broutin, no. 56, fols. 667–74, 29 November 1802.

95. Oath of Allegiance Given by Company of Free Pardos and Morenos, SJR, 20 September 1769; Nonwhite Baptisms, book 2a, 22 October 1778; Acts of F. Broutin, no. 25, fol. 144, 22 May 1793.

96. Acts of Almonester y Roxas, fol. 459, 27 August 1779.

97. Acts of Ximénez, no. 18, fol. 9, 22 January 1801; 1801 Militia Rosters.

98. "Autos hechos por fin y muerte de Juan Bta. Hugón," SJR, 8 August 1792.

99. Ibid.; Nonwhite Baptisms, books 2a, 3a, 4a, 5a, 6a, and 7a, 1777–1804; 1801 Militia Rosters.

100. Nonwhite Marriages, book 1, no. 49a, 7 March 1799; Nonwhite Burials, [book 3], 26 March 1799; Nonwhite Baptisms, books 3a, 4a, 5a, 1783–98; 1801 Militia Rosters.

101. Funerals of Whites and Nonwhites, [book 1], March 1772 and September 1796; Nonwhite Baptisms, books 2a, 3a, 4a, 5a, 6a, and 7a, 1777–1804; Acts of Pedesclaux, no. 12, fol. 275, 2 May 1791; 1801 Militia Rosters.

102. Letter from the Free Black Militia to the Cabildo, PDLC, book 4088, doc. 367, 24 October 1800; RDC, vol. 4, no. 4, 14 August and 18 September 1801. The free black militia also acted as a corporate political body when its members signed an oath of allegiance to the Spanish government in 1769 and a petition to the United States government in 1804 requesting continued existence and equal treatment as guaranteed to all Louisiana citizens under the transfer agreement ("Address from the Free People of Color," January 1804, in Carter, *Territorial Papers of the United States,* 9:174–75).

103. Acts of Ximénez, no. 14, fol. 227, 26 April 1799.

104. McAlister, *Spain and Portugal in the New World,* pp. 45, 79–82.

105. Holmes, *Honor and Fidelity,* pp. 57–59, 74; McConnell, "Louisiana's Black Military History," pp. 37–62, and *Negro Troops,* pp. 33–55.

106. Klein, *African Slavery,* p. 233.

Chapter 5: Cultural and Political Activities

1. Brasseaux, Fontenot, and Oubre (*Creoles of Color in the Bayou Country*) and Mills (*The Forgotten People*) see similar trends of increasing isolation and withdrawal after the Civil War among rural free black communities in north and south Louisiana.

2. As Hall, Usner, and other scholars have shown, all elements of the population interacted and contributed ingredients to Louisiana's unique cultural "gumbo" (Hall, *Africans in Colonial Louisiana,* and Usner, *Indians, Settlers, and Slaves,* pp. 191–218).

3. The 1778 and 1791 censuses of New Orleans recorded households by street rather than by quarter; like the 1795 and 1803 censuses, they, too, pointed to a lack of racial segregation.

4. The morena libre Prudencia Cheval, for example, leased the top floor of the house on Calle de los Almacenes that she inherited from Don Francisco Cheval to Señor Don Manuel de Justis y Calvo at the rate of six pesos per month for eighteen months and then eight pesos per month for an additional eighteen months (Acts of Ximénez, no. 6, fol. 162, 25 April 1794). Don Pedro Cázelar rented a house to his free parda consort, Carlota Wiltz, for eight pesos monthly. Wiltz also owned houses on the property next to this rented house (Acts of Perdomo, fol. 401, 27 October 1782; Acts of F. Broutin, no. 46, fol. 118, 17 June 1797).

Although not analyzed in detail here, the census of 1778 has been databased by Gwendolyn Midlo Hall and made available for use at The Historic New Orleans Collection in New Orleans. The census is very valuable, because it provides information for each household member rather than just its head; the original is located in the AGI (PC 191) but is badly deteriorated and still in the process of conservation.

5. Christian Schultz, *Travels on an Inland Voyage through the States of New York, Pennsylvania, Virginia, Ohio, Kentucky, and Tennessee, and through the Territories of Indiana, Louisiana, Mississippi, and New Orleans, Performed in the Years 1807 and 1808; Including a Tour of Nearly Six Thousand Miles,* 2 vols. (New York: Isaac Ripley, 1810), 2:197.

6. Quoted in Henry A. Kmen, *Music in New Orleans: The Formative Years, 1791–1841* (Baton Rouge: Louisiana State University Press, 1966), pp. 226–27.

7. Alliot, "Historical and Political Reflections," p. 77.

8. Fiehrer, "African Presence," p. 23.

9. Robin, *Voyages,* 2:72.

10. "Resumen de los Libros de Colecturía de Blancos, como de Pardos, y Morenos," Records of the Diocese of Louisiana and the Floridas, roll 4, 15 January 1796.

11. As with the very low median age at death for libre males noted in chapter 1, I cannot account for these differential death rates by racial and status group. One

possible explanation is that many whites in New Orleans at this time were foreign-born and unacclimated to its environment, whereas libres were primarily creoles.

12. Father Theodoro Thirso Henríquez to Henrique, Records of the Diocese of Louisiana and the Floridas, roll 3, 10 December 1792; Acts of Ximénez, volume of various notaries, fols. 246–63, 28 May 1804.

13. Court Proceedings of Quiñones, no. 6, 10 September 1793; Acts of N. Broutin, no. 3, fol. 78, 5 March 1801.

14. Bishop Peñalver y Cárdenas to the Cabildo, Records of the Diocese of Louisiana and the Floridas, roll 5, 5 February 1796; Acts of N. Broutin, no. 3, fol. 78, 5 March 1801.

15. Schultz, *Travels on an Inland Voyage*, p. 196.

16. Natalie Zemon Davis, *Society and Culture in Early Modern France* (Stanford: Stanford University Press, 1975), pp. xvi, 97.

17. Schultz, *Travels on an Inland Voyage*, p. 195. Earlier in 1804 Paul Alliot observed that "since there are two different castes, divided by color, each has its own hall" (Alliot, "Historical and Political Reflections," p. 77).

18. Berquin-Duvallon, *Vue*, p. 185.

19. Miró's Bando, article 12, RDC, vol. 3, no. 1, 2 June 1786.

20. Acts of Ximénez, no. 9, fol. 178, 14 March 1795.

21. Berquin-Duvallon, *Vue*, p. 28.

22. Schultz, *Travels on an Inland Voyage*, p. 193.

23. René J. Le Gardeur Jr., *The First New Orleans Theatre, 1792–1803* (New Orleans: Leeward Books, 1963), pp. 10–14.

24. Alfred N. Hunt, *Haiti's Influence on Antebellum America: Slumbering Volcano in the Caribbean* (Baton Rouge: Louisiana State University Press, 1988), pp. 67–68; Schultz, *Travels on an Inland Voyage*, p. 196.

25. RDC, vol. 4, no. 3, 8 and 21 February 1800.

26. Berquin-Duvallon, *Vue*, p. 297; Miró's Bando, articles 3 and 10, RDC, vol. 3, no. 1, 2 June 1786.

27. See, for example, RDC, vol. 4, no. 3, 21 February 1800; RDC vol. 4, no. 4, 14 August and 18 September 1801; Kmen, *Music in New Orleans*, pp. 42–46.

28. Kmen, *Music in New Orleans*, pp. 42–48.

29. RDC, vol. 2, 19 January 1781; Berquin-Duvallon, *Vue*, pp. 32–33.

30. RDC, vol. 2, 19 January 1781; RDC, vol. 4, no. 3, 7 and 13 February 1800; James Pitot, *Observations on the Colony of Louisiana from 1796 to 1802*, trans. Henry C. Pitot (Baton Rouge: Louisiana State University Press for The Historic New Orleans Collection, 1979), p. 29.

31. "Criminales seguidos de oficio contra el Pardo Libre Pedro Bahy," SJR, 7 October 1791.

32. "Información producida por Juan Bautista Gómez, pardo Libre," SJR, 24 April 1794.

33. Berquin-Duvallon, *Vue*, p. 185.

34. Ibid.

35. Schultz, *Travels on an Inland Voyage*, pp. 195–96.

36. Miró's Bando, articles 7 and 11, RDC, vol. 3, no. 1, 2 June 1786; Pitot, *Observations*, p. 29.

37. Berquin-Duvallon, *Vue*, p. 40.

38. "Criminales seguidos de oficio contra Pedro Alarcón sobre consentir Juegos prohividos en su casa," SJR, 21 March 1791.

39. "Auto Levantado por el señor don Juan Ventura Morales contra Juan Freyre (el Gallego) sobre haver dado a Jugar a Juegos prohibidos a los Negros mulatos y blancos," SJR, 16 August 1791.

40. "Autos seguidos de oficio contra varios Individuos por haverse encontrado jugando a juegos prohibidos," SJR, 21 May 1792.

41. "Autos seguidos de oficio contra varios individuos que se encontraron jugando a juegos prohividos en casa de Agustín Díaz, maestro de zapertero," SJR, 15 February 1793.

42. See articles 52 and 53 of the French Code noir as applied to Louisiana in 1724 and Bowser, "Colonial Spanish America," pp. 40–42.

43. "Criminales Seguidos por don Pedro Fabrot contra María Cofinie, parda libre, sobre palabras infuriosas," SJR, 8 June 1795.

44. Court documents never state his name, but the boy was either Juan Isidoro, who was nine years old at the time and died in 1812 at the age of twenty-six, or Pedro, who was five and a half years old (Nonwhite Baptisms, book 3a, 20 July 1786, and book 4a, 19 March 1790; Nonwhite Burials, [book 5], 1 October 1812).

45. Cofignie bore eight children during the Spanish period, the first in 1785 and the last in 1801; of these, three died in their youth. She had another daughter in 1806. The father of only one of Cofignie's children was identified; Josef Urra, a cuarterón libre born November 1797, was described in his baptismal record as the illegitimate son of Manuel Urra and the parda libre María Cofignie (Nonwhite Baptisms, books 3a, 4a, 5a, 6a, 7a, 8a, and 9a, 1785–1806).

46. Cofignie did not give up fighting for what she believed to be just causes, however. During the same month in which Favrot brought charges against her, she petitioned a tribunal for the freedom of her brother, Antonio Cofignie, a slave of her own former mistress, the widow of her and Antonio's white father, Don Claudio Cofignie. It appears that Don Claudio had verbally promised to give each of his three illegitimate children—María, Feliciana, and Antonio—by his grifa slave Luison four hundred pesos to purchase his or her freedom. The girls had done so prior to Cofignie's death in 1786, but Antonio had not, and now the widow refused to free him for that amount, demanding instead what María claimed to be an exorbitant sum. While María was in the process of seeking retribution, Antonio took matters into his own hands and ran away. His mistress then accused María of assisting Antonio and hiding him; ironically María, who obviously placed much faith in the legal system, was thrown in jail once again, where she again called on the mercy of the court as a "pobre mujer" to release her so she could support her family. Finally, a white planter in Opelousas, whose ties to the Cofignies are not clear, paid

1,100 pesos for the fugitive, with the promise that María would reimburse him that sum if her brother ever reappeared. And the case concluded ("Promovido por María Cofiny Parda Libre sobre que se estime su hermano Antonio Esclavo de doña Francisca Monget para su Libertad," SJR, 23 June 1795).

47. The two Bailly trials are "Criminales seguidos de oficio contra el Pardo Libre Pedro Bahy," SJR, 7 October 1791, and "Testimonio de la Sumaria contra el Mulato libre Pedro Bailly, Theniente de las Milicias de Pardos de esta Ciudad, por haver prorrumpido especies contra el Govierno Español, y haverse manifestado adicto a las máximas de los Franceses rebeldes," AGI Estado 14, no. 60, 11 February 1794.

48. David Geggus, "Racial Equality, Slavery, and Colonial Secession during the Constituent Assembly," *American Historical Review* 94:5 (December 1989): 1290–1308.

49. For more on the spread of the French Revolution in Louisiana and activities of various groups see Hall, *Africans in Colonial Louisiana,* pp. 316–74; Hanger, "Conflicting Loyalties" and "A Privilege and Honor to Serve: The Free Black Militia of Spanish New Orleans," *Military History of the Southwest* 21:1 (spring 1991): 80–82; Lachance, "Politics of Fear"; Liljegren, "Jacobinism in Spanish Louisiana."

50. An informative overview of free blacks in the Caribbean is Cohen and Greene, introduction to *Neither Slave nor Free,* pp. 1–18. Free black military service in Louisiana is discussed in Holmes, *Honor and Fidelity,* and McConnell, *Negro Troops.* See also chapter 4 of this work.

51. Foner, "Free People of Color," p. 420.

52. Foner, "Free People of Color." For information on the incidence of collusion between free blacks and slaves throughout the Americas see Cohen and Greene, *Neither Slave nor Free.*

53. Lachance, "Politics of Fear," pp. 173–74; Liljegren, "Jacobinism in Spanish Louisiana."

54. Carondelet quoted in Hunt, *Haiti's Influence,* pp. 26–27.

55. For further discussion of these activities see Hall, *Africans in Colonial Louisiana,* pp. 316–74, and Liljegren, "Jacobinism in Spanish Louisiana."

56. The following discussion and assessment of Bailly's activities in 1791 and 1793–94 are derived from testimony in the two trials, cited in note 47 above.

57. As noted in chapter 4, Dorville always included his militia rank in every document to which he was a party. In census records he defined his occupation as captain of the pardo militia, even though he primarily was a vendor. He obviously was very proud to be a militia officer.

58. Account of Bailly's Life and Career by Dorville and Simón, AGI Estado 14, no. 60, fols. 40–52, 12 February 1794. After an extensive search no other documents have been located to support Dorville's and Simón's claims. Bailly appears as present on all extant militia rosters. As noted in the following text, it is possible that Dorville and Simón made up the whole story. After all, Bailly, like the Pointe Coupée slaves, had been acquitted in 1791 under Miró's jurisdiction; more intense fear of slave revolt and free black–slave collusion most likely would affect Carondelet's de-

cision. Maybe astute free blacks like Dorville and Simón, who had several personal and material reasons for attacking Bailly, perceived that the paranoid Carondelet would convict Bailly this time around. In the 1795 case, unlike the 1791 one, there were several white as well as free black witnesses to Bailly's actions.

59. See Archer, *The Army of Bourbon Mexico;* Campbell, "Changing Racial and Administrative Structure"; Holmes, *Honor and Fidelity;* Klein, "The Colored Milita of Cuba"; Kuethe, "Status of the Free Pardo"; Landers, "Gracia Real de Santa Teresa de Mose"; McAlister, *"Fuero Militar";* and Sánchez, "African Freedmen" for further analysis of the prestige a military title conferred upon individuals in the colonies and Spain. Several court proceedings demonstrate the extent of Dorville's economic woes. See Court Proceedings of F. Broutin, no. 5, June–August 1791; no. 11, March–April 1792; no. 12, April–June 1792; no. 16, January–March 1793. Both Dorville and Simón continued to serve as militia officers well into the period of United States rule. Dorville was even involved in the 1806 free black–Spanish conspiracy revealed by Stephen and discussed in the epilogue of this work. Frustrated by United States reluctance to recognize the free black militia, Dorville "flaunted a Spanish cockade" and signed notarized records with the appendage "commandante de mulatos que en Tiempo de la Dominación Española" (McConnell, *Negro Troops,* p. 42).

60. Court Proceedings of F. Broutin, no. 8, fols. 75–92, 93–100, 12 September 1791.

61. "Pedro Bailly solicitando que don Luis Lalande Daprémont le satisfago el Almazenage de una partida de hierro que atenido en su Almazén de la pertenenda de dicho Daprémont," SJR, 13 October 1791.

62. Cap Français is now known as Cap Haitien. El Guarico was the name the Spaniards gave to Le Cap; however, as with other principal cities in Spanish parlance, it sometimes stood as a synecdoche for the colony as a whole, or at least the northern part.

63. Bailly probably referred to the period when the Jacobins dominated French politics. In 1792 the National Assembly decreed full civil rights as Frenchmen for all free persons of color in the colonies (Hunt, *Haiti's Influence,* p. 22).

64. Declouet was the son of Don Alexandro Declouet (colonel of the Fixed Infantry Regiment of Louisiana and a native of France) and Doña Luisa Favrot (native of Louisiana). He was a native of Louisiana and a tobacco merchant. In 1791 Declouet was twenty-five years old and lived on St. Peter Street. He had a common-law relationship with and later married Clara López de Peña, a free mulata or mestiza who eventually passed as white (a fuller discussion of the Declouet family can be found in chapter 3).

65. As of May 1796 Bailly was still imprisoned in Havana, and he does not appear in New Orleans notarial registers until a few months later. Unlike four other white prisoners from New Orleans, he was not released in December 1795 (Don Luis de las Casas to Señor Príncipe de la Paz, Havana, AGI Estado 5, no. 107, 8 May 1796; El Señor Príncipe de la Paz to el Señor Governador del Consejo, Aránjuez, AGI Estado 5, no. 107, 15 May 1796; el Ph.e Obpo de Salamanca to el Señor Príncipe de la

Paz, Madrid, AGI Estado 5, no. 107, 21 May 1796). When Bailly was jailed, he conferred a power of attorney on his wife Naneta Cadis, and she sold land in his name (Acts of Pedesclaux, no. 20, fol. 135, 11 February 1794, and no. 23, fol. 5, 3 January 1795). In 1796 Naneta petitioned the crown to free her husband, stating her need for him to support their family. Like many women in New Orleans' patriarchal society, Naneta stressed her inability as a "pobre mujer" to care for the family's needs so that she could gain the court's sympathy. She obviously could and did do well on her own, despite being "reduced to misery" (AGI PC 211-A, 1796).

66. The notarial records indicate that Bailly continued buying and selling slaves with persons of all colors. He frequently borrowed and loaned large sums of money. For example, Don Antonio Cavelier repaid him 2,230 pesos in 1801, and he gave power of attorney to another white person to collect a debt of 3,214 pesos (Acts of N. Broutin, no. 3, fol. 94, 23 March 1801, and no. 4, fol. 56, 5 February 1802). For the registration of Bailly's promotion see Acts of F. Broutin, no. 47, fol. 31, 12 March 1798. Also see Census of Faubourg Ste. Marie, 1798, AGI PC 215-A; "Address from the Free People of Color," January 1804, in Carter, *Territorial Papers of the United States,* 9:174–75). Bailly also was involved in the Batture case of 1807 (McConnell, *Negro Troops,* pp. 28–29).

67. Testimony Given by Esteban Lalande, in "Criminales seguidos de oficio contra el Pardo Libre Pedro Bahy," SJR, 7 October 1791.

68. Baade, "Law of Slavery"; Berlin, *Slaves without Masters;* John W. Blassingame, *Black New Orleans, 1860–1880* (Chicago: University of Chicago Press, 1973); McConnell, *Negro Troops;* and Schafer, " 'Open and Notorious Concubinage,' " along with other works cited in the epilogue of this book, examine the declining status of free people of color in antebellum New Orleans and Louisiana. See Caryn Cossé Bell's *Revolution, Romanticism, and the Afro-Creole Protest Tradition in Louisiana, 1718–1868* (Baton Rouge: Louisiana State University Press, 1997) for the most recent assessment of free black activism, a political and intellectual heritage that originated in the colonial period and continued to develop during the antebellum, Civil War, and Reconstruction eras.

Epilogue

1. Fiehrer, "African Presence," pp. 23–24. Fiehrer and other recent scholars of Louisiana emphasize the "continuity of Caribbean culture."

2. Lachance, "Formation of a Three-Caste Society."

3. For further discussion of Creoles of Color and their activities in the nineteenth century, see Bell, *Revolution, Romanticism, and the Afro-Creole Protest Tradition;* Brasseaux, Fontenot, and Oubre, *Creoles of Color in the Bayou Country;* Mills, *The Forgotten People;* and Tregle, "Creoles and Americans."

4. Clark, *New Orleans,* pp. 275–329; Fiehrer, "African Presence," p. 4; Geggus, *Slavery, War, and Revolution,* p. 21; James E. Winston, "Notes of the Economic His-

tory of New Orleans, 1803–1836," *Mississippi Valley Historical Review* 11:2 (September 1924): 200–226.

5. Everett, "Emigres and Militiamen: Free Persons of Color in New Orleans, 1803–1815," *Journal of Negro History* 38:4 (October 1953): 377–94; McConnell, *Negro Troops*, pp. 33–55; Winston, "The Free Negro in New Orleans, 1803–1860," *LHQ* 21:4 (October 1938): 1075–79.

6. "Address from the Free People of Color," January 1804, in Carter, *Territorial Papers of the United States*, 9:174–75. Interestingly, the militia members addressed Claiborne as "Governor General and Intendant of Louisiana," the title given to *Spanish* governors.

7. Recent research by Judith Kelleher Schafer has revealed, however, that New Orleans officials, lower-court judges in particular, did not always follow or enforce these or other laws pertaining to African Americans (*Slavery, the Civil Law, and the Supreme Court of Louisiana* [Baton Rouge: Louisiana State University Press, 1994]).

8. Everett, "Emigres and Militiamen," p. 385; Lachance, "The 1809 Immigration"; McConnell, *Negro Troops*, pp. 46–47.

9. Fiehrer, "African Presence," p. 5.

10. Everett, "Emigres and Militiamen," pp. 383–84; McConnell, *Negro Troops*, pp. 41–42.

11. Glenn R. Conrad, "Summary of Trial Proceedings of Those Accused of Participating in the Slave Uprising of January, 1811," *Louisiana History* 18:4 (fall 1977): 472–73; James H. Dorman, "Persistent Specter: Slave Rebellion in Territorial Louisiana," *Louisiana History* 18:4 (fall 1977): 398–404; McConnell, *Negro Troops*, pp. 48–49. As seen below, Louisiana's propertied free persons of color offered their services to the Confederacy on the eve of the Civil War.

12. McConnell, *Negro Troops*, pp. 49–53.

13. Ibid., p. 53.

14. Ibid., pp. 63–64.

15. Ibid., pp. 91–115. McConnell provides the poem, translated into English, on pages 107–8:

The Campaign of 1814–15

I remember that, one day, during my childhood,
A beautiful morning, my mother, while sighing,
Said to me: "Child, emblem of innocence,
"You do not know the future that awaits thee.
"You believe that you see your country under this beautiful sky
"Renounce thy error, my tender child,
"And believe above all your beloved mother. . . .
"Here, thou art but an object of scorn."

Ten years later, upon our vast frontiers,
One heard the English cannon,

And then these words: "Come, let us conquer, my brothers,
"We were all born of Louisiana blood."
At these sweet words, and embracing my mother,
I followed you, repeating your cries,
Not thinking, in my pursuit of battle,
That I was but an object of scorn.

Arriving upon the field of battle,
I fought like a brave warrior;
Neither the bullets nor the shrapnel,
Could ever fill me with fear.
I fought with great valor
With the hope of serving my country,
Not thinking that for recompense
I would be the object of scorn.

After having gained the victory,
In this terrible and glorious combat,
All of you shared a drink with me
And called me a valiant soldier.
And I, without regret, and with a sincere heart,
Helas! I drank, believing you to be my friends,
Not thinking, in my fleeting joy
That I was but an object of scorn.

But today I sigh sadly
Because I perceive a change in you:
I no longer see that gracious smile
Which showed itself, in other times, so often
Upon your honeyed lips.
Have you become my enemies?
Ah! I see it in your fierce looks,
I am but an object of your scorn.

16. Foner, "Free People of Color"; John Garrigus, "Blue and Brown: Contraband Indigo and the Rise of a Free Colored Planter Class in French Saint-Domingue," *The Americas* 50:2 (October 1993): 233–63; Geggus, *Slavery, War, and Revolution,* pp. 19–20; Knight, *Slave Society in Cuba* and "Cuba," in Cohen and Greene, *Neither Slave nor Free,* pp. 289–305. Geggus observes that as sugar cultivation intensified "during the eighteenth century a body of racist legislation was built up from both local and metropolitan enactments that was perhaps unequalled in the West Indies" (*Slavery, War, and Revolution,* p. 21).

17. Fiehrer, "African Presence," p. 22.

18. Landers, "Black Society," p. 23. Knight also states that in Cuba's preplanta-

tion phase "social and legal divisions between the racial groups tended to be flexible" ("Cuba," p. 300).

19. Geggus, *Slavery, War, and Revolution,* pp. 20–21; Klein, *African Slavery,* p. 234.

20. Berlin, *Slaves without Masters,* pp. 118–29; Blassingame, *Black New Orleans,* pp. 1–22; Cohen and Greene, introduction to *Neither Slave nor Free,* pp. 15–16; Curry, *The Free Black in Urban America;* Foner, "Free People of Color"; Geggus, *Slavery, War, and Revolution,* pp. 20–21. For example, "by the late 1830's a Negro Philharmonic Society was organized with over one hundred members. Its purpose was to provide formal music for those who objected to sitting in segregated sections in the theaters" (Kmen, *Music in New Orleans,* p. 234).

21. Quotation from Baade, "Law of Slavery," p. 47. Domínguez, *White by Definition,* pp. 116–17; Schweninger, *Black Property Owners in the South* and "Prosperous Blacks in the South."

22. Frances Trollope, *Domestic Manners of the Americans,* ed. Richard Mullen (Oxford: Oxford University Press, 1984), pp. 9–10.

23. Charles Lyell, *A Second Visit to the United States of North America,* 2 vols. (London: John Murray, 1849), 2:130; Paul Wilhelm, *Travels in North America, 1822–1824,* trans. W. Robert Nitske (Norman: University of Oklahoma Press, 1973), p. 33.

24. Quote from Klein, *African Slavery,* p. 237; Garrigus, "Blue and Brown." Using United States census returns for 1850, 1860, and 1870, Schweninger calculates that Louisiana had the greatest number of libres holding at least $2,000 in real estate and having the highest average value of real estate holdings in the Lower and Upper South (with the one exception that in 1870 freedmen in Missouri had a slightly higher average real property holdings value equaling $6,100). The Civil War devastated Louisiana's free black property holders; their real property holdings fell from an average of $10,311 in 1860 to $5,730 in 1870, even though the number of them having at least $2,000 in real estate rose from 472 to 510 ("Prosperous Blacks in the South," pp. 39, 46, 50, 52).

25. New Orleans *Daily Delta,* 28 December 1860.

26. For example, Karasch argues that "Cariocan slaves joined the ranks of the freed not because 'benevolent' masters kindly gave it to them, but because they *earned* it" (*Slave Life in Rio,* pp. 336–37).

Appendix: Regulations Governing the Free Black Militia

1. See McAlister's definition of urban and provincial militias in his "Reorganization of the Army," p. 4.

2. Holmes, *Honor and Fidelity,* p. 51.

3. Kuethe, "Status of the Free Pardo," p. 113; Sánchez, "African Freedmen," p. 168.

4. AGI SD 2553, 12 June 1789.

5. AGI PC 160-A, 1 September 1801.

6. Reglamento para las milicias de infantería . . . , AGI PC 160-A, fol. 312–35,

13 April 1801. Some of these ordinances included royal orders found in AGI SD 2566, 12 December 1796 and 18 January 1797, and in AGI SD 2568, 21 August 1797.

7. For example, see tables of officials and enlisted personnel, 1801 Militia Rosters.

8. This description differs from the one given by McConnell in "Louisiana's Black Military History," p. 38.

Glossary

ahijado godchild

alcalde magistrate and member of the cabildo

arpent French linear and area measure; in lineal terms equivalent to 190 feet

audiencia high or superior court

ayudante aide, assistant

bando edict; decree

bozal slave newly arrived from Africa

cabildo town council or corporation

carta de libertad certificate of manumission

casta mixed-race; person of mixed racial ancestry

cédula decree

coartación self-purchase of manumission

compadrazgo godparenthood; fictive or ritual kinship

cuarterón(a) person with one-fourth black and three-fourths white ancestry

faubourg/arrabal suburb

fuero militar privileges accorded to military personnel

graciosa/graciosamente gratis or freely without conditions (as in the case of manumission)

grifo(a) offspring of a moreno(a) and a parda(o); sometimes refers to the offspring of a black and a Native American

habitación plantation; large landholding

hijo(a) natural natural child (illegitimate but recognized by the parents)

hojas de servicio military service records

jornal daily wage

ladino African who had been "seasoned" in the Americas

libre free; in this work meaning a free person of African descent

madrina godmother

mercader shopkeeper, retail merchant

mestizo(a) offspring of a white and a Native American

miliciano militiaman

moreno(a) a dark-skinned person of African descent

padrino godfather (in plural form means godparents)

palabras infuriosas "violent words"; slander

pardo(a) a light-skinned person of African descent

parentela patron-client relationship

peso Spanish monetary unit on which U.S. dollar was based as its equivalent

peso fuerte peso in hard currency rather than paper; generally more valuable and steady in value than fluctuating paper currency

plana mayor headquarter command and staff group

Plaza de Armas parade ground; in New Orleans, modern day Jackson Square

procurador general attorney general

real Spanish monetary unit in which eight reales were equivalent to one peso

reglamento regulations; rules

soldado soldier

tasador appraiser

vasallo subject; vassal

vecino resident; inhabitant; citizen of a town

Bibliography

Primary Sources

Manuscript Collections
Archives of the Archdiocese of New Orleans, New Orleans, La.
    Nonwhite Baptisms, St. Louis Parish, books 2a–13a, 1777–1814
    Nonwhite Marriages, St. Louis Parish, book 1, 1777–1830
    White and Nonwhite Burials, St. Louis Parish, [book 1], 1772–90
    Nonwhite Burials, St. Louis Parish, [books 2–5], 1790–1815
Archivo General de Indias, Seville, Spain
    Audiencia de Santo Domingo
    Estado
    Papeles Procedentes de la Isla de Cuba
Archivo General de Simancas, Simancas, Spain
    Guerra Moderna
The Historic New Orleans Collection, New Orleans, La.
    L. Durand Letter
    Free Persons of Color in Louisiana Collection
    Records of the Diocese of Louisiana and the Floridas
    Spanish Colonial Land Grant Papers
Historical Center, Louisiana State Museum, New Orleans, La.
    Miscellaneous, Record Group 68
    Spanish Judicial Records, Record Group 2
    French Judicial Records, Record Group 1
Howard-Tilton Memorial Library, Tulane University, New Orleans, La.
    Favrot Papers
    Rosemond E. and Emile Kuntz Collection
    New Orleans Municipal Papers
    John Minor Wisdom Collection
Louisiana and Lower Mississippi Valley Collections, Louisiana State University,
        Baton Rouge, La.
    Cabildo Records, Miscellaneous
    Laura L. Porteous Collection
    Charles L. Thompson Collection
Louisiana Division, New Orleans Public Library, New Orleans, La.
    Census of New Orleans, 6 November 1791
    Inventory of the Notarial Office of Carlos Ximénez, 1768–70
    Inventory of the Notarial Office of Pedro Pedesclaux, 1770–1804

Petitions, Letters, and Decrees of the Cabildo, 1770–99
Records and Deliberations of the Cabildo, 1769–1803
Orleans Parish Notarial Archives, New Orleans, La.
Acts of Andrés Almonester y Roxas, 1771–82
Acts of Juan Bautista Garic, 1771–79
Acts of Rafael Perdomo, 1782–90
Acts of Leonardo Mazange, 1779–83
Acts of Fernando Rodríguez, 1783–87
Acts and Court Proceedings of Pedro Pedesclaux, 1788–1803
Acts and Court Proceedings of Carlos Ximénez, 1790–1803
Acts and Court Proceedings of Francisco Broutin, 1790–99
Acts and Court Proceedings of Narciso Broutin, 1799–1804
Court Proceedings of C. Ximénez, R. Perdomo, F. Broutin, and N. Broutin, 1784–1803
Acts and Court Proceedings of Esteban de Quiñones, 1778–1802

Published Works

Carter, Clarence Edwin, ed. *The Territorial Papers of the United States.* 28 vols. Vol. 9, *The Territory of Orleans, 1803–1812.* Washington, D.C.: United States Government Printing Office, 1940.

Din, Gilbert C., ed. *Louisiana in 1776: A Memoria of Francisco Bouligny.* Louisiana Collection Series, 3. New Orleans: Holmes, 1977.

Faye, Stanely, ed. "Louis Declouet's Memorial to the Spanish Government, December 7, 1814." *LHQ* 22:3 (July 1939): 795–818.

Flannery, Matthew, comp. *New Orleans in 1805: A Directory and a Census Together with Resolutions Authorizing Same Now Printed for the First Time.* New Orleans: Pelican Gallery, 1936.

Forsyth, Hewitt L., trans. and comp. *First Book of Confirmations of this Parish of St. Louis of New Orleans, Containing Folios from the Beginning to the Present.* New Orleans: Genealogical Research Society of New Orleans, 1967.

Holmes, Jack D. L., trans. and ed. "O'Reilly's Regulations on Booze, Boarding Houses, and Billiards." *Louisiana History* 6:3 (summer 1965): 293–300.

———, trans. and ed. "O'Reilly's 1769 Commission: A Personal View." *Louisiana History* 24:3 (summer 1983): 307–13.

Kinnaird, Lawrence. *Spain in the Mississippi Valley, 1765–1794.* 4 vols. Washington, D.C.: American Historical Association, 1946–49.

Morazán, Ronald R. "La Semana Santa in New Orleans, 1800." *Louisiana History* 12:1 (winter 1971): 67.

Porteous, Laura L., trans. "The Spanish Procedure in Louisiana in 1800 for Licensing Doctors and Surgeons." *LHQ* 14:2 (April 1931): 204–7.

Robertson, James Alexander, trans. and ed. *Louisiana under the Rule of Spain, France, and the United States, 1785–1807: Social, Economic, and Political Conditions of the Territory Represented in the Louisiana Purchase.* 2 vols. Cleveland: Arthur H. Clark, 1911.

Woods, Msgr. Earl C., and Charles Nolan, eds. *Sacramental Records of the Roman Catholic Church of the Archdiocese of New Orleans.* 10 vols. New Orleans: Archdiocese of New Orleans, 1987–95.

Contemporary Accounts

Alliot, Paul. "Historical and Political Reflections." In Robertson, *Louisiana under the Rule*, 1:29–143.

Ashe, Thomas. *Travels in America Performed in 1806.* 3 vols. London: Richard Phillips, 1808.

Bartram, William. *The Travels of William Bartram.* Edited by Mark Van Doren. New York: Dover Publications, 1928.

Beer, William, ed. "New Orleans and Bayou St. John in 1766: Extract from the Journal of an Expedition along the Ohio and Mississippi by Captain Harry Gordon, 1766, p. 17." *LHQ* 6:1 (January 1923): 19–20.

Berquin-Duvallon, Pierre-Louis. *Vue de la colonie espagnole du Mississipi, ou des provinces de Louisiane et Floride occidentale, en l'année 1802.* Paris: Imprimerie Expédite, 1803.

Bossu, Jean-Bernard. *Travels in the Interior of North America, 1751–1762.* Translated and edited by Seymour Feiler. Norman: University of Oklahoma Press, 1962.

Darby, William. *A Geographical Description of the State of Louisiana, the Southern Part of the State of Mississippi, and Territory of Alabama.* Philadelphia: John Melish, 1816.

Hall, A. Oakey. *The Manhattaner in New Orleans; or, Phases of "Crescent City" Life.* New Orleans: J. C. Morgan, 1851.

Lyell, Charles. *A Second Visit to the United States of North America.* 2 vols. London: John Murray, 1849.

Perrin du Lac, M. *Voyage dans les deux Louisianes.* Paris: Imprimerie Expédite, 1805.

Pintard, John. "New Orleans, 1801: An Account by John Pintard." Edited by David Lee Sterling. *LHQ* 34:3 (July 1951): 217–33.

Pitot, James. *Observations on the Colony of Louisiana from 1796 to 1802.* Translated by Henry C. Pitot. Baton Rouge: Louisiana State University Press for The Historic New Orleans Collection, 1979.

Pittman, Philip. *The Present State of the European Settlements on the Mississippi.* London: J. Nourse, 1770.

Pope, John. *A Tour through the Southern and Western Territories of the United States of North America.* Reprint ed. Gainesville: University Presses of Florida, 1979.

Robin, Claude C. *Voyages dans l'intérieur de la Louisiane, de la Floride occidentale, et dans les isles de la Martinique et de Saint-Domingue pendant les années 1802, 1803, 1804, 1805 et 1806.* 3 vols. Paris: F. Buisson, 1807.

Schultz, Christian. *Travels on an Inland Voyage through the States of New York, Pennsylvania, Virginia, Ohio, Kentucky, and Tennessee, and through the Territories of Indiana, Louisiana, Mississippi and New Orleans, Performed in the Years 1807 and 1808; Including a Tour of Nearly Six Thousand Miles.* 2 vols. New York: Isaac Ripley, 1810.

Trollope, Frances. *Domestic Manners of the Americans.* Edited by Richard Mullen. Oxford: Oxford University Press, 1984.

Troth, Henry. "Journal of Henry Troth, 1799." Transcribed by Clinton Lee Brooke and Tyrrell Willcox Brooke. July 1970. LHC.

Wilhelm, Paul. *Travels in North America, 1822–1824.* Translated by W. Robert Nitske. Norman: University of Oklahoma Press, 1973.

Guides

Beers, Henry Putney. *French and Spanish Records of Louisiana: A Bibliographical Guide to Archive and Manuscript Sources.* Baton Rouge: Louisiana State University Press, 1989.

Casey, Powell A. *Encyclopedia of Forts, Posts, Named Camps, and Other Military Installations in Louisiana, 1700-1981.* Baton Rouge: Claitor's Publishing Division, n.d.

Cummins, Light Townsend, and Glen Jeansonne, eds. *A Guide to the History of Louisiana.* Westport, Conn.: Greenwood Press, 1982.

Holmes, Jack D. L. *A Guide to Spanish Louisiana, 1762-1806.* New Orleans: A. F. Laborde, 1970.

McAvoy, Thomas T. *Guide to the Microfilm Edition of the Records of the Diocese of Louisiana and the Floridas, 1576-1803.* Notre Dame: University of Notre Dame Archives, 1967.

Secondary Sources

Books

Acosta Rodríguez, Antonio. *La Población de Luisiana española (1763-1803).* Madrid: Ministerio de Asuntos Exteriores, 1979.

Albi, Julio. *La Defensa de las Indias (1764-1799).* Madrid: Instituto de Cooperación Iberoamericana, 1987.

Alexander, Adele Logan. *Ambiguous Lives: Free Women of Color in Rural Georgia, 1789-1879.* Fayetteville: University of Arkansas Press, 1991.

Allain, Mathé. *"Not Worth a Straw": French Colonial Policy and the Early Years of Louisiana.* Lafayette: Center for Louisiana Studies, 1988.

Andreu Ocariz, Juan José. *Movimientos rebeldes de los esclavos negros durante el dominio español en Luisiana.* Zaragosa, Spain: Cagisa, 1977.

Andrews, George Reid. *The Afro-Argentines of Buenos Aires, 1800-1900.* Madison: University of Wisconsin Press, 1980.

———. *Blacks and Whites in São Paulo, Brazil, 1888-1988.* Madison: University of Wisconsin Press, 1991.

Archer, Christon I. *The Army of Bourbon Mexico, 1760-1810.* Albuquerque: University of New Mexico Press, 1977.

Barbier, Jacques A., and Allan J. Kuethe, eds. *The North American Role in the Spanish Imperial Economy, 1760-1819.* Dover, N.H.: Manchester University Press, 1984.

Baudier, Roger. *The Catholic Church in Louisiana.* New Orleans: Author, 1939.

Bell, Caryn Cossé. *Revolution, Romanticism, and the Afro-Creole Protest Tradition in Louisiana, 1718-1868.* Baton Rouge: Louisiana State University Press, 1997.

Berlin, Ira. *Slaves without Masters: The Free Negro in the Antebellum South.* New York: Pantheon Books, 1974.

Blanchard, Peter. *Slavery and Abolition in Early Republican Peru.* Wilmington, Del.: Scholarly Resources, 1992.

Blassingame, John W. *Black New Orleans, 1860-1880.* Chicago: University of Chicago Press, 1973.

Blume, Helmut. *The German Coast during the Colonial Era, 1722-1803.* Destrehan, La.: German Acadian Coast Historical and Genealogical Society, 1990.

Bowser, Frederick P. *The African Slave in Colonial Peru, 1524–1650.* Stanford: Stanford University Press, 1974.

Brasseaux, Carl A. *Denis-Nicolas Foucault and the New Orleans Rebellion of 1768.* Ruston, La.: McGinty Publications, 1987.

Brasseaux, Carl A., Keith P. Fontenot, and Claude F. Oubre. *Creoles of Color in the Bayou Country.* Jackson: University Press of Mississippi, 1994.

Burson, Caroline Maude. *The Stewardship of Don Esteban Miró, 1782–1792.* New Orleans: American Printing, 1940.

Bush, Barbara. *Slave Women in Caribbean Society, 1650–1838.* Bloomington: Indiana University Press, 1990.

Carroll, Patrick James. *Blacks in Colonial Veracruz: Race, Ethnicity, and Regional Development.* Austin: University of Texas Press, 1991.

Clark, John G. *New Orleans, 1718–1812: An Economic History.* Baton Rouge: Louisiana State University Press, 1970.

Clendinnen, Inga. *Ambivalent Conquests: Maya and Spaniard in Yucatan, 1517–1570.* New York: Cambridge University Press, 1987.

Coker, William S., and Hazel P. Coker. *The Seige of Mobile, 1780, in Maps with Data on Troop Strength, Military Units, Ships, Casualties, and Prisoners of War Including a Brief History of Fort Charlotte (Conde).* Pensacola: Perdido Bay Press, 1982.

———. *The Seige of Pensacola, 1781, in Maps, with Data on Troop Strength, Military Units, Ships, Casualties, and Related Statistics.* Pensacola: Perdido Bay Press, 1981.

Coker, William S., and Thomas D. Watson. *Indian Traders of the Southeastern Spanish Borderlands: Panton, Leslie and Company and John Forbes and Company, 1783–1847.* Pensacola: University of West Florida Press, 1986.

Cox, Edward L. *Free Coloreds in the Slave Societies of St. Kitts and Grenada, 1763–1833.* Knoxville: University of Tennessee Press, 1984.

Crété, Lilian. *Daily Life in Louisiana, 1815–1830.* Translated by Patrick Gregory. Baton Rouge: Louisiana State University Press, 1981.

Cummins, Light Townsend. *Spanish Observers and the American Revolution, 1775–1783.* Baton Rouge: Louisiana State University Press, 1991.

Curry, Leonard P. *The Free Black in Urban America, 1800–1850: The Shadows of a Dream.* Chicago: University of Chicago Press, 1981.

Davis, David Brion. *The Problem of Slavery in Western Culture.* Ithaca: Cornell University Press, 1966.

Davis, Natalie Zemon. *Society and Culture in Early Modern France.* Stanford: Stanford University Press, 1975.

Dawson, Joseph G., III, ed. *The Louisiana Governors: From Iberville to Edwards.* Baton Rouge: Louisiana State University Press, 1990.

Degler, Carl N. *Neither Black nor White: Slavery and Race Relations in Brazil and the United States.* New York: Macmillan, 1971.

Din, Gilbert C. *The Canary Islanders of Louisiana.* Baton Rouge: Louisiana State University Press, 1988.

———. *Francisco Bouligny: A Bourbon Soldier in Spanish Louisiana.* Baton Rouge: Louisiana State University Press, 1993.

Domínguez, Virginia R. *White by Definition: Social Classification in Creole Louisiana.* New Brunswick, N.J.: Rutgers University Press, 1986.

Elkins, Stanley. *Slavery: A Problem in American Institutional and Intellectual Life.* Chicago: University of Chicago Press, 1959.

Fabel, Robin F. A. *The Economy of British West Florida, 1763–1783.* Tuscaloosa: University of Alabama Press, 1988.

Franklin, John Hope. *The Free Negro in North Carolina, 1790–1860.* Chapel Hill: University of North Carolina Press, 1943.

Frey, Silvia R. *Water from the Rock: Black Resistance in a Revolutionary Age.* Princeton: Princeton University Press, 1991.

Freyre, Gilberto. *Casa grande e senzala, formação da familia brasileira sob o regimen de economia patriarchal.* Rio de Janeiro: Livario José Olympio Editora, 1933.

———. *Sobrados e mucambos: Decadencia do patriarchado rural no Brasil.* São Paulo: Livario José Olympio Editora, 1936.

Gaspar, David Barry. *Bondmen and Rebels: A Study of Master-Slave Relations in Antigua, with Implications for Colonial British America.* Baltimore: Johns Hopkins University Press, 1985.

Geggus, David P. *Slavery, War, and Revolution: The British Occupation of St. Domingue, 1793–1798.* New York: Oxford University Press, 1982.

Gehman, Mary. *The Free People of Color of New Orleans: An Introduction.* New Orleans: Margaret Media, 1994.

Gutiérrez, Ramón A. *When Jesus Came, the Corn Mothers Went Away: Marriage, Sexuality, and Power in New Mexico, 1500–1846.* Stanford: Stanford University Press, 1991.

Hall, Gwendolyn Midlo. *Africans in Colonial Louisiana: The Development of Afro-Creole Culture in the Eighteenth Century.* Baton Rouge: Louisiana State University Press, 1992.

———. *Social Control in Slave Plantation Societies: A Comparison of St. Domingue and Cuba.* Baltimore: Johns Hopkins University Press, 1971.

Handler, Jerome S. *The Unappropriated People: Freedmen in the Slave Society of Barbados.* Baltimore: Johns Hopkins University Press, 1974.

Harris, Marvin. *Patterns of Race in the Americas.* New York: Walker and Co., 1964.

Heuman, Gad. *Between Black and White: Race, Politics, and the Free Coloureds in Jamaica, 1792–1865.* Westport, Conn.: Greenwood Press, 1981.

Hoetink, Harry. *The Two Variants of Caribbean Race Relations: A Contribution to the Sociology of Segmented Societies.* London: Alfred A. Knopf, 1947.

Holmes, Jack D. L. *Gayoso: The Life of a Spanish Governor in the Mississippi Valley, 1789–1799.* Baton Rouge: Louisiana State University Press, 1965.

———. *Honor and Fidelity: The Louisiana Infantry Regiment and the Louisiana Militia Companies, 1766–1821.* Birmingham: Author, 1965.

Holt, Thomas C. *The Problem of Freedom: Race, Labor, and Politics in Jamaica and Britain, 1832–1938.* Baltimore: Johns Hopkins University Press, 1992.

Horton, James Oliver. *Free People of Color: Inside the African American Community.* Washington, D.C.: Smithsonian Institution Press, 1993.

Huber, Leonard V., and Samuel Wilson Jr. *Baroness Pontalba's Buildings: Their Site and the Remarkable Woman Who Built Them.* New Orleans: Friends of the Cabildo, 1964.

Hünefeldt, Christine. *Paying the Price of Freedom: Family and Labor among Lima's Slaves, 1800–1854.* Berkeley: University of California Press, 1994.

Hunt, Alfred N. *Haiti's Influence on Antebellum America: Slumbering Volcano in the Caribbean*. Baton Rouge: Louisiana State University Press, 1988.

James, C. L. R. *The Black Jacobins: Toussaint Louverture and the San Domingo Revolt*. New York: Dial Press, 1938.

Johnson, Michael P., and James L. Roark. *Black Masters: A Free Family of Color in the Old South*. New York: W. W. Norton, 1974.

Karasch, Mary C. *Slave Life in Rio de Janeiro, 1808–1850*. Princeton: Princeton University Press, 1987.

Kerr, Derek Noel. *Petty Felony, Slave Defiance, and Frontier Villainy: Crime and Criminal Justice in Spanish Louisiana, 1770–1803*. New York: Garland, 1993.

Kinser, Samuel. *Carnival, American Style: Mardi Gras at New Orleans and Mobile*. Chicago: University of Chicago Press, 1990.

Klein, Herbert S. *African Slavery in Latin America and the Caribbean*. New York: Oxford University Press, 1986.

———. *Slavery in the Americas: A Comparative Study of Cuba and Virginia*. Chicago: University of Chicago Press, 1967.

Kmen, Henry A. *Music in New Orleans: The Formative Years, 1791–1841*. Baton Rouge: Louisiana State University Press, 1966.

Knight, Franklin W. *Slave Society in Cuba during the Nineteenth Century*. Madison: University of Wisconsin Press, 1970.

Koger, Larry. *Black Slaveowners: Free Black Slave Masters in South Carolina, 1790–1860*. Columbia: University of South Carolina Press, 1985.

Kolchin, Peter. *American Slavery, 1619–1877*. New York: Hill and Wang, 1993.

Kuethe, Allan J. *Military Reform and Society in New Granada, 1773–1808*. Gainesville: University Presses of Florida, 1978.

Le Gardeur, René J., Jr. *The First New Orleans Theatre, 1792–1803*. New Orleans: Leeward Books, 1963.

Martin, François-Xavier. *History of Louisiana*. 2 vols. New Orleans: Lyman and Beardslee, 1827.

Martínez-Alier, Verena. *Marriage, Class, and Colour in Nineteenth-Century Cuba: A Study of Racial Attitudes and Sexual Values in a Slave Society*. 2nd ed. Ann Arbor: University of Michigan Press, 1989.

McAlister, Lyle N. *The "Fuero Militar" in New Spain, 1764–1800*. Gainesville: University Presses of Florida, 1957.

———. *Spain and Portugal in the New World, 1492–1700*. Minneapolis: University of Minnesota Press, 1984.

McConnell, Roland C. *Negro Troops in Antebellum Louisiana: A History of the Battalion of Free Men of Color*. Baton Rouge: Louisiana State University Press, 1968.

Menn, Joseph Karl. *The Large Slaveholders of Louisiana—1860*. New Orleans: Pelican Publishing, 1964.

Mills, Gary B. *The Forgotten People: Cane River's Creoles of Color*. Baton Rouge: Louisiana State University Press, 1977.

Montero de Pedro, José. *Españoles en Nueva Orleans y Luisiana*. Madrid: Ediciones Cultura Hispánica del Centro Iberoamericano de Cooperación, 1979.

Moreno Fraginals, Manuel. *El Ingenio: Complejo económico social cubano del azúcar*. 3 vols. Havana: Editorial de Ciencias Sociales, 1978.

Mörner, Magnus. *Race Mixture in the History of Latin America.* Boston: Little, Brown and Co., 1967.

Mullin, Gerald W. *Flight and Rebellion: Slave Resistance in Eighteenth-Century Virginia.* New York: Oxford University Press, 1972.

Nolan, Charles E. *A Southern Catholic Heritage.* Vol. 1, *Colonial Period, 1704–1813.* New Orleans: Archdiocese of New Orleans, 1976.

Nutini, Hugo G., and Betty Bell. *Ritual Kinship: The Structure and Historical Development of the Compadrazgo System in Rural Tlaxcala.* Princeton: Princeton University Press, 1980.

Ott, Thomas. *The Haitian Revolution, 1789–1804.* Knoxville: University of Tennessee Press, 1973.

Palmer, Colin A. *Slaves of the White God: Blacks in Mexico, 1570–1650.* Cambridge: Harvard University Press, 1976.

Quarles, Benjamin. *The Negro in the American Revolution.* New York: W. W. Norton, 1973.

Reis, João José. *Slave Rebellion in Brazil: The Muslim Uprising of 1835 in Bahia.* Translated by Arthur Brakel. Baltimore: Johns Hopkins University Press, 1993.

Roussève, Charles B. *The Negro in Louisiana: Aspects of His History and His Literature.* New Orleans: Xavier University Press, 1937.

———. *The Negro in New Orleans.* New York: Archives of Negro History, 1969.

Russell-Wood, A. J. R. *The Black Man in Slavery and Freedom in Colonial Brazil.* New York: St. Martin's Press, 1982.

Schafer, Judith Kelleher. *Slavery, the Civil Law, and the Supreme Court of Louisiana.* Baton Rouge: Louisiana State University Press, 1994.

Schwartz, Stuart B. *Slaves, Peasants, and Rebels: Reconsidering Brazilian Slavery.* Urbana: University of Illinois Press, 1992.

Schweninger, Loren. *Black Property Owners in the South, 1790–1915.* Urbana: University of Illinois Press, 1991.

Scott, Rebecca J. *Slave Emancipation in Cuba: The Transition to Free Labor, 1860–1899.* Princeton: Princeton University Press, 1985.

Seed, Patricia. *To Love, Honor, and Obey in Colonial Mexico: Conflicts over Marriage Choice, 1574–1821.* Stanford: Stanford University Press, 1988.

Sharp, William F. *Slavery on the Spanish Frontier: The Colombian Chocó, 1680–1810.* Norman: University of Oklahoma Press, 1976.

Sitterson, J. Carlyle. *Sugar Country: The Cane Sugar Industry in the South, 1753–1950.* Lexington: University of Kentucky Press, 1953.

Sterkx, H. E. *The Free Negro in Ante-bellum Louisiana.* Rutherford, N.J.: Fairleigh Dickenson University Press, 1972.

Tannebaum, Frank. *Slave and Citizen: The Negro in the Americas.* New York: Alfred A. Knopf, 1947.

Taylor, Joe Gray. *Louisiana: A Bicentennial History.* New York: W. W. Norton, 1976.

———. *Negro Slavery in Louisiana.* Baton Rouge: Louisiana Historical Association, 1963.

Torres Ramírez, Bibiano. *Alejandro O'Reilly en las Indias.* Seville: Escuela de Estudios Hispano-Americanos, 1969.

Usner, Daniel H., Jr. *Indians, Settlers, and Slaves in a Frontier Exchange Economy: The Lower Mississippi Valley before 1783.* Chapel Hill: University of North Carolina Press for the Institute of Early American History and Culture, 1992.

Whitaker, Arthur Preston. *The Spanish-American Frontier: 1783-1795, the Westward Movement and the Spanish Retreat in the Mississippi Valley.* Gloucester, Mass.: Peter Smith, 1962.

White, Richard. *The Middle Ground: Indians, Empires, and Republics in the Great Lakes Region, 1650-1815.* New York: Cambridge University Press, 1991.

Woodson, Carter G. *Free Negro Owners of Slaves in the United States in 1830.* New York: Negro Universities Press, 1924.

Articles

Aguirre Beltrán, Gonzalo. "African Influences in the Development of Regional Cultures in the New World." In *Plantation Systems of the New World,* pp. 64-72. Washington, D.C.: Pan American Union, 1959.

Allain, Mathé. "Slave Policies in French Louisiana." *Louisiana History* 21:2 (spring 1980): 127-37.

Arena, C. Richard. "Landholding and Political Power in Spanish Louisiana." *LHQ* 38:4 (October 1955): 23-39.

————. "Philadelphia–Spanish New Orleans Trade in the 1790s." *Louisiana History* 2:4 (fall 1961): 429-45.

Baade, Anne A. "Slave Indemnities: A German Coast Response, 1795." *Louisiana History* 20:1 (winter 1979): 102-9.

Baade, Hans W. "The Law of Slavery in Spanish Louisiana, 1769-1803." In Haas, *Louisiana's Legal Heritage,* pp. 43-86.

Bennett, Herman L. "A Research Note: Race, Slavery, and the Ambiguity of Corporate Consciousness." *Colonial Latin American Historical Review* 3:2 (spring 1994): 207-13.

Bowser, Frederick P. "Colonial Spanish America." In Cohen and Greene, *Neither Slave nor Free,* pp. 19-58.

Brasseaux, Carl A. "The Administration of Slave Regulations in French Louisiana, 1724-1766." *Louisiana History* 21:2 (spring 1980): 139-58.

Brewer, James R. "Negro Property Owners in Seventeenth-Century Virginia." In *The Making of Black America: Essays in Negro Life and History,* edited by August Meier and Elliott Rudwick, pp. 201-5. New York: Atheneum, 1969.

Campbell, Leon. "The Changing Racial and Administrative Structure of the Peruvian Military under the Late Bourbons." *The Americas* 32:1 (July 1975): 117-33.

Clark, John G. "New Orleans: Its First Century of Economic Development." *Louisiana History* 10:1 (winter 1969): 35-47.

Conrad, Glenn R. "Summary of Trial Proceedings of Those Accused of Participating in the Slave Uprising of January, 1811." *Louisiana History* 18:4 (fall 1977): 472-73.

Coutts, Brian E. "Flax and Hemp in Spanish Louisiana, 1777-1783." *Louisiana History* 26:2 (spring 1985): 129-39.

Couturier, Edith. "Women and the Family in Eighteenth-Century Mexico: Law and Practice." *Journal of Family History* 10:3 (fall 1985): 294-304.

Cruzat, Heloise Hulse. "The Ursulines of Louisiana." *LHQ* 2:1 (January 1919): 5-23.

Dart, Henry Plauche. "Courts and Law in Colonial Louisiana." *LHQ* 4:3 (July 1921): 255–89.

———. "The Place of the Civil Law in Louisiana." *Tulane Law Review* 4:1 (February 1930): 163–77.

———. "Public Education in New Orleans in 1800." *LHQ* 11:2 (April 1928): 24–52.

DeConde, Alexander. "Napoleon and the Louisiana Purchase." In *Napoleon and America,* edited by Robert B. Holtman, pp. 100–136. Pensacola: Perdido Bay Press for the Louisiana State Museum, 1988.

Din, Gilbert C. "*Cimarrones* and the San Malo Band in Spanish Louisiana." *Louisiana History* 21:3 (summer 1980): 237–62.

———. "Proposals and Plans for Colonization in Spanish Louisiana." *Louisiana History* 11:3 (summer 1970): 197–213.

Dorman, James H. "Persistent Specter: Slave Rebellion in Territorial Louisiana." *Louisiana History* 18:4 (fall 1977): 398–404.

Dunbar-Nelson, Alice. "People of Color in Louisiana." *Journal of Negro History* 1:4 (October 1916): 361–76.

Elisabeth, Léo. "The French Antilles." In Cohen and Greene, *Neither Slave nor Free,* pp. 134–71.

Everett, Donald E. "Emigres and Militiamen: Free Persons of Color in New Orleans, 1803–1815." *Journal of Negro History* 38:4 (October 1953): 377–402.

———. "Free Persons of Color in Colonial Louisiana." *Louisiana History* 7:1 (winter 1966): 21–50.

Fiehrer, Thomas Marc. "The African Presence in Colonial Louisiana: An Essay on the Continuity of Caribbean Culture." In Macdonald, Kemp, and Haas, *Louisiana's Black Heritage,* pp. 3–31.

Fitchett, E. Horace. "The Traditions of the Free Negro in Charleston, South Carolina." *Journal of Negro History* 25:2 (April 1940): 139–52.

Foner, Laura. "The Free People of Color in Louisiana and St. Domingue: A Comparative Portrait of Two Three-Caste Slave Societies." *Journal of Social History* 3:4 (summer 1970): 406–30.

Fredrickson, George. "Comparative History." In *The Past before Us,* edited by Michael Kammen, pp. 457–73. Ithaca: Cornell University Press, 1980.

Garrigus, John. "Blue and Brown: Contraband Indigo and the Rise of a Free Colored Planter Class in French Saint-Domingue." *The Americas* 50:2 (October 1993): 233–63.

Geggus, David. "Racial Equality, Slavery, and Colonial Secession during the Constituent Assembly." *American Historical Review* 94:5 (December 1989): 1290–1308.

Genovese, Eugene D. "Materialism and Idealism in the History of Negro Slavery in the Americas." *Journal of Social History* 1:4 (summer 1968): 371–94.

———. "The Slave States in North America." In Cohen and Greene, *Neither Slave nor Free,* pp. 258–77.

———. "The Treatment of Slaves in Different Countries: Problems in the Application of the Comparative Method." In *Slavery in the Americas: A Comparative Reader,* edited by Genovese and Laura Foner, pp. 202–10. Englewood Cliffs, N.J.: Prentiss-Hall, 1969.

Gould, L. Virginia. "Urban Slavery-Urban Freedom: The Manumission of Jacqueline

Lemelle." In *More Than Chattel: Black Women and Slavery in the Americas,* edited by David Barry Gaspar and Darlene Clark Hine, pp. 298–314. Bloomington: Indiana University Press, 1996.

Gudeman, Stephen, and Stuart B. Schwartz. "Cleansing Original Sin: Godparenthood and the Baptism of Slaves in Eighteenth-Century Bahia." In *Kinship Ideology and Practice in Latin America,* edited by Raymond Smith, pp. 35–58. Chapel Hill: University of North Carolina Press, 1984.

Hall, Gwendolyn Midlo. "Saint Domingue." In Cohen and Greene, *Neither Slave nor Free,* pp. 172–92.

Handler, Jerome S., and Arnold A. Sio. "Barbados." In Cohen and Greene, *Neither Slave nor Free,* pp. 214–57.

Hanger, Kimberly S. " 'Almost All Have Callings': Free Blacks at Work in Spanish New Orleans." *Colonial Latin American Historical Review* 3:2 (spring 1994): 141–64.

———. "Avenues to Freedom Open to New Orleans' Black Population, 1769–1779." *Louisiana History* 31:3 (summer 1990): 237–64.

———. "Conflicting Loyalties: The French Revolution and Free People of Color in Spanish New Orleans." *Louisiana History* 34:1 (winter 1993): 5–33.

———. " 'The Fortunes of Women in America': Spanish New Orleans's Free Women of African Descent and Their Relations with Slave Women." In *Discovering the Women in Slavery: Emancipating Perspectives on the American Past,* edited by Patricia Morton, pp. 153–78. Athens: University of Georgia Press, 1996.

———. "Household and Community Structure among the Free Population of Spanish New Orleans, 1778." *Louisiana History* 30:1 (winter 1989): 63–79.

———. "Origins of New Orleans's Free Creoles of Color." In *Creoles of Color of the Gulf South,* edited by James H. Dormon, pp. 1–27. Knoxville: University of Tennessee Press, 1996.

———. "Patronage, Property, and Persistence: The Emergence of a Free Black Elite in Spanish New Orleans." *Slavery and Abolition* 17:1 (April 1996): 44–64.

———. "A Privilege and Honor to Serve: The Free Black Militia of Spanish New Orleans." *Military History of the Southwest* 21:1 (spring 1991): 59–86.

———. "Protecting Property, Family, and Self in the Circum-Caribbean: The *Mujeres Libres* of Colonial New Orleans." *Revista/Review Interamericana* 22:1/2 (spring/summer 1992): 126–50.

Holmes, Jack D. L. "The Abortive Slave Revolt at Pointe Coupée, Louisiana, 1795." *Louisiana History* 11:4 (fall 1970): 341–62.

———. "Do It! Don't Do It! Spanish Laws on Sex and Marriage." In Haas, *Louisiana's Legal Heritage,* pp. 19–42.

———. "Indigo in Colonial Louisiana and the Floridas." *Louisiana History* 8:4 (fall 1967): 329–49.

———. "Spanish Regulation of the Tavern and the Liquor Trade in the Mississippi Valley." In McDermott, *The Spanish in the Mississippi Valley,* pp. 149–82.

Ingersoll, Thomas N. "Free Blacks in a Slave Society: New Orleans, 1718–1812." *William and Mary Quarterly* 48:2 (April 1991): 173–200.

Johnson, Lyman. "The Impact of Racial Discrimination on Black Artisans in Colonial Buenos Aires." *Social History* 6:3 (1981): 301–16.

Kendall, John S. "New Orleans' 'Peculiar Institution.'" *LHQ* 23:3 (July 1940): 864–86.

Klein, Herbert S. "The Colored Militia of Cuba: 1568–1868." *Caribbean Studies* 6 (July 1966): 17–27.

Knight, Franklin W. "Cuba." In Cohen and Greene, *Neither Slave nor Free,* pp. 278–308.

Kuethe, Allan J. "The Status of the Free Pardo in the Disciplined Militia of New Granada." *Journal of Negro History* 56:2 (April 1971): 105–17.

Lachance, Paul F. "The 1809 Immigration of Saint-Domingue Refugees to New Orleans: Reception, Integration, and Impact." *Louisiana History* 29:2 (spring 1988): 109–41.

———. "The Formation of a Three-Caste Society: Evidence from Wills in Antebellum New Orleans." *Social Science History* 18:2 (summer 1994): 211–42.

———. "Intermarriage and French Cultural Persistence in Late Spanish and Early American New Orleans." *Histoire Sociale/Social History* 15:2 (May 1982): 47–81.

———. "The Politics of Fear: French Louisianians and the Slave Trade, 1786–1809." *Plantation Society in the Americas* 1:2 (June 1979): 162–97.

Landers, Jane. "Gracia Real de Santa Teresa de Mose: A Free Black Town in Spanish Colonial Florida." *American Historical Review* 95:1 (February 1990): 9–30.

Liljegren, Ernest R. "Jacobinism in Spanish Louisiana, 1792–1797." *LHQ* 22:1 (January 1939): 47–97.

McAlister, Lyle N. "The Reorganization of the Army of New Spain, 1763–1767." *HAHR* 33:1 (February 1953): 1–32.

McConnell, Roland C. "Louisiana's Black Military History, 1729–1865." In Macdonald, Kemp, and Haas, *Louisiana's Black Heritage,* pp. 32–62.

McCutcheon, Roger Philip. "Libraries in New Orleans, 1771–1833." *LHQ* 20:1 (January 1937): 152–58.

Miller, W. James. "The Militia System of Spanish Louisiana, 1769–1783." In *The Military Presence on the Gulf Coast,* edited by William S. Coker, pp. 36–63. Pensacola: Perdido Bay Press, 1975.

Mintz, Sidney W., and Eric Wolf. "An Analysis of Ritual Co-Parenthood (Compadrazgo)." *Southwestern Journal of Anthropology* 6 (winter 1950): 341–67.

Moore, John Hebron. "The Cypress Lumber Industry of the Lower Mississippi Valley during the Colonial Period." *Louisiana History* 24:1 (winter 1983): 25–47.

Porteous, Laura L. "Sanitary Conditions in New Orleans under the Spanish Regime, 1799–1800." *LHQ* 15:4 (October 1932): 610–17.

Price, Jacob. "Economic Function and the Growth of American Port Towns in the Eighteenth Century." *Perspectives in American History* 8 (1974): 123–86.

Rankin, David C. "The Tannenbaum Thesis Reconsidered: Slavery and Race Relations in Antebellum Louisiana." *Southern Studies* 18:1 (spring 1979): 5–31.

Ricard, Ulysses S., Jr. "Pierre Belly and Rose: More Forgotten People." *Chicory Review* 1:1 (fall 1988): 2–17.

Rojas, Lauro A. de. "The Great Fire of 1788 in New Orleans." *LHQ* 20:3 (July 1937): 578–89.

Russell, John H. "Colored Freemen as Slave Owners in Virginia." *Journal of Negro History* 1:3 (July 1916): 233–42.

Sánchez, Joseph P. "African Freedmen and the *Fuero Militar:* A Historical Overview of *Pardo* and *Moreno* Militiamen in the Late Spanish Empire." *Colonial Latin American Historical Review* 3:2 (spring 1994): 165–84.

Schafer, Judith K. "'Open and Notorious Concubinage': The Emancipation of Slave Mistresses by Will and the Supreme Court in Antebellum Louisiana." *Louisiana History* 28:2 (spring 1987): 165–82.

Schwartz, Stuart B. "The Manumission of Slaves in Colonial Brazil: Bahia, 1684–1745." *HAHR* 54:4 (November 1974): 603–35.

Schweninger, Loren. "Prosperous Blacks in the South, 1790–1880." *American Historical Review* 95:1 (February 1990): 31–56.

Scott, Rebecca J. "Defining the Boundaries of Freedom in the World of Cane: Cuba, Brazil, and Louisiana after Emancipation." *American Historical Review* 99:1 (February 1994): 70–102.

Seed, Patricia. "Social Dimensions of Race: Mexico City, 1753." *HAHR* 62:4 (November 1982): 569–606.

Sio, Arnold A. "Marginality and Free Coloured Identity in Caribbean Slave Society." In *Caribbean Slave Society and Economy,* edited by Hilary Beckles and Verene Shepherd, pp. 150–59. Kingston, Jamaica: Ian Randle Publishers, 1991.

Tregle, Joseph G., Jr. "Creoles and Americans." In Hirsch and Logsdon, *Creole New Orleans,* pp. 136–41.

———. "Early New Orleans Society: A Reappraisal." *Journal of Southern History* 18:1 (February 1952): 20–36.

Twinam, Ann. "Honor, Sexuality, and Illegitimacy in Colonial Spanish America." In Lavrin, *Sexuality and Marriage,* pp. 118–55.

Usner, Daniel H., Jr. "From African Captivity to American Slavery: The Introduction of Black Laborers to Colonial Louisiana." *Louisiana History* 20:1 (winter 1979): 25–48.

———. "The Frontier Exchange Economy of the Lower Mississippi Valley in the Eighteenth Century." *William and Mary Quarterly* 44:3 (April 1987): 165–92.

Waldron, Kathy. "The Sinners and the Bishop in Colonial Venezuela: The *Visita* of Bishop Mariano Martí, 1771–1784." In Lavrin, *Sexuality and Marriage,* pp. 156–77.

Weber, David. "John Francis Bannon and the Historiography of the Spanish Borderlands." *Journal of the Southwest* 29:4 (winter 1987): 331–63.

Webre, Stephen. "The Problem of Indian Slavery in Spanish Louisiana, 1769–1803." *Louisiana History* 25:2 (spring 1984): 117–35.

Winston, James E. "The Free Negro in New Orleans, 1803–1860." *LHQ* 21:4 (October 1938): 1075–85.

———. "Notes on the Economic History of New Orleans, 1803–1836." *Mississippi Valley Historical Review* 11:2 (September 1924): 200–226.

Wood, Minter. "Life in New Orleans in the Spanish Period." *LHQ* 22:3 (July 1939): 642–709.

Wu, Cecilia. "The Population of the City of Querétaro in 1791." *Journal of Latin American Studies* 16:2 (November 1984): 277–307.

Collected Works

Berlin, Ira, and Ronald Hoffman, eds. *Slavery and Freedom in the Age of the American Revolution*. Charlottesville: University of Virginia Press, 1983.

Cohen, David W., and Jack P. Greene, eds. *Neither Slave nor Free: The Freedmen of African Descent in the Slave Societies of the New World*. Baltimore: Johns Hopkins University Press, 1972.

Haas, Edward F., ed. *Louisiana's Legal Heritage*. Pensacola: Perdido Bay Press for the Louisiana State Museum, 1983.

Hirsch, Arnold R., and Joseph Logsdon, eds. *Creole New Orleans: Race and Americanization*. Baton Rouge: Louisiana State University Press, 1992.

Lavrin, Ascunción, ed. *Sexuality and Marriage in Colonial Latin America*. Lincoln: University of Nebraska Press, 1989.

Macdonald, Robert R., John R. Kemp, and Edward F. Haas, eds. *Louisiana's Black Heritage*. New Orleans: Louisiana State Museum, 1979.

McDermott, John Francis, ed. *The Spanish in the Mississippi Valley, 1762–1804*. Urbana: University of Illinois Press, 1974.

Theses and Dissertations

Garrigus, John David. "A Struggle for Respect: The Free Coloreds of Pre-Revolutionary Saint Dominigue, 1760–1769." Ph.D. dissertation, Johns Hopkins University, 1988.

Gould, L. Virginia Meacham. "In Full Enjoyment of Their Liberty: The Free Women of Color of the Gulf Ports of New Orleans, Mobile, and Pensacola, 1769–1860." Ph.D. dissertation, Emory University, 1991.

Greene, Karen. "The Ursuline Mission in Colonial Louisiana." M.A. thesis, Louisiana State University, 1982.

Hanger, Kimberly S. "*Personas de varias clases y colores:* Free People of Color in Spanish New Orleans, 1769–1803." Ph.D. dissertation, University of Florida, 1991.

Ingersoll, Thomas H. "Old New Orleans: Race, Class, Sex, and Order in the Early Deep South, 1718–1819." Ph.D. dissertation, University of California, Los Angeles, 1990.

Kerr, Derek Noel. "Petty Felony, Slave Defiance, and Frontier Villainy: Crime and Criminal Justice in Spanish Louisiana, 1770–1803." Ph.D. dissertation, Tulane University, 1983.

Landers, Jane. "Black Society in Spanish St. Augustine, 1784–1821." Ph.D. dissertation, University of Florida, 1988.

McGowan, James Thomas. "Creation of a Slave Society: Louisiana Plantations in the Eighteenth Century." Ph.D. dissertation, University of Rochester, 1976.

Index

Kimberly S. Hanger is Assistant Professor of History
at the University of Tulsa.

Library of Congress Cataloging-in-Publication Data
Hanger, Kimberly S.
Bounded lives, bounded places : free Black society in colonial New
Orleans, 1769–1803 / Kimberly S. Hanger.
    p. cm.
  Includes bibliographical references (p.   ) and index.
  ISBN 0-8223-1906-3 (alk. paper). —
  ISBN 0-8223-1898-9 (pbk. : alk. paper)
1. Free Afro-Americans—Louisiana—New Orleans—History—18th
century. 2. Spaniards—Louisiana—New Orleans—History—18th
century. 3. New Orleans (La.)—History. 4. Louisiana—History—
To 1803. I. Title.
F379.N59N44 1997
976.3'00496073—dc20   96-33332